Mike Brearley OBE was educated at Cambridge, where he read classics and moral sciences, and captained the university. He played for Middlesex County Cricket Club intermittently from 1961 to 1983, captaining the team from 1971 to 1982. He first played for England in 1976 and captained the side from 1977 to 1980, winning eighteen test matches and losing only four. He was recalled to the captaincy in 1981 for the Ashes home series, leading England to one of their most famous victories. Since retiring from cricket in 1982, he trained and continues to work as a psychoanalyst, and is a lecturer on leadership and motivation. He is the author of the bestselling *The Art of Captaincy* and *On Form*, and has written on cricket and the psychology of sport for the *Sunday Times*, *Observer* and most recently *The Times*. He lives in London.

Praise for *On Cricket*

'Brearley is at his best in these quirky, delightful essays when he is exploring the human qualities of humbler players . . . Brearley's admiration for his friends' decency, craftsmanship and modesty seems to recall a golden age of country cricket'

Michael Henderson, *The Times*

'Mike Brearley is a cultured and intelligent man . . . able elegantly to assess his colleagues and predecessors, as he does with customary grace in his latest volume'

Robert Crampton, *The Times*

'Brearley speaks with understated authority on the matter. His words are all the more powerful for that'

Sunday Express

'A treasure of recollections and reactions, talking heroes, controversies and big themes'

ON CRICKET

Mike Brearley

Dear Elliot,

Leather + willow = cricket!
Happy 9th anniversary! This gift
comes with a promise of a day
at a match next season.

All my love
Caroline

CONSTABLE

CONSTABLE

First published in Great Britain in 2018 by Constable
This paperback edition published in 2019 by Constable

1 3 5 7 9 10 8 6 4 2

A CIP catalogue record for this book
is available from the British Library.

ISBN: 978-1-47212-946-8

Typeset in Electra by SX Composing DTP, Rayleigh, Essex SS6 7EF
Printed and bound in Great Britain by Clays Ltd, Elcograf S.p.A

Papers used by Constable are from well-managed forests
and other responsible sources.

MIX
Paper from
responsible sources
FSC® C104740

Constable
An imprint of
Little, Brown Book Group
Carmelite House
50 Victoria Embankment
London EC4Y 0DZ

An Hachette UK Company
www.hachette.co.uk

www.littlebrown.co.uk

In memory of Horace and Midge, who set me on this track

and
to Luka, Alia and Maia, who will find their own paths

CONTENTS

'Are We Going to the Same Place?'   xi

PART 1: FROM HECKMONDWIKE TO LORD'S

1   The Football Cap   3
2   'Then I Knew We Had a Chance'   14
3   The Darling Buds of May   22

PART 2: THE ASHES

4   The Gnawed Umbrella Handle and the Burned Bail   33
5   Raking Through the Ashes   36
6   A Late Developer (or: My Lucky Breaks)   43
7   Almost Losing a Dominion   48
8   Four Images from the 2006–7 Series   60
9   Giants   66

PART 3: HEROES

10   What Makes a Hero?   75
11   'In My Opinion'   80
12   'Michael Boy'   84
13   From Wot to Fot   90
14   Whispering Death   100
15   Caleb Garth: the Craftsman   108

vii

PART 4: CRICKET AND RACE

16	Crises in Cricket	119
17	'Batting like a Gorilla'	124
18	'Nice Bonking Pace'	128
19	'We Picked Him'	135
20	'Half a Good Night'	146
21	Bible and Passion	153
22	The Zimbabwe Affair	158
23	Cometh the Hour	166

PART 5: CHEATING AND CORRUPTION

24	Not Common-or-Garden Cheating	183
25	Ball Tampering: Disenchantment	191
26	The Sting: Lord's 2010	198
27	The Spirit of Cricket	205

PART 6: GAME CHANGERS

28	Scoops, Switch-hits and Helmets at Short Mid-on	219
29	Father of Reverse Swing	227
30	The Doosra and the Splint	234
31	'Naaaaaagh, That's No Good!'	241

PART 7: INDIAN BATSMANSHIP

32	Supping with the Devil	251
33	'When I First Saw the English Bowling'	260
34	The Indian Bradman	267
35	The Bridge	273

PART 8: COMMENTATORS

36	From the Commentary Box	283
37	'Desperately Good'	285
38	'Another Time, Another Time'	293
39	Endgame	298
40	'They've Not Got the Singles Going'	303
41	What Do They Know of Cricket . . .	308

PART 9: WICKET-KEEPERS

42	Behind the Timbers	323
43	Elegance	326
44	'What Do You Think This Is, Randall?'	332
45	The Flea	338
46	Not Yet the King of Albania	345

PART 10: AESTHETICS

47	The Art of the Masses	353
48	The Beautiful Game	361

PART 11: BACK TO THE BEGINNING

49	Summer County	383

Notes and References	388
Acknowledgements	397
Image Credits	399
Index	401

'ARE WE GOING TO THE SAME PLACE?'

In 1964, I opened the batting with Geoffrey Boycott at Salisbury, as Harare was then called, in the first match of the MCC tour of South Africa. We were both young hopefuls, though as things quickly panned out, my hopes were less firmly grounded than his. The game was a two-day friendly match. The pavilion was at mid-wicket in relation to the pitch. Geoffrey and I were each 20 or so not out in the fifty minutes' batting we had before tea. He played the last ball and marched off towards the pavilion without waiting for me to join him. I had to run a few paces to catch up with him. I said, cheerfully I think, but perhaps also sarcastically, 'Are we going to the same place?' He turned on me, snapping, 'None of your egghead intellectual stuff.' The name 'egghead' stuck, at least for a while, though I don't think of myself as an intellectual, let alone as an egghead.

Looking back, it's tempting to see outcomes in matches and careers as inevitable and to read events and people as simpler than they are and more sharply edged – Perth rather than Mumbai. In life we nose our way forwards, uncertain about the future, and indeed with only vague and patchy knowledge of the present and the past.

One of the benefits of becoming an expert (of a kind) in one sphere, however narrow the sphere might be, is that we are in a position to know how little we understand of other spheres (or polyhedrons for that matter). It's hard to really look and see. We are hindered by partial viewpoints, by the complexity of events; by lack of thought, and by over-thinking. (Expectation gets in the way of seeing; as the philosopher Ludwig Wittgenstein said: 'Don't think, look'; and it is necessary to attempt to suspend and question some of our assumptions if we are to see what is in front of us.)

As I wrote in my book *On Form*, I think that writing, like playing cricket, like, in fact, many activities of life, involves at best a benign sort of marriage between discipline and spontaneity, between hard work and playfulness, between letting go of conscious control and the application of sometimes critical thought.

What follows is a collection of pieces on the game, portraits of players and issues that have interested me and continue to do so. It is not meant to be exhaustive. There is nothing, for instance, on captaincy, on retirement and depression, or on county cricket. Little on umpiring, on DRS, on grounds, on Middlesex colleagues; even on the future of the game. Some are pieces written originally for newspapers – mostly for the *Sunday Times, Observer* or *The Times* – over the past forty years. I have contextualized, and at least tampered with, them all. Twenty-five are new, or virtually so.

I started this brief pipe-opener with a tiny episode from the tour of South Africa. One continuing area of interest has been race, including apartheid, in cricket (that tour opened my eyes to the horrors of that system and the way it entered every area of people's lives) and the question of whether it is legitimate to speak of physiological, cultural, racial and social differences in cricketing technique and character. I discuss at some length the D'Oliveira affair, and some of the personalities involved in that episode (perhaps the most significant in terms of broader influence in life beyond sport of any during my lifetime); the protest by Andy Flower and Henry Olonga at Mugabe's Zimbabwe; and C. L. R. James's account of the campaign for the election of a black captain (Frank Worrell) of the West Indies team. And I examine some quirks and special skills of the great Indian batsmen,

Ranjitsinhji, Pataudi, Sachin Tendulkar and Virat Kohli. Differences of physiology, social customs and personality are to be celebrated and not denied (for reasons of political correctness) or scorned (for reasons of prejudice), but neither are they to be exempt from criticism.

There are many other topics, from John Arlott and Harold Pinter to Alan Knott and Kumar Sangakkara, from being pushed into a rose bush at the cricket ground at Burton upon Trent by an irate Middlesex supporter to conspiring with Philippe Edmonds to put the helmet at short mid-on to tempt Yorkshire batsmen into error in the search for five penalty runs. And there is something on the Ashes – including the prediction, almost correct, that Douglas Jardine would win the Ashes but lose a Dominion – and on corruption, as in attempts to fix matches or passages of play by Hansie Cronje and by Pakistan players lured by the *News of the World* sting, as opposed to common-or-garden cheating (including ball tampering).

If a sufficient number of people enjoy the book, and if I live long enough, there may even be a sequel. You may take this as a warning or a promise.

PART 1

FROM HECKMONDWIKE TO LORD'S

1

THE FOOTBALL CAP

'Please can you bring me a football, a football jersey, some football gloves, some football boots, some football socks, a football cap, and a football shirt. Good bye until next Christmas': Extract from letter to Father Christmas, 1948. (I also politely wished him a very happy Christmas and hoped 'you won't get too "tied" when you go on your "raindeas" [sic] down every chimney'.)

This six-year-old me, or I, had a one-track mind. Note the football gloves and cap; these were what the Brentham goalie, Paul Swann, wore when facing west late on a winter day. When play was safely down the other end, Paul would chat with this obsessive little boy by his goalpost. Then the players would come sweeping towards his goal, the thud of studs surging like a herd of Father Christmas's reindeer, the swirling male bodies barging against each other.

Paul and his brother John were, along with my earthbound father, Horace, my heroes, John particularly. Intermediate in age between my father and myself, he was an excellent footballer and an even better cricketer. He played both games for Brentham, near our home in Ealing, West London, along with my father. He was a capped Middlesex Second XI player, and also played four first-class games for the county between 1949 and 1951.

Smartly turned out, with his upturned collar (did I unconsciously copy him?), John was a correct and classical left-hand batsman, a fine fielder, especially in the covers, and a skilful and reliable leg-spin bowler. He was elegant in everything he did. On the football field I remember him as an athletic, forthright inside-forward.

I can picture him playing a ball just short of a length wide of mid-on with a straight bat, from a sideways-on position, and moving smoothly for a quick single. As a bowler he didn't turn the ball much, but he drifted it in, and was accurate. He had a high action, perhaps too high for a real leg-spinner.

John was offered a contract by Middlesex, but, aware of the uncertainties of such a move, which would involve giving up his job as a draughtsman in an aircraft company, decided against.

My image of him was of someone who always gave his best, was entirely straightforward, and would never blame others. If his partner called him for a run, John would trust him, put his head down, and go for the crease as hard as he could. His demeanour was modest. He would accept a decision without a hint of visible disappointment, let alone

4

dissent. John was quiet, but with a nice sense of humour. He was an admirable model for a young cricketer. He had a motorbike and sidecar, which seemed glamorous to me then, but rather precarious now.

Later, like John Swann and my father, I too played for Brentham and Middlesex.

Another significant influence was Middleton Sports Club, in Sussex. It was three miles from Bognor, where we went on holiday each August over ten years. As a small boy, I would go along Bognor beach asking to join cricket games in progress. I'm told that they would sometimes get fed up with me when they couldn't get me out, but I don't remember that. We discovered Middleton when I was ten. Mr Leigh-Breeze ran the cricket for the sports events held on three days a week, and the team for a whole week's colts' cricket against other teams. My first proper game of cricket was when I was ten. The colts team had boys as old as eighteen. We were one short. My main anxiety before the match was that my pair of long whites, due to be sent by my aunt, wouldn't arrive in time, and I'd have to play in shorts. Batting at number ten on the day, proudly trousered, I scored 5 not out. A hook and an off-drive. Next match, at Chichester, I was put in first. The opening bowler was a giant left-arm bowler. When he bowled me a slower ball, I thought: 'I wish he'd bowl slower balls all the time.' This kind of feeling remained with me for much of the next thirty years.

In one match a few years later, I faced John Snow, opening the bowling for Bognor Colts. The colts week was followed by three weeks of men's cricket. As I grew older, I wanted to play as often as possible, almost every day. A Middleton Sunday XI played at often picturesque village grounds across Sussex. At Wisborough Green, I first encountered the Nawab of Pataudi.

Freddie Brown, England captain not long before, occasionally played against Middleton. I was too timid to be one of the boys bowling at him on the outfield before the game. He belched spectacularly after lunch and port. When I was about fifteen I batted against him in a match, and remember hitting him through the covers for four off the back foot. Billy Griffith (ex-England wicket-keeper and batsman) and his son Mike also played for Middleton. I once opened the batting with my father, but was so excited and anxious I got bowled for 0, rushing down the wicket to an off-spinner.

My father, born in Heckmondwike, near Dewsbury, in Yorkshire's West Riding, was the youngest of eight children. His father Joseph was an engine fitter, who would travel across the north of England repairing and fitting crucial mill engines. His mother Lydia-Anne, daughter of the publican at the Shoulder of Mutton in Liversedge, was a determined woman, whom my father would remember playing bridge, and bidding, rebidding and re-re-rebidding spades. There is a story about her spending the whole of a £50 legacy that came to her – a huge amount for that time and that family – on a piano. To get it into the house the windows upstairs had to be taken out and a crane brought in to lift the piano up.

Horace was an excellent all-round sportsman (my mother too: she played netball for London University, and later tennis). He was good at cricket, football, hockey, water-polo, swimming – to name only a few. He played cricket for Yorkshire Seconds for three years, at a time when Yorkshire were the best team in the country. He captained the Combined British Universities team. And he played once for Yorkshire, against, as it happened, Middlesex, at Bramall Lane, Sheffield, in 1937.

Some of England's greatest players were playing in this match: for Yorkshire, Len Hutton, Herbert Sutcliffe, Hedley Verity and Bill Bowes; for Middlesex, Denis Compton, Bill Edrich, Patsy Hendren and Walter Robins. Middlesex had three international leg-spinners, Jim Sims, 'Tuppy' Owen-Smith and Robins, a breed of bowling not trusted in Yorkshire, and hardly ever met with by someone (like my father) brought up in the northern leagues.

Coming in at number five, he scored 8 and 9. In the second innings, he batted with Len Hutton, who was due to play his first Test match a few days later. I think it was typical of the Yorkshire Horace that he complained of Hutton pinching the bowling; a mere Southerner would have been pleased to stay watching from the non-striking end while Hutton did his stuff, but there is a sort of Yorkshire pride that comes through saying, 'I refuse to kow-tow to anyone.'

It was not only Yorkshire's league players who struggled against leg-spin. Their professionals too were often disconcerted by this form of bowling. The chilly, damp climate doesn't help; and psychologically Yorkshiremen were traditionally too suspicious of a tribe whose members inevitably bowl the odd long hop or full toss. In 1967 I played a season for Cambridgeshire, keeping wicket. One of the great pleasures was keeping to Johnny Wardle, especially when he bowled Chinamen and googlies. I asked him about Len. He told me:

> I once bowled to him in a pre-season middle practice at Headingley. I'm honestly not boasting when I say: I have never seen so great a player so bamboozled. Yet as captain of England he wouldn't risk the odd boundary. He wanted me to bowl defensively, orthodox slow-left-arm, to give the fast bowlers a rest.

In only his second game for Middlesex, in 1965, Middlesex leg-spinner Harry Latchman took 6 for 52 against Yorkshire at Lord's. Len came into our dressing room after play. J. T. Murray, the Middlesex wicket-keeper, ribbed him: 'What is it about your lot, Len, that they can't play leg-spin?' Leonard paused, characteristically, having us all wait for his words of wisdom. 'You see,' he eventually said, pointing upwards with his finger by his head, 'the further north you go, the slower they get.' (He meant the batsmen, not the leg-spinners.)

Hutton bowled leg-breaks himself, by the way; in 1939 he took 44 wickets at 18.88, finishing eighth in the national bowling averages. But he was suspicious of wrist spinners on his own side, partly because, notwithstanding Wardle's encounter with him, he played

Sonny Ramadhin and Jack Iverson, both fine international leg-spinners, so well himself (treating them both as off-spinners, I gather).

Perhaps this was not so much a Yorkshire failing as a north country one. The cricket writer Stephen Chalke tells me that the Yorkshire player Ken Taylor, who played leg-spin as well as anyone, told him that Lancashire and England batsman Cyril Washbrook was hopelessly at sea against this type of bowler. He used to stay at the other end when Doug Wright was bowling for Kent, and 'didn't know whether it was Christmas or Easter' against Wardle.

Yorkshiremen traditionally were brought up not to be too pleased with themselves, not to get ahead of themselves. 'Don't get your feet too far under the table too soon' was my father's only advice to me for potential romantic relationships. They were at the same time stolidly averse to being treated as anyone's inferior.

Once when my father came off the field after scoring a hundred at Heckmondwike, an old chap in the pavilion said, 'Well played young man, but tha' wouldn't have scored a 'oondred if thi' father [the 'a' rhyming with 'fat', not with the second 'a' in 'palaver'] had been bowling [rhyming with 'howling']. To my mind this captures something fundamental to the Yorkshire mentality – give praise, but stint it: don't let the young fellow get above himself: the old days were better.

When I was about fourteen, I remember my father telling me off, quietly, for boasting. I felt and can still feel the shame. I had been both arrogant and falsely modest, commenting to Mike Griffith and my father that my wicket-keeping was 'not quite as good as Mike's on the leg-side'. I remember exactly where this conversation occurred, as we walked round the Middleton boundary.

On the rare occasions when we had a chance to play table tennis, Horace would allow me to get to a 20–16 lead before he won 22–20. I remembered this during my second game for Cambridge, aged nineteen. I hooked the great Fred Trueman for four (it was a slow, damp pitch). 'Good shot, son,' he said, 'but tha' won't do it again.' And indeed, two balls later, a second short ball was several miles an hour faster, and I had to take hasty evasive action.

You weren't allowed to elevate yourself too much in that world. Don't think you're the only pebble on the beach. Don't be one of those who fancy the sun shines out of their backsides.

As the youngest child, Horace was able to stay on at school to do his A-levels, as the older children were by then bringing money into the home. He got a scholarship to Leeds University to read maths. The practice of taking the hat round for a collection if you scored fifty made quite a difference to his financial well-being during these years.

After the war, there was Brentham. He played in a local derby the day my younger sister Margy was born, in 1946, scoring 50 against Ealing. An entry in my school workbook from 1948 reads: 'when daddy takes me to away crickett match-is [sic] I like it. His hiest scor this yeara is 73. That is not-bad.' (Even then I had a penchant for hyphens.) And, later: 'I went-to brentham crickit-field and watchet daddy play crickit, he got 50 runs I scored everey-man until he was-out, nobodey got ass-menny runs as 50. I did not scor the boling becase I can not do the boling.'

When I was thirteen, I was drafted in to play for Brentham at Malden Wanderers ground, when they were one short. I came in at number ten, playing for a draw, and scored three not out, batting against a bowler who seemed quick to me (Harry Edney, his name, and I can still remember his quaintly dance-like side-step as he started his run-up.) At the other end was a leg-spinner who played for Kent 2nd XI, named Keith Walker. I learned later that the opposition were miffed at my presence, since they could not, they felt, bowl short at this boy.

By chance I recently met Michael Burns, who played in the match, himself only sixteen. He recalled bowling with another spinner at Brentham against my father and John Swann, right hander and left hander. As the bowlers alternated between over and round the wicket depending on whether a left hander or right hander was facing, the batsmen insisted on having the (single) sight screen moved (by the fielders) at each change. He also remembered my father being grumpy at the 'loud' and youthful Malden team. My father didn't hide his feelings.

He also played for Middlesex II, and twice for the county team when Middlesex were depleted due to Test calls. These two matches, in 1949, were at Bath and Swansea. The first of them was also the debut of Fred Titmus, aged sixteen. In my last year as a professional cricketer, 1982, we pulled in Fred, aged forty-nine, to play for Middlesex against Surrey at Lord's at the end of August, when he'd dropped in to the dressing room to say hello and to watch the start. He took four wickets in the match, which effectively won us the Championship. Fred said: 'I saw the father in, and the son out'.

Horace was warm and affectionate. He was very encouraging and supportive. He would spend hours making me dive for catches, or bowling to me. Mind, if we were playing catch up-hill, he'd be at the higher point, so if I missed it I've have to go all the way to the bottom of the hill to get the ball. When he bowled at me on Bognor beach, he'd bowl with the wind, and when he acceded to my imploring him to take me to the recreation ground near the house we rented on the Chichester Road, I would have to run to fetch the ball whether I missed it or hit it. There was a premium on defensive shots played straight back down the pitch.

In those days, if you were to play for Yorkshire you had to be born in the county (there was one perhaps mythical exception, on moral grounds it seems, for an individual careless enough to have been born on a plane, who got special dispensation to be eligible for the county on the grounds that his parents were trying so hard to get back to give birth in the promised land). My father used to joke that he should have got my mother onto the train north for my birth. But times were hard in 1942.

So, beyond the local influences and heroes, there were Middlesex and Yorkshire. Middlesex foremost. The year my father played for the county, 1949, was the first in which I followed first-class cricket. It was also the season when Middlesex and Yorkshire shared the County Championship. The first four Middlesex batsmen were Jack Robertson, Sid Brown, Edrich and Compton. But I chose Robertson as my hero, rather than either of the more flamboyant and dramatic pair. Jack opened the batting, was a correct, neat player, quick on his feet. I find it interesting that I preferred him, especially in light of the kind of player I became, and the more modest, Robertson-like role I played. Oddly, our career averages were virtually identical. Perhaps my choosing him had something to do with his scoring 331 not out, in a day, at Worcester in 1949, a wondrous feat to a seven-year-old fan.

When I was ten, I went to the City of London School, next to Blackfriars Bridge, where my father taught maths and cricket, and sang in the choir. (His first teaching job in London after the war had been at Sloane Grammar School. The headmaster ran the choir and was a good musician. Horace wanted to join the choir. The head told him he'd have to audition. 'All right,' said Horace, 'I'll sing to you if you sing to me.' So they happily sang to each other, and my father got the job and joined the choir.)

At eleven I scored my first century, against Forest School. And around that time, I was able to bowl leg-breaks and googlies, once taking 8 wickets for 21 against Dulwich College. But as I grew, I could no longer spin or control the ball.

When I was fifteen, the school employed Reg Routledge, an ex-Middlesex professional, to do some coaching. He taught me to allow my hands to flow through the shot, enabling me to hit the ball on the up on the non-deviating, skiddy, composite pitches recently installed in the playground.

A year or two later I had my first playing link with Lord's, though I had been there a few times, once watching Compton score 70 or so against Worcestershire; I remember only one ball of that innings. Roly Jenkins, the leg-spinner, was bowling from the Nursery End. Compton came yards down the wicket, but misjudged the length. Jenkins must have thought at last he had him, but as the ball went past him, Compton brilliantly late cut it. I once saw Robertson score a century at Lord's, too.

I also went to a Test match against Australia, and while it rained, bought for a shilling a little booklet with scorecards of all the Tests played between the countries up to then. Thus names like Spofforth and Bannerman became known to me. (Earlier, aged five, I had dug a hole in the back garden to get to Australia.)

But now, at sixteen, on Monday evenings (an extra bonus being that I thereby got out of the compulsory Combined Cadet Force) I was coached by Jim Sims, who had played in that Yorkshire vs Middlesex match at Sheffield in 1937.

Jim was a strange, kindly man, with a confidential manner. His advice to a young cricketer, as I recall, was a mixture of platitudes, patiently reinforced, and obscurities. For instance: 'A straight ball, Michael, has a certain lethal quality about it.' (Pause for effect.) 'If you miss it you've 'ad it.' And then: 'Do you follow me, Michael?' Or: 'I once took eight wickets against Sussex at Lord's. The *Evening News* report said, "Sims took eight wickets, six of them from long-'ops." What they didn't say,

Michael, was that five of them long-'ops were straight long-'ops.' He once asked me why 'Bloodnut' (Bob Hurst, a slow left-armer on the Middlesex staff) 'would never make a first-class cricketer'. When I admitted I had no idea, he revealed, enigmatically, 'Because he's not properly shod.' Sometimes I didn't follow Jim.

Jim told me that he was sure I'd play for Middlesex. He was not quite sure if I'd play for England. His judgement was accurate and might easily have been how things turned out. By 1959 I was playing for Middlesex Young Amateurs (as they were called) and the next year for Middlesex Second XI.

Jim was a strange mixture of the canny and the naïve. In the 1970s he became Middlesex scorer. He would arrive for lunch at the Players' Dining Room at Lord's in his long beige raincoat, with capacious pockets. These he would fill with cans of beer (still then placed on the lunch table as routine refreshment for players in the middle of a day's play). He needed warming up in the draughty scorebox on cold days, and cooling down on hot ones. One of the many stories told about him referred to his teenage years on the ground staff at Lord's. Occasionally these youngsters would be included in MCC out-matches against schools and clubs. In his first match, smartly dressed in blazer and tie, he was asked his name by the captain. 'Sims,' he said; 'Jim Sims.' 'OK, Sims,' said the captain, 'you can bat at number ten.' Next match he again turned up early, impeccably dressed. The captain asked him his name. 'Morton-Sims, sir; James Morton-Sims.' 'Ah, Morton-Sims,' said the captain, deferentially, 'would you care to bat at number three?'

2

'THEN I KNEW WE HAD A CHANCE'

In 1962, Tony Lewis was captain, and I was Secretary, of Cambridge University Cricket Club. A first-year undergraduate had recently played his first games. His father invited Tony and me to dinner at the Garden House Hotel. The father was Sir Leonard Hutton, the son, Richard, who later followed his father in playing for Yorkshire and England.

Len's generosity had its motives. 'You've not yet seen the best of our Richard,' he said. 'It's this Economics he's reading. It's not easy. I've looked at his books.' Over the succeeding years, Len came to watch Richard, and Cambridge, play, and I would sometimes drive Richard to his home, near Kingston, from matches. When he failed to direct me or follow the map, Richard would complain in a baleful way about how 'In the south of England all the roads look alike', as if there were no similar roads in the north.

Thus I came to know Len, and became fond of the family.

But first, something about his cricket. Herbert Sutcliffe, who played in the match my father played in, in 1937, said of his young opening partner: 'I'm only setting up these records for Hutton to break them.'

I don't remember seeing him bat, which is a sadness. I've seen those rather miserly and distant clips of him during his 364 at the Oval in 1938. He looks relaxed, flowing, careful. He moved easily between the wickets. He had what we would now call 'soft hands'.

According to cricket correspondent, John Woodcock, he was as natural a player, as capable of playing appropriately in the situation, as Joe Root, though of course the latter plays in a lot of different contexts from those Len played in. In 2002, Micky Stewart, the Surrey and England opener, compared Michael Vaughan (then at his best) to Hutton. 'When running between the wickets, he even carries his bat under his left arm, just like Len.'

There seem to be different accounts of the changes made by the six years of war, and the broken arm and bone grafts from the injury in the gym that led to Hutton's left arm being two inches shorter than the right one. After the war, by all accounts, he didn't hook; and some said he was more cautious. But he had also been criticized for slow scoring before 1939. I imagine that he got used to his shorter arm, and was not much hampered by it. He did get a 50 per cent disability pension for his injury, which must have pleased him.

Picked out by the Australians for special treatment, as the key England batsman, he had to face Ray Lindwall and Keith Miller in their prime. Richie Benaud and Alan Davidson said of him that they never saw anyone with a better technique.

He was also a genius at playing on uncovered pitches. I remember listening to the crackly radio broadcast from Brisbane in 1950. Having won the toss, Australia were all out for 228. That night there was a storm, and a leaky tarpaulin. On the resultant 'sticky dog', England captain Freddie Brown held Hutton back to number 6, and declared on 68 for 7, Hutton not out 8. (In retrospect I can't understand this; you leave your best player to number six and then declare when he is still batting? In fact the situation was even more bizarre; Brown had Hutton down to go in number five from the start, and had picked reserve wicket-keeper Arthur McIntyre as a specialist batsman.) Alec Bedser and Trevor Bailey reduced Australia to 32 for 7, when they in turn declared. Set 193 to win, on an obviously near-unplayable pitch, but one that was going to get slightly easier when drier the next morning, Hutton (again) and Compton were held back, eventually going in at eight and nine. That evening, McIntyre was run out for 7 going for a fourth run. This was to my highly critical eight-year-old mind, the greatest cricketing sin I'd heard of. Run out, for a fourth, when his job was to stay in as long as he could until the pitch eased out! England were 30 for 6 overnight. McIntyre never got over his chagrin. 'Christ,' he said decades later, 'if I could have walked off the ground the other way and not had to face Freddie Brown, I would have done.'

Next morning Hutton scored 62 not out of the 92 runs that England's last four wickets managed. Of the last-wicket partnership of 45 with Hutton, Doug Wright scored 2. Jack Fingleton wrote: 'England lost because they had only one Hutton. Just half another Hutton would have been sufficient.'

In 1963 the Gillette Cup was introduced. For the first time, professional cricket teams played limited-overs cricket, 65 overs each side, soon coming down to 60. Richard Hutton was scathing about it. Definitively, as if it were an eternal truth, he pronounced: 'It's not cricket.' (Though when

Yorkshire won in 1965, thanks to Geoff Boycott's remarkable 146, Richard, opening the bowling with Fred Trueman, bowled 8 overs for 17 runs and Yorkshire won by the comfortable margin of 175 runs, so Richard was probably unwilling to consider this match, at least, 'not cricket.')

Richard's bluntness was almost the opposite of his father's characteristically faltering, apparently naïve, uncertainty. Len's take on one-day cricket around the same time was: 'In this limited-overs cricket, the thing is, it doesn't matter if you get out. Fancy that, batting without worrying about getting out.' For Len, this did seem to contradict the first law of batting. You owed it to your side, you owed it to yourself, to stay in. On his slender shoulders the England batting often rested.

Apart from his batting, Len was England's first professional captain. Colin Cowdrey writes an appreciative and perceptive account of the tour of Australia in 1954–5, which Len captained. He was an extraordinary mixture of the shrewd and the naïve. On landing at Perth, he was asked about the prospects for the tour. 'Actually we've come out here to learn a thing or two from you . . . We've got one or two batsmen, I suppose. We've not got much bowling, really. We've got these young chaps, what's their names? Statham, Tyson, but they've 'ardly bowled.' A masterly performance.

Len had a healthy regard for sheer speed. In the run-up to the first Test, at Sydney against New South Wales, Len said: 'Neil Harvey – he could play a bit, Harvey, you know – had to take his pad off to rub his leg, when Frank [Tyson] hit him on the shin. That's when I knew we had a chance.'

And I love his studied ploy when the young Benaud came in to bat. Hutton knew he wasn't good against Tyson. Early in his innings, when Benaud was facing, Hutton would allow the fielders to get into their positions. As the bowler was about to run in for the first ball, Hutton would hold his hand up, and say, 'Hang on a minute, where's Frank?' He'd look round the field as if unable to locate him, despite his being at his usual fine leg or third man. 'Come and have a bowl, Frank.' Poor Benaud must have been quaking in his boots.

He also surprised Cowdrey when the latter was batting shortly before lunch in one Test, by sending twelfth man Vic Wilson out to the middle in his MCC blazer, carrying a silver salver with a bunch of bananas on it. 'What's all this about?' asked the bewildered Cowdrey. 'I rather think the captain doesn't want you to get out before lunch,' said Wilson, drily. 'He wonders if you're hungry.'

Len was sparing with his words, especially when anxious about captaincy. He did, I'm told, respond to requests for a cricketing chat from his players, but he could also go days hardly speaking. Geoffrey Howard, manager of that tour, who knew him as well as anyone in the cricket world, described him as an enigma: 'so often when alone he switches on the radio and sits looking at the wall'. One evening he knocked on the door of Brian Statham's and Frank Tyson's room. They were having a drink with two young women. Len said: 'Better get ready for tomorrow's Test. Good night.' The girls left immediately.

On a different note, he was paternal and kind to Cowdrey on that tour. The latter's father had died while they were on-board ship, and he had received the news in Colombo. Hutton took him under his wing.

When Len retired from first-class cricket in 1955, Alan Ross wrote a fine piece called 'Hutton departs'. He records conversations with Len on the topic mentioned above: on his longing to play without having to worry about getting out.

Ross describes Hutton's classicism:

Self-sufficiency, I suppose, is one of the true marks of the artist, and Hutton has been self-sufficient as a cricketer to the point of often seeming disinterested. He seemed at moments unutterably wearied by it. The context of Hutton's cricket, the bleak decade when he almost alone – Compton and Bedser were allies – preserved its dignity, has been such that grace and levity seemed almost excluded as indecencies. Compton, born under a warmer star, has combined these attributes as if in defiance. His genius is romantic and individual. Hutton never made such an appeal, His art has existed within precise technical limits. It would have been as unthinkable for Hutton the man to step outside the figure of Hutton the batsman, as it would have been for Nijinsky suddenly to assert his own personality while dancing the faun.

He continues:

It is in precisely this subservience of the personal to the impersonal, this sacrificing the imp of human impulse to the demands of the situation, that classicism consists. Hutton has been the embodiment of so many classical ideas – discipline, restraint, concentration, correctness and elegance of execution – that he came to be thought of as an abstraction, infallible and incapable of improvisation.

He was not, Ross goes on, either infallible or unable to improvise. In 1948, he 'conquered majestically a fallibility against fast hostile bowling': in 1946–7 in Australia he showed, when forced to it, 'powers of improvisation never hitherto suspected, of an order of which only the greatest are capable'.

He could, of course, play every stroke – except perhaps the hook, but then the hook is a luxury and Hutton's technical vocabulary, though complete, was spare in character – but he showed flashes during his great post-war seasons, flashes as rewarding as his own smile, the lightening of his eyes – those amazingly light wide eyes, revealing perhaps his Moravian ancestry – he took pleasure in playing the rare more dangerous ones. Only however when necessary; it remained an axiom of Hutton's batting that economy was all, that flourishes were an indulgence and no part of perfection, no matter how esoteric and complex perfection may be adjudged to be.

And here Alan Ross makes a wonderful link, quoting a remark of Hutton's that was echoed a decade later when he spoke to me of not having to worry about getting out: 'I refrain from saying too much', he had written to Ross not long before he retired. 'I am Yorkshire-bred and born, you know. I have bought a drink but not too often.'

And when he was already out of Test cricket, but not scoring too many runs, he once said to Ross: 'A hundred or two will put me right, a few runs' – and he looked up quizzically, as if he found them strange words to say, 'made just for fun'.

One word Ross applies to Len's batting was 'ascetic'. It seems right. It went against his grain to play 'for fun', it was indulgent to have too much of a flourish. He was classic, in his restraint, in his orthodoxy, in his care. His appeal lay in this elegant near-perfection of restraint. And yet somewhere he did long to play when 'it doesn't matter if you get out', to play, at least once or twice, with abandon; 'for fun'. For Len I imagine batting was more often work than play, hard work, more discipline than improvisation, more control than spontaneity.

He was born under a different star from Compton. He once went to meet Compton in the middle of the pitch when Lindwall and Miller were bowling. His dry comment was: 'There must be easier ways of earning a living than this.' Compton was an entertainer. At a less important game, he'd say to his batting partner, 'There aren't many people here . . . I shan't be out here long'. It would have been unimaginable for Hutton to say this.

At Adelaide in 1954–5, Tyson, Statham and Bob Appleyard bowled Australia out for 111 in the second innings, leaving England 97 to win. Miller took three early wickets, including Hutton's; England were 18 for 3. Len was reputed to have said, morosely: The 'boogers 'ave done us again.' Compton about to go in, standing next to him, said: 'But I haven't been in yet.' 'Ah know, ah know,' said Len. In the event, Compton saw England home by five wickets, scoring 34 not out.

Hutton and Compton never really got on.

Doug Insole recalled, however, an occasion in the summer of 1990. Both these great players were in a box at Lord's. They had a drink, and at lunch went to the buffet at the back of the box to fill their plates. And then sat down next to each other, and talked. They didn't get up till after tea, talking just to each other. When one left, the other said, 'See you next time.' A month later Len was dead. But they had that long afternoon of rapprochement.

Not long before, Insole had been sitting with Len and his wife Dorothy at Lord's when Graham Gooch scored his triple century against India. As Gooch approached and then passed 300, Len got more and more silent. He was an occasional smoker, but on this occasion he smoked non-stop, puffing quickly on each cigarette, and then stubbing it out. The pile of long cigarette ends became a small pyramid on the ash-tray. At one point, Dorothy said: 'Leonard, if he does score 365, the cameras will be trained on you; they all know you're here. You'd better look a bit pleased, and then say the right thing.' Len said nothing, but went on leaning back in his chair, chain-smoking, filling the ash-tray. At last Gooch got out, for 333. At this moment, Doug says, Leonard leaped out his chair, saying for all to hear, 'He's a very fine player, a very fine player, what an innings!'

3

THE DARLING BUDS OF MAY

Shall I compare thee to a summer's day?
Thou art more lovely and more temperate:
Rough winds do shake the darling buds of May,
And summer's lease hath all too short a date . . .

If, after the war, cricket meant to millions of English people the return of normality, Denis Compton and Bill Edrich represented the arrival of a brand new spring, the rebirth of flamboyance, instinct and pleasure in a grey world of bombsites, ration-cards and austerity. They were indeed the darling buds of May.

Compton particularly soon became a household name and face, to an extent shared in those days only by film stars. During the 1946 season, a visitor to the Middlesex dressing room, Bagenal Harvey, saw three thousand unopened letters addressed to Compton scattered on ledges and window sills. Harvey offered to manage Compton's affairs, and get the letters answered. Thus began the first sportsman/promoter-manager relationship, with 10 per cent (or more) commission and the expansion of image from back page to bill board. Compton, ironically the least mercenary of men, became the first English cricketer to use his association with a commercial product – Brylcreem – that was unrelated to the game. He was a natural for stardom, primarily because of his sheer brilliance and skill as a sportsman, but also because of

his boyish good looks, personal charm, and a capacity to treat as old friends people he had forgotten.

Compton handled success with unforced modesty. His contemporaries, their amused affection tinged with awe, recall him without envy or resentment. There was 'nothing to dislike him for'. He 'never played for himself'. He was 'marvellously easy, helpful in a delightful way,' said George Mann, captain of Middlesex in 1948 and 1949.

He could fail to appreciate the problems experienced by the ordinary player: 'Why don't you get on with it, Harry?' he said to Harry Sharp, later Middlesex scorer, whose connection with him went back to 1933, when he joined Denis on the ground staff at Lord's. 'But I can't, Denis.' In this failing, though, he was not more than momentarily unthinking, never carping or judgemental. And he was characteristically generous to lesser players. Mike Murray, who played as an amateur in the 1950s, recalls Denis coming in to the dressing room from the balcony when Murray got out to give him some tips about moving later against the swinging ball. He 'went out of his way to help'. On the other hand, his son Patrick is reported to have said that Denis would tell him that he was coming to see him play when he was at Marlborough School, and regularly not appear.

Even his reputation for being a shocking caller and runner between the wickets was exaggerated. According to Sharp, the Middlesex scorer, his 'running between the wickets was not as bad as it was made out to be; far better than Mike Gatting's'. Fred Titmus, the Middlesex and England all-rounder, adds that many of the run-outs occurred largely because the rest of the team were terrified of causing his dismissal, so they would not send him back firmly when there was a dubious call.

As a batsman, his wonderful improvisations were founded on a basic copy-book technique. If his batting had a limitation, it was perhaps in his rarely hitting straight; yet when Walter Robins, the captain, once teased him at the tea interval about having boringly omitted to hit the ball back over the bowler's head, he took care to remedy the omission in the over after tea, even nominating, correctly, which ball was to end up in the pavilion.

He had his occasional struggles, too. In 1946, he scored ten runs in five innings. In the next innings, against Warwickshire, before he'd scored, the ball trickled back onto his off-stump without dislodging a bail. In relief and desperation Compton decided that, come what may, the next ball would have to go. He smashed spinner Eric Hollies over the top, scored a century, and for the next five years forgot about struggling. Rough winds did shake him again in 1950–1, when he averaged less than ten in the series in Australia, a tour in which the famous knee, injured in the Cup Final the previous May, troubled him continuously.

I asked Denis if he premeditated any of his audacious strokes. He couldn't tell me. What he did say was that he 'looked to go on the back foot against the quickest bowlers'. But it was rare that Compton had to worry, or think his way out of trouble. His pre-season practice was said to consist of playing a few 'air-shots' in the dressing room half an hour before play on the first day of the season, his sole preparation. (He himself claimed to have enjoyed knocking up for ten minutes on the outfield and practising on the slip cradle.) He 'simply', as John Arlott wrote in 1947, 'plays – like a boy striking at a rubber ball with a paling from a fence – for fun'. Indeed, though he never used a paling, stories abounded of his borrowing any bat – someone's discard, perhaps – left in the bottom of a Lord's locker – and putting it to magical use. (He even once borrowed mine, in a match at the Lord's Nursery Ground in about 1958, when I was still at school. I was more worried about my bat than honoured by the identity of the borrower.)

Fellow Middlesex-cricketer, and later coach, Don Bennett, recalled an innings against Sussex on a drying pitch at Lord's in 1955: 'The shot that just was not on in such conditions was the cover drive "on the up"; Compo kept hitting fours past cover, on the up. He scored 150 out of 206 all out. The next highest scorer was tail-ender John Warr, with 13.'

Titmus agreed. Batting at the other end, he would feel, '"You can't do that!", until the scoreboard showed Compton 120 not out and we had to say, "*You* can."'

For the record, Compton scored 38,942 runs in 839 innings at an average of 51.85. He scored 123 centuries. His Test average was 50.06.

He also took 622 wickets with his flowing Chinamen and googlies.

Warr, captain of Middlesex in the 1950s, tells of an August Bank Holiday match at Hove. Flustered, Denis arrived on the field at 12.55, an hour and a half late, ingenuously surprised by the amount of traffic. Sussex were 70 for 1. Robins barked at him, 'Now you've turned up you'd better have a bowl.' In the half-hour to lunch, bowling in gym-shoes, he took three wickets.

Denis was always modest about his beginnings. He acknowledged the support he had from his sports master at Bell Lane School, Hendon; and from his father, who had a small painting-and-decorating business and was a keen amateur sportsman. At fourteen, he was, he said, 'lucky enough' to score a hundred for the Elementary Schools against the Public Schools. Pelham Warner, watching the match, offered him, through his parents, a contract on the Lord's ground staff for the next season. His mother, who thought the Civil Service a sounder bet, refused, asking, 'What about the other eight months?' Soon the answer came: Arsenal offered him a winter contract as a footballer. Thus was the Civil Service saved from Denis Compton!

He served his apprenticeship at Lord's, bowling at members in the nets ('the new boys got the one who didn't give tips!', he told me), playing on Sundays and in MCC out-matches. He was not, Sharp said, much good at selling scorecards. For Middlesex II, Denis recalled a partnership of 98 against Kent with Jim Swanton, of which Swanton, improbably, scored more than half. At eighteen, in 1936, he was picked for the first team as a bowler, batting (for the last time in his life) at number 11. When he came in to join 'Old Gubby' (Allen, then 33 years old), Middlesex needed 25 for a first-innings lead. They got them, but

Maurice Tate was 'past his best' and he was 'lucky'. (Tate's analysis in the innings was, incidentally: 30 overs, 6 wickets for 48.)

Denis himself rated his 76 not out against Australia at Lord's in 1938 as his best-ever innings. He came in on a hard pitch whose top had been softened by rain, in a crisis, with the score 76 for 5. With typical modesty, he dwelt not on his innings but on the match, which 'we nearly won, and would have if Bradman had been given out lbw off Edrich, plumb in front on the back foot'.

He didn't bear grudges. Wally Hammond was said not to have much encouraged the younger player, perhaps out of envy. But the worst Denis had to say about him was that, when Hammond, the tour captain in Australia in 1946–7, after some months at last gave him a match off (for the up-country game at Bendigo), it 'didn't go down too well when I was named twelfth man!'

Compton was not only a modest and generous genius; he was also courageous and unselfish. He was never afraid. His batting may often have been delicate and impudent, charmingly insouciant. But it was also tough and resolute, as he showed in what many judged to be his finest innings, when he scored 145 not out at Old Trafford in 1948. The pitch was continually topped up and enlivened by showers, the bowlers freshened by delays, the light bad. For much of his innings he had stitches in his head, cut by a Lindwall bouncer. Here he was not just 'playing for fun'.

As for his unselfishness, Titmus attested that, though Compton was not averse to getting more than his share of the strike, he never, unlike many a fine player, avoided the rough end; he took it all, and the younger players were able to watch him from the bowler's end.

I wondered how this born sportsman coped with the inevitable decline of nature's gifts: with life after his sporting career. Denis agreed it *was* a problem; at the time he knew only that he did not want to coach. He did commentate, on TV and in the papers. But his main work was, and continued to be, in advertising. As he put it, he did 'quite enjoy it'. In Warr's words, he rode it well, and for the rest of his life people gravitated towards him when he entered a room. But it cannot have been easy, and perhaps the strain showed.

At times, his gold complexion dimmed by one or two too many gins, he was unable to bear gladly a later generation of cricketing fools. In the 1970s he once loudly voiced his disappointment at the incompetence of the current Middlesex players. Some of us found this hard to take, especially from the man who was forever acclaimed as the epitome of the county's Golden Age. His views on life became fixed, politically somewhere to the right of the MCC Committee (which had itself, not so long before, been described by Lord Monckton as making the Conservative Cabinet look like a 'bunch of pinkos').

To me, he volunteered, on the subject of his birthplace, that it was 'next door to Margaret Thatcher's constituency'. His championing of South Africa during the years of its sporting exclusion was so bellicose that his old friend Allen asked him please to talk about anything other than South Africa. Nick Cosh, who played for Cambridge after me, wrote to tell me of meeting Compton before an English Schools tour of South Africa in 1965. 'I must', he continued, 'have made a comment about apartheid. This prompted Compton to say: "That's the trouble with you and Brearley, you Cambridge intellectuals . . ."' I once outraged him at a party at New Zealand House in the Haymarket for not knowing that it was St George's Day, and for not being particularly roused by the information. (I wonder which way Compton would have voted on Brexit?)

It must have been galling to him not to be invited to the celebrations of South African cricket, in 1991, presumably because his support would have been embarrassing to the new South Africa.

When I interviewed him he had been unwell. As Colin Ingleby-Mackenzie, captain of Hampshire from 1958 to 1965, put it, this illness was a 'salutary shot across the bows, which should help him to steam staunchly into his 90s'. Compton had by then a young family: two daughters aged fifteen and eight, by his third wife. Five years before, at his seventieth birthday party, his nineteen-year-old South African grandson, meeting Denis's daughter (then aged four) said, 'I suppose I'd better call you auntie.' No doubt his daughters kept him lively.

Ingleby-Mackenzie told me of their first meeting, in 1952 at Portsmouth, when he himself, aged nineteen and just out of Eton, was about to play his fifth match for Hampshire. When the great man generously calmed his nerves over coffee, the youth addressed him as 'Sir'. As he walked off towards the dressing room, Denis called after him. 'Young man, two things. One, never call me "Sir" again; and, two, may I borrow your *Sporting Life*?' That memorable day, Ingleby was bowled by Compton for 61; the three horses picked by Edrich and the two of them all won; and the 'young man' drank late into the night with his two heroes. Forty years on, they continued their joint celebration of their sporting life.

PART 2

THE ASH

PART 2

THE ASHES

4

THE GNAWED UMBRELLA HANDLE AND
THE BURNED BAIL

Nineteen of my 39 Tests were against Australia, 18 of them as captain. Fifteen were designated as Ashes Tests, that is, for the (virtual) possession of the little urn. The three in 1979–80 were not so designated, as they did not constitute a full series, which has always been a feature. Nor of course was the Centenary Test, in 1977.

Every two years Ashes series are scheduled, in alternating countries. And each time people want to read or hear Ashes stories. What is it like to play in them? What is it like to play in Australia? What is different in captaining in an Ashes series? Ten/twenty/thirty years on, tell us about the 1981 series.

I suspect that this fascination is similar to that of children's bedtime stories. We all want to hear the familiar stories that excited us in the past. There may be new revelations; but basically it's the same old narratives retold. We know the outcome, but can relive the tension in the light of known, and sometimes reassuring, finales. We re-read heroic sagas of old, of the irascible Goose tearing downhill at Headingley to take 8 wickets for 43 in 1981, for instance. Families delight in sharing again and again the same old stories, mixtures of history and myth: 'You remember the time the front wheel came off the old Ford, and rolled off down the hill ahead of the car?!'

My foreword to Ian Botham's autobiography (1994) started

somewhat like this: 'Once upon a time, when giants were giants, there was a Giant. On ordinary days he was a friendly giant, but some days he became an ogre, eating Australians, Pakistanis, Indians and New Zealanders for breakfast . . . He was not choosy about his menu, though he was less good at catching West Indians, and Pakistanis he maintained were a bit stringy.'

And, of course, there is the element of myth, derived from the Greek word which simply means 'story' but which has the overtones of supernatural events, of fantasies that are formative of our ideas about our tribe (and of course of rival tribes). The events of 1981 fit in with our national mythology of winning against the odds, of the darkest hour, of the Battle of Britain.

The long Ashes history, beginning in 1882 (though the first Test match was in 1877), uninterrupted except for world wars, has of course a lot to do with it. So has colonialism, the larrikins paying back their snobbish rulers, the raw harshness of the outback alternating with the elegance and superiority of class-conscious Lord's, baking heat erupting occasionally into sub-tropical storms on one side, against drizzle, cloud and visits by the Queen on the other.

And the story of the origin of the word 'Ashes', and the urn with its alleged contents of the burned bails, is quite a tale. It starts with the *Sporting Times*'s mock obituary on English cricket after the Oval Test in 1882, in which Australia had the effrontery to beat England on home soil by seven runs, a match featuring the umbrella handle bitten through by an agonized English spectator, an umbrella as famous as that of the assassin of a Bulgarian on Waterloo Bridge with a poison-infected blade hidden in its Cold War point.

The story is developed by Scyld Berry and Rupert Peploe in their book *Cricket's Burning Passion*. There we read about the Hon. Ivo Bligh, captaining England on their subsequent tour, during which he fell in love with Florence, a young governess living with a family at Rupertswood, near Melbourne. (It has everything, the Ashes story.)

So tell us a story, Daddy. That one about Headingley. Or the (invented) one about the Giant walking into the lamppost at 4 a.m. in the town square in Brisbane, and the city demanding payment for damage done to its property. Or of the luggage handlers at Perth saying 'Welcome to 'Strylia. If Lillee don't get yer, Thommo will. And carry your own bags.'

Wilfred Bion, who became after the Second World War a leading British psychoanalyst, in 1917 had to go out onto duckboards in no-man's land to see if the tank he commanded might be salvageable from the mud in which it had got stuck. When he asked what the sounds he heard there were, he was told they were the gasps and cries of men drowning in the mud. Decades later, he imagines a child (or a part of himself) saying, 'Don't go down into the mud, don't go down into the unconscious, Daddy.'

Other stories, other horrors. 'Mike, Mike,' five-year-old Richard Scholar told me, stammering with apprehension after seeing TV highlights of an MCC tour of Australia I had been on, 'some of those balls were . . . were . . . were . . . absolutely shocking.' I could only agree.

So this section alludes to some of these stories, these myths that heighten expectation and a sense of significance, tending to reduce the degree of luck involved in it all. History is done backwards, life is lived forwards.

I comment on (probably) the greatest ever series (2005), as well as on 1981. I include a piece on Douglas Jardine and the Bodyline series – how he won the Ashes but almost lost a Dominion. And I end with a piece comparing Botham with the other great fast-bowling all-rounders of the past sixty years.

5

RAKING THROUGH THE ASHES

An Ashes series must be not only the most sustained but also the most anticipated bilateral international fixture in any sport. Football is the bigger game, but there is none of the regularity of meetings between, say, England and Germany, or Italy and Brazil, that we have in cricket. And Lions rugby tours of South Africa, Australia and New Zealand, which have the éclat of regular but not too frequent series, don't quite have the history or mythology to inflate them.

As Ian Botham once said: 'It's been going on for a long, long time; we still hate each other, and it's wonderful!'

Two series in my time stand out, especially in beleaguered and often-defeated England, as reinforcing the mythic quality of the Ashes. One was England's win in 2005, captained by Michael Vaughan.

The other was 1981, Botham's Ashes (though also Willis's). I captained the last four Tests in this series, which we eventually won 3–1, with two matches drawn.

How difficult it is now to look back without rosy tints in one's glasses. How difficult to remember afresh that summer and its extraordinary games, to free myself from the habitual and no doubt cliché-ridden versions of them – think how hard it is to recall cherished holidays from long ago in a newly detailed way.

In retrospect it's tempting to see the chain of events as not only inevitable but morally appropriate. We were bound to win; we won because we deserved to, and we deserved to because of some ineffable quality or spirit lacking in the opposition. Through lenses of nostalgia and historical determinism, we easily feel that things could not have been different.

Yet how different it might have been! How small the margins in each of the first two of the Tests we won: at Headingley (Ian Botham 149 not out, Bob Willis 8 for 43), a mere 19 runs; at Edgbaston (Botham 5 wickets for 1 run), 29 runs.

And how many times at Headingley did Botham play and miss on what was a horrible pitch for batting, or carve the ball over the slips? What if Rod Marsh had got an eighth of an inch more bat on the hook that Graham Dilley caught a yard inside the fine-leg boundary on that last afternoon, or if Mike Gatting and Botham himself had not caught excellent catches an inch or two off the ground in the over before lunch on the same day?

Indeed, on the evening of the first day at Headingley, also my first day back as captain, when Australia were 210 for 3, I was convinced I – or we – had made a serious error in picking four seamers and omitting our only specialist spinner, John Emburey. I'd been picked for my captaincy, and I was convinced the first decision I'd made was wrong.

Moreover, if we had done the conventional thing and picked Emburey, the person who might well have been left out was none other than my old friend Willis, who had been suffering from a virus, an infection of no-balls, and loss of form.

So, luck plays a huge part.

Compare 2005. England won at Edgbaston by two runs. On the first morning of the match, the great Glenn McGrath trod on a ball in the outfield, turned his ankle over, and was unfit to play. For want of a nail a kingdom is lost. For the random placing of a stationary ball a hero is removed from the battlefield. And of course that was not the only chance event. How many thousands of moments might have made that two or three run difference? Take just one ball, the penultimate

one of the match. Steve Harmison had bowled magnificently. With Australia needing only four runs for victory, he attempted a yorker to Brett Lee. Instead, he was a couple of feet off the right length, and a few inches off the right line, which meant that he presented the batsman with any tail-ender's dream ball – a low full toss outside off-stump. It's hard to get out to such a ball, it's even hard not to score off it. Lee met it with the full face of the bat; the ball sped towards the boundary over the fast turf, but as chance had it, within easy reach of deep cover. Five yards either side and the match was over. One run, not four. Death not glory!

Next ball, a short one, brushed the glove of number eleven batsman, Michael Kasprowicz, was caught by keeper Geraint Jones, and the game was over – though here too luck played a further part: close-up replays showed that the gloved hand was not on the bat at the moment when the ball hit it. Kasprowicz should not have been given out.

A moment later, Andrew Flintoff, England's fine all-rounder, left the huddle of his own team celebrating victory (and relief), to put his arm round a disconsolate Lee, crouching beside the pitch, who had himself batted with courage and panache to get Australia so close.

However, not everything is entirely down to the vagaries of chance, or to the particular, unpredictable actions of individuals when they find themselves in the cauldron of conflict. Morale and strategies – even the strategy of being suspicious of strategies – also need fostering, nurturing. We need not necessarily go along with Fred Trueman's judgement at the end of the Headingley Test, that Botham's performance came one match too late; that is, that it was simply fortuitous that he happened on success in his first match after being relieved of, or relieving himself of, the captaincy. I don't agree.

Botham had captained England in the previous twelve Tests, nine against the West Indies at more or less the height of their powers, and three against Australia, probably the next best side in the world at that time. I wrote to him when he was in Jamaica with a piece of advice: he should try captaining England against someone else.

In my view, he had lost confidence with ball and bat since being under the added pressure of captaincy for fourteen months. It wasn't accidental that it was only when he was no longer captain that he did so well. I have no doubt that, for match-winning performances to become, once again, possible for him, he needed someone to bounce off, someone who would bear the responsibility and anxiety of being in charge, and who would both provoke and encourage him.

At Headingley in 1981 I remember the interchange I had with him about his bowling on the first day of the match. I took him off after three nondescript overs. He was outraged. 'How can I bowl in three-over spells?' he demanded. 'And how can I keep you on if you bowl medium-paced half-volleys?' I retorted. This exchange, along with my calling him the Sidestep Queen (for his exaggerated step-in towards the stumps in the hope of making the ball swing, an uncharacteristic shimmy, which took away his directness and speed), stirred him into a more purposive and vigorous forcefulness when bowling. He took six

39

wickets in that Australian first innings.

When he batted in our first innings, after playing an attacking shot at a ball from Dennis Lillee that flew past his gloves from just short of a length, he looked up to where I was sitting on the players' balcony. I think he was nervous that I might be critical of his boldness. Instead, I gave him full licence to hit out, to play with exuberance; he could be the blacksmith on the village green. He was not called upon to mimic the squirearchy in batting respectability.

It would also, I think, have been hard for anyone other than me, as captain, at that point, to interact with him so directly and provocatively. I had been his first Test captain. And it would have been even more difficult for anyone to speak with that sort of frankness to Botham when he himself was captain.

I feel confident that he could not have batted or bowled as he did had he continued as captain. Not that Botham agrees with this now, any more than he would have then! He, I imagine, shares Trueman's view.

Does anything new come into the mind after all these years? Or is memory stuck? Are we limited to versions already imposed?

One thing that occasionally carries me back to that strange summer of 1981 is the BBC's video *Botham's Ashes*, with its own particular take on the series. At the moment in the film when Ian is acknowledging the applause for his remarkable century, the camera pans to the players' balcony, and focuses on my gesture to the batsmen. I am pointing in an angry, determined, insistent way. What did this mean?

In his commentary Richie Benaud generously gives me the credit for telling Chris Old to play his shots. I think what I meant was more complex. I was in favour of that, but I also wanted someone to rivet Old's back foot before it made its involuntary jerk backwards. I wanted Ian, too, to see that we had this real though outside chance of actually winning the match. At the same time, I did not at all want him suddenly to start taking himself solemnly. It's as if I was saying: 'This is now serious, it is no longer a gallant, moving but ultimately useless gesture or frolic in the face of defeat, like that of the sailor in the war film who, at the instant before the curtain falls on his life, and he disappears forever beneath the freezing Baltic in the aftermath of the sinking of his ship, raises his hat and bows with mock gallantry.' I did indeed want Old to fashion his own style, which he did to vital effect in scoring 29 and adding 67 runs with Botham, enlarging our meagre lead from 25 (for 8, in effect) to 92, a target that would, when amplified by the last-wicket stand of 39, give us just that sniff of hope. But I fear that my gesture also betrayed a more restrictive attitude than Benaud suggested. It was not so clear-cut a message.

Another puzzle about this match lies in the transformation in Willis's bowling between one innings and the next. Several of us did talk with him on the night before the last day. My memory is that it was Graham Gooch and Gatting, supported by Botham and me, who encouraged Willis to forget about no-balls (with which he had recently been plagued), and simply bowl as fast and straight as he could. It was, in dressing-room parlance, a shit-or-bust scenario. Without the desperate hope of an almost lost cause, and the chance to redeem ourselves (rather as had almost happened at Trent Bridge in the first Test of the series, when England lost, but by only two wickets, after Australia had been set, on another unreliable pitch, a target of 132 to win, just two more than their eventual target at Headingley), I doubt if Willis would have recovered his élan. He had been miserable about the way things had been going. Eighteen months before, in Australia, he had looked stiff, uncoordinated, not fully fit. He had not gone to the Caribbean for the series Botham captained. He was out of sorts. When Bob's timing was off, there were few saving graces, no sheer strength in his bowling, nor agile fielding or muscular batting to catch the eye. Not a natural athlete, à la Lilley or Holding, he looked ordinary when lacking rhythm. What one saw was a man who looked past his best. So without that last chance for glory, so triumphantly taken by him on that memorable day, I think it likely that his Test career would have come to an end.

So much for the inexorability of fate.

And as for fresh memories, it's all a bit of a re-hash. But as a friend's child said recently, 'Mum, when are we going to have left-overs for dinner again?' We may not do much with them, push them around the frying pan, add a bit of garlic, spice them up a bit. But occasionally they taste even better second or third time round.

6

A LATE DEVELOPER
(OR: MY LUCKY BREAKS)

Raymond Illingworth, when asked if I was the best England captain, replied: 'The luckiest, more like.'

Well I don't know about luckiest, but I do agree about lucky. And as in other walks of life, but perhaps more dramatically in a role like this, you need a fair share of it, and at the right times.

I was lucky to play for England at all. My first Test came in 1976 when I was thirty-four (an age at which many cricketers are retiring from Test cricket), and was based on a questionable theory of Tony Greig's. He had watched Australia beat the West Indies in 1975–6 by five Tests to one, and was impressed by the way batsmen Ian Redpath and Ian Chappell, with the aid of sound defence and plenty of grit, had blunted the raw but impressive fast-bowling attack led by Andy Roberts and Michael Holding. Greig concluded that he needed batsmen who were hardened by long experience. Thus, for the first Test in 1976, he picked John Edrich (aged thirty-nine), Brian Close (forty-five) David Steele (thirty-four) and me. Since 1949, Close, ever the optimist, had put the Test matches and their venues in his diary at the beginning of each season; 1976 was the first time he had not done so. Even Close must have been surprised to be called up to the trenches.

A few weeks earlier, I had required another piece of luck to get into the frame at all; on the day before the MCC vs West Indies match in late May, Yorkshire opener Richard Lumb dropped out because of injury, and I (no doubt as a result of Greig's theory) was selected to take his place. So instead of going from Cambridge to Chelmsford to play in a Benson and Hedges one-day match, I went to Lord's to open the batting with Dennis Amiss (thirty-three). Early in our innings, Dennis was hit on the back of the head by a Roberts bouncer, but I batted a long time, against the fastest and most lethal bowling I remember facing before or after. Hence two Tests, one at Nottingham, one at Lord's.

On the day before the first of these, I went with Tony Greig to meet Bill Swanwick, who constructed protective headgear for children suffering from epilepsy. He made us each a small plastic skullcap to go under our caps, with extra protection over the temples. I wore mine against Australia in 1977, in the wake of yet another chain of unpredictable events: after the Centenary Test in Melbourne earlier that year, Greig revealed that he had been acting as a recruiting agent for Kerry Packer's forthcoming World Series revolution. He was sacked as captain, and replaced by me. Without that particular timing, my Test careeer would probably have quietly died and been forgotten (though not by me).

So, I played in five Tests against Australia in 1977, wearing the skullcap, believing that the tough Australians must have been scornful towards this open display of vulnerability, only to discover that their attitude to the idea was sensible but the product inadequate. By the next year, cricketers round the world were wearing substantial helmets not unlike the current ones.

So, here was one lesson: don't allow Australian cricketers to be taken at their own valuation, don't be over-impressed by their macho exteriors. Marsh and Dennis Lillee are, I've discovered, kind and genial men, full of emotion. As international sportsmen they were indeed tough. They did not think of a Test match as an occasion for cheery banter. They were, however, and are, also sentimental. Like other international cricketers, Australian players love Lord's, with its ambience and traditions (years later Steve Waugh was proud to wear the distinctive orange-and-yellow-striped tie when given honorary membership; and their cricketers speak with much feeling and pride about walking out to play for their country on what they regard as hallowed turf). Now I count Lillee and Marsh among my friends.

To go back. In the Centenary Test at Melbourne in 1977, Lillee took 11 wickets, Derek Randall scored 174 in the second innings, and England lost, heroically in the end, by 45 runs, chasing a last-innings target of 463. By a strange chance, the result – and the margin – were exactly the same as in the first Test match 100 years before.

At Headingley in the home series later that year, Randall celebrated making the catch that won the Ashes by doing a cartwheel on the field. In 1978–9, we toured Australia at the same time as World Series Cricket was on. Randall was a central actor in one of my most prominent memories from that tour, of the fourth Test, at Sydney. We had made a hash of the first innings, being bowled out for 152. At one stage, with Willis ill and off the field, Australia were 126 for 1. The temperature was a claustrophobia-inducing 34 degrees centigrade. Yet, after we had restricted them to a lead of 142, Randall, after being within a whisker of lbw to Geoff Dymock when he'd scored only three, again made a magnificent century in the second innings: 150 this time. We then bowled Australia out (seven wickets shared between Geoff Miller and John Emburey) for 111, to win by 93 runs and find ourselves 3–1 up in the series rather than being pegged back to 2–2. Another set of chances had prolonged my career as captain.

In the next year, 1979–80, there was a hastily arranged tour of Australia as part of the deal done by the Australian Board with Packer, which put an end to World Series Cricket. We lost 3–0, having declined to put the Ashes at stake for a mere three-match series. Before the second of these Tests, again at Sydney, due to start on 4 January, the ground staff had gone off for their party on New Year's Eve. They omitted to cover the pitch, and it rained more or less non-stop for four days. The pitch was therefore wet and likely to be lethal. We had Derek Underwood in our side, the world's greatest bowler on rain-affected pitches. I gambled on winning the toss, putting Australia in, and bowling when the pitch was at its worst. I thought if we had that stroke of luck, we would then win, and that even if we lost the toss we might scrape through. So when the umpires took the captains – Greg Chappell and me, to look at the conditions, I argued that the pitch was fit to play sooner than it really was.

We lost the toss (bad luck), and the match. But I always felt that had Greg Chappell been given out caught behind in their second innings, when the score was 98 for 3 (Australia needing 216 to win), we would have had a fifty-fifty chance of winning. (Twenty years later I asked him if he did in fact edge the ball; he said, 'Yes, but it was a very thin one. I was amazed when you all appealed!') We lost by six wickets, Chappell ending 98 not out.

And finally, there was 1981. Luckiest captain? Probably so. First, to have Ian Botham in his pomp, and for Bob Willis to bowl the spell of his life, taking 8 for 43. And not only Headingley! This match was followed by Edgbaston (Botham's spell of five wickets for one run causing a collapse and a win by another narrow margin), and then Old Trafford (where Botham scored 117 in an innings of unusually cultured brutality). This little month was a time-out from ordinary life, now framed by a no doubt sentimental memory like a wish-fulfilling dream. For the Australians involved it must still be a not quite believable nightmare.

And being invited to captain England in 1981? That too had been, I discovered years later, in the lap of the gods (or certainly of the selectors), when I heard that it was a toss-up between Keith Fletcher and me. The glory – or the disappointment – might just as well have been his.

7

ALMOST LOSING A DOMINION

In a touching foreword to the first edition of this strangely appealing book, R. C. N. Palairet, Joint Manager of the MCC Team on the 1932–3 tour, warmly praises the captain (and writer), Douglas Jardine, for his leadership. This, he writes, 'contributed more than anything else to [our] success. Your determination, your imperturbability, your calmness when things were going wrong, and your magnanimity when things were going right excited the warmest admiration of all but the most violent partisans.'

But violent partisans there were in plenty, who dubbed this the 'Bodyline' series, and famously accused Jardine and his team of unsportsmanlike behaviour for systematically targeting the batsman's body, with a packed leg-side field, a form of attack called 'leg-theory'.

Jardine the writer plunges straight into the controversy. His Preface opens with an interview with a South African magistrate (a Mr Hotson of Cape Town), whose opinions on the series are quoted at length. The reader wonders why this apparently random item is included, especially in so prominent a place. Who is Mr Hotson? How much credit should we give his opinion, favourable to Jardine, especially when, having conceded that '[Harold] Larwood occasionally did bump', he continues, 'but [Don] Bradman especially, and even [Bill] Woodfull, quite often "ducked" to balls that barely rose above the wicket? In some cases this was done obviously for the benefit of the gallery'. I doubt the truth of this last statement. Could anyone imagine deliberately ducking into 90 mph deliveries barely rising above the height of the wicket, simply for the benefit of the gallery? Quite apart from the physical risk, there is the obvious danger of getting out. As MCC's vice-captain Bob Wyatt argued in his book *Fighting Cricket*, many of the problems caused by short, leg-theory bowling were due to the variable bounce of the wickets. Not impressive testimony from Mr Hotson, and one feels Jardine must have known better.

However, the blunt fact is that *In Quest of the Ashes* is Jardine's defence – his '*apologia pro vita sua*' – and one imagines that, if he were found guilty and invited to nomimate a penalty, he might well have proposed, like Socrates, that he should be fed at the city's expense for the rest of his days.

Jardine goes on to maintain that Test cricket was 'at the crossroads'. He lays the blame for this unhappy state of affairs on the behaviour of crowds, the press, and the Australian Cricket Board. It is their 'invasion' of the arena hitherto sacred to eleven players on either side [that] well may prove the death knell of cricket for those happy ones who still regard it as a survival from the days of chivalry, and a modern substitute for the tourney of Knights, that was played on the same green turf.

Jardine develops at some length his notion of the ideal cricket match, in which there are: 'Great deeds done in so knightly a fashion that there is no arrogance in triumph, no chagrin in defeat, but only calm of mind, all passion spent.' The spectators have no real place in this knightly encounter: 'The great deeds, the lack of arrogance, and the ability to take defeat philosophically . . . may safely be left to the players.'

Jardine's case against crowds is amplified by reference to the Australian tendency to consider that 'when England play Australia the whole of their national prestige [is] at stake'. This is confirmed by an unnamed Australian acquaintance, who opines that 'If it were only a game of tiddleywinks and there were 50,000 people watching, the whole atmosphere in Australia would become changed; public competition charges the air with partisan electricity.' The atmosphere was also intensified by telegraph, telephone, newspapers and wireless. Add the intensity of crowd mentality generally, and the fact of the Australians being 'persistent, courageous but inveterate gamblers', and you were left with 'no game . . . [but] . . . warfare'.

Jardine's argument suggests that the shift from game to warfare, from chivalry to cut-throat competition, had nothing whatever to do with the tactics employed by him and his team, nothing to do with the employment of leg-theory, and the relentless bowling of fast and often short-pitched bowling at the body, with six or seven fielders on the leg-side, but was entirely the outcome of the Australian mentality, and of the vociferous partisan barracking of the crowd. If the crowd had been demure, chivalry would never have been in question. He strikes me as not unlike the highwayman who blames the darkness of the roads, or the reactions of the public, for hold-ups. Perhaps part of Jardine's extreme loathing of the Australian public was down to their forcing him to examine (and even at some level to doubt) his own supposed 'chivalry'.

As to the question of whether a chivalrous approach is fundamentally compatible with keen competition, I believe that it is, although the lines are hard to draw and depend to some extent on the particular customs and standards of the day, in cricket as in other areas of life. However strongly Jardine felt that he was behaving within the (chivalrous) spirit of cricket, he was scorning its customs and standards.

In the book, Jardine is at pains to establish the respectability of 'leg-theory' (he rejects the term Bodyline). This he does partly by reference to its longevity. He dates it back at least twenty-five years, to George Hirst (of Yorkshire and England), the fast-medium left-arm in-swing bowler, and W. W. Armstrong, the Australian leg-spinner, pointing out that, however irritating such tactics might have been, no one accused the perpetrators of being unfair. Bowling has two aims, he notes: to get the batsman out or to restrict his scoring – and no sane captain would dream of using his fast bowlers for the latter purpose, especially in the heat of Australia. The charge that any of the English bowlers in 1932 or 1933 had another aim – that of threatening physical harm to the batsman – he ridicules as patently untrue and stupid.

In my view this is disingenuous. Fast bowlers rarely (I think) have the physical injury of the batsman as their prime goal, though they have not always been above adopting it in the heat of battle, or when particularly riled. But Jardine knew perfectly well that the realistic threat of physical harm is part of the fast bowler's armoury. The purpose of persistent short-pitched bowling aimed at the batsman's body is not – usually – to hit or hurt, but to soften up, to shake up, to disrupt the batsman's technique. This is part of the explanation of the fact that eighteen of Larwood's thirty-three wickets in the series were either lbw or bowled (which Jardine uses as evidence that he generally bowled at the wicket: another claim which seems to me disingenuous). The ordinary word for such bowling is intimidation, and an element of it is part and parcel of the game. Jardine, however, took intimidation to a new level.

Another aspect of Jardine's case for leg-theory is that Australian conditions and changes in batting technique had tended to make off-theory – that is bowing wide of the off stump with a packed off-side field – both boring as a spectacle and unproductive as a tactic. The ball lost its shine rapidly in Australia, and thus was far less prone to swing. Batsmen consequently tended to let more and more balls go, and to move further across in front of the stumps. Moreover, the then current lbw law stipulated that the batsman could not be given out lbw if the ball had pitched outside the off-stump. Leg-theory, on the other hand (he argues), did not limit the batsman's stroke-play, and in fact Jardine maintains that he would not have deployed it on a rain-affected pitch, for fear of giving away too many runs. He quotes Jack Ryder and Arthur Mailey, both former Australian Test players; both supporting the legitimacy of leg-theory, the latter celebrating the electric thrill of anticipation that heralded each ball bowled by Larwood. Jardine also cites the view of the twenty-four-year-old prodigy Archie Jackson, expressed not long before his poignant death from tuberculosis at Brisbane during the fourth Test then being played in that city. Jackson commented that, if Bill Ponsford and Jack Fingleton had been battered about the body, 'that [was] mostly their own fault', and urged that, 'for the sake of Australia's sporting traditions, it may be left to the players themselves to furnish the only answer to the legitimate tactics employed by the Englishmen'.

As to the origins of the tactic as it was used in 1932–3, Jardine denies that it was devised solely to limit Bradman. It was true that he had heard on all sides of Bradman's having been 'far from convincing on the leg stump while there was any life in the wicket' during the Oval Test of 1930, and indeed he remarks that this was 'in very marked contrast to Jackson, who was batting at the other end'. But he felt it to be a reasonable assumption that 'a weakness in one of Australia's premier batsmen might find more than a replica in a good many of his contemporaries'. Elsewhere he mentions not only Australian batsmen who were troubled by leg-theory – Ponsford, Alan Kippax and Bradman himself – but also others who thrived on it or were more bothered by an off-stump line – Fingleton, Stan McCabe and Arthur Richardson. He also suggests that, having witnessed Larwood trying a few overs of leg-theory in 1928–9, he had not been inclined to 'rate [its] possibilities very highly' at the start of the tour. Indeed, he had 'never imagined that it would stand such a test as would prove its effectiveness throughout a whole tour, but . . . did hope that it might occasionally provide a profitable variation when two batsmen were set'.

In *Fighting Cricketer*, vice-captain Wyatt gives a somewhat different account of the early use and justification of leg-theory on the 1932–3 tour. He suggests that it was first used in the match he himself captained at Melbourne, against an Australian XI, as a means of countering the Australian technique of moving right across their stumps and playing straight balls through the leg-side. This match was played, Wyatt wrote, on a very quick pitch, on which good-length balls were still rising as they reached the keeper. Bradman was dismissed twice by Larwood relatively cheaply. While this little drama occurred, Jardine was 200 miles away fishing in the Bogong Valley.

Jardine also avoids mentioning his alleged meeting, months before the tour began, with A. W. Carr, Larwood's and Bill Voce's captain at Nottinghamshire, at which leg-theory was apparently discussed. According to 'Gubby' Allen, one of England's fast bowlers on the tour, the theory was first mooted after the early match at Perth against a Combined Australian XI, when, on a drying pitch, Bradman was made to look very uncomfortable by Allen and was dismissed by him for 10 (without leg-theory). Jardine, however, is generally keen to underplay the significance of Bradman in his policy decisions; my reading is that he wants very much to reduce him to the dimensions of the ordinary mortal, and to underplay his special significance for England's bowling tactics.

The chief causes of trouble for the Australians in 1932–3 were, Jardine maintains, the speed and accuracy of Larwood and Voce. He does not deny that, in certain conditions – for instance, on a bumpy park pitch with a big eighteen-year-old bowling fast leg-theory to a younger batsman – such tactics might be 'rather strong meat'. But strong meat, in his view, is what Test cricket is about. If batsmen couldn't deal with bouncers by avoidance or with the bat, then they should 'consider the desirability of giving way to younger talent'. To the objection that the ball often lifted from a good length, he replies that in that case credit should be given to the bowler, and that batsmen need courage. No one would seriously contend that cricket should not be played on drying pitches. Otherwise we might as well, Jardine suggests, give up the idea of playing with a hard ball.

What then are we to make of the controversy? I have no doubt that Jardine is right in much of what he says. Test cricket should be 'strong meat'. And if England had used it to less effect, there would have been little or no opposition. If Australia had won, the offence would have been minimal. If it had been used as an occasional variation, no one would have made much of a fuss.

Does this exonerate him? Not entirely. For there is something about the sheer relentlessness of Jardine that sets him apart – for instance, in his use of the method so early in an innings, or in his alleged refusal of *one* extra fielder on the leg-side for Bowes, yet his willingness to place *four* extra men there instead. This relentlessness entailed the belief that the end justified the means. It entailed following through his course of action (and his argument) to its logical, or fanatical, conclusion. Compunction, concern, self-doubt – the glimmerings of conscience – would in Jardine's system of values appear as signs of weakness, both to others and perhaps also to himself.

He was positively bloody-minded in his timing. Immediately after Woodfull was hit on the chest at Adelaide, Jardine switched over to leg-theory field-placing. As for his claim that, had he 'realized the misrepresentation to which we [he and Larwood] were to be subjected, neither of us would have set that particular field for that particular over', this seems to me *faux-naif.* I think Jardine knew full well the significance of the move. If he found the Australian crowds provocative in their barracking, they had reason to find him provocative both in his timing and in his attitude. In fact this is exactly Wyatt's view. He felt that the use of persistent short-pitched leg-theory was against the spirit of the game, and not good for cricket. I agree.

One of the features of Jardine's conception of chivalrous cricket was, it will be remembered, the lack of arrogance in the winners, and he may have achieved this, at least according to his lights. However, what Jardine shows no sign of appreciating is the extent to which he came across to Australians (and to some others) as superior, unbending and arrogant. His book shows, I think, something of the hatred and contempt he had for the common Australian, at least for the latter's incarnation within a Test cricket crowd. Jardine's stiff manner, his Harlequin cap, his standoffishness before the spectators, notoriously aroused the ire of the Australians.

I offer two examples. One was conveyed to me by Doug Insole, who heard it from Wyatt in conversation; the other I was told personally by Larwood. The first occurred when, while fielding in Larwood's leg-trap, Jardine was hit on the shin by a full-blooded hook from McCabe. A ball or two later, blood could be seen seeping out over his boot. Wyatt suggested the skipper should go off for treatment. The response was: 'What? And let 90,000 convicts know I'm hurt?'

The second came before the last Test, with the Ashes secure. There was a question as to whether Larwood was fit to play. Larwood himself was in doubt. Jardine would not even consider leaving him out. 'We've got them down. Now we tread on them,' he told his fast bowler.

I too was accused of arrogance by some Australians. The ex-Prime Minister of Australia, Labour Party leader Bob Hawke, gave me some friendly advice one day in Melbourne, after I had been loudly booed by sections of the crowd. 'They're not bad fellows – many of them voted for me,' he said, before counselling me: 'They want a response. Give them a wave, laugh a bit, relax. They see your stiffness as colonialist arrogance.' There was a contrast between my rather taut attitude and the more genial, confraternal, sometimes crude, posturing of my predecessor, Tony Greig, which may have been paralleled by the similar contrast between former England captain, Percy Chapman (who had a bet with a Perth docker within a few minutes of landing in the country) and Jardine. But – and I may of course be biased – I have the impression that Jardine placed himself a good few degrees to the colder end of the scale than I did.

In a letter from Australia to his parents, Allen wrote: 'Douglas Jardine is loathed; and, between you and me, rightly, more than any German who fought in any war. I am fed up with anything to do with cricket . . . He seems too damn stupid and he whines away if he doesn't have everything he wants . . . Some days I feel I should like to kill him and today is one of those days.'

Another amateur, a man who opposed bodyline, refusing to field in the leg-trap, the Nawab of Pataudi, of whom Jardine said, 'I see His Highness is a conscientious objector', remarked towards the end of the tour: 'I am told he has his good points. In three months, I have yet to see them.'

On the other hand, Stephen Chalke knew Hedley Verity's son, who was born in June 1933, not long after the players returned from Australia. According to Chalke: 'Hedley Verity was an upstanding character, a Methodist lay preacher of integrity and sportsmanship. One county cricketer of the 1930s told me that in that respect he stood out as a gentleman in the Yorkshire side of the time. Verity christened his son Douglas.'

And I have some sympathy for Jardine's cool, defiant way of reacting to the provocations of media and public in Australia. His message was: 'nothing you can say or do will affect me one jot'. And whatever else one might say of him, he was not, at least in public, a whinger. In 1933 the West Indies used their leg-theory with fast bowlers Manny Martindale and Learie Constantine. Patsy Hendren came in to bat against them for MCC at Lord's wearing a 'three-peaked' helmet, made by his wife. As far as I know, no one complained about the nature of the bowling, least of all Jardine.

But I find Jardine's account of leg-theory insufficiently detailed and frank. He leaves a lot out. He fails to mention, for example, that Allen, his fellow-amateur and one of his main fast bowlers, refused to bowl leg-theory, or that the Nawab of Pataudi, another amateur, refused to field in the leg-trap, and was dropped two Tests after scoring a century. One of the book's polemical aims is to imply that the Australian players were on the whole unmoved by the idea that the tactic was unsporting. Hence he also refrains from including any mention of Bradman's proposal that a complaint be made against Jardine's tactic after Australia had levelled the series by winning the second Test at Melbourne. Similarly, he nowhere alludes to the famous remark made by Woodfull, the Australian captain, to P. F. Warner, the England manager, at Adelaide, to the effect that 'there are two teams out there, and only one is playing cricket'.

The book is not only about Bodyline, of course. There are chapters on each Test, as well as others of a more reflective nature. The style is dry: at times preparatory for a 'Hear, hear' from the reader, at times circumlocutorily humorous. Too often for a modern reader he leaves out details that one craves, but perhaps this was a feature of a time when people were less eager to know the inside story or the specifics of human relations or tactics.

To give two examples of my frustration: I wanted to know how many balls an over Larwood and Voce bowled that bounced to rib-height.

And I wanted to know what sort of a shot led Bradman to offer 'an easy chance off Larwood to Allen, who was standing close in at forward square leg'. Was it a bouncer? And how did he play it, when so often his response to leg-theory was to get to the leg-side of the ball and hit through the vacant off-side?

But Jardine is a better writer than this implies. I enjoyed his obliquely frank and telling account of captaining his main spin bowler:

> Verity is one of the most interesting bowlers whom I have had the privilege of observing at close quarters, for I would frequently stand at mid-off when he was bowling, offering him encouragement and advice. I believe that Verity prefers to bowl without advice, but he certainly accepted it with very good grace. Once or twice we registered a doubly satisfying success, though in all probability he would have done as well, if not better, had I been fielding in the deep!

On tactics, I was interested in how flexible Jardine's batting order was. I admire this, as I used to meet resistance in batsmen to the idea that they might be moved around from the position they had come to feel was their own. Perhaps Jardine's autocracy outweighed any such scruples.

I was impressed by how much he claims to have consulted on tactics, especially with Herbert Sutcliffe and Wally Hammond. I admired too his clarity about the roles of different bowlers, his recognition of the job done by the less dramatic bowling of, say, Verity in keeping an end tied up, so that his fast bowlers stayed fresh for short spells downwind. Towards the end of the series the side had clearly allocated roles for batsmen too, Hammond and Maurice Leyland being deputed to get on top of Bill O'Reilly and Bert Ironmonger.

But there is no getting away from it: 1932–3 will always be remembered as the Bodyline series. As his cricket master at Winchester,

Rockley Wilson, who had toured Australia with MCC in 1920–1, so presciently put it on hearing of his selection: 'Oh, Jardine will probably win us back the Ashes, but he may also lose us a Dominion!' He was right on the first count, and nearly right on the second.

8

FOUR IMAGES FROM
THE 2006–7 SERIES

My first image is of captain Andrew Flintoff, playing a forward defensive shot, inside the line of the ball. He looks uncharacteristically studious. The bowler could have been either Stuart Clark or Glenn McGrath. The second: Flintoff's field placings to Andrew Symonds in Melbourne – no one in close on the leg-side when he first came in, Australia on 84 for 5, Steve Harmison bowling well with his tail up. Shortly after, defensive sweepers are in place on both sides of the wicket; for Monty Panesar, mid-off and mid-on are back near the boundary. Third: Geraint Jones's fumble at Perth, when Monty Panesar had beaten Michael Clarke's outside edge, allowing the key batsman to scramble back into his ground and avoid being stumped. Fourth: Duncan Fletcher, that most tight-lipped of publicists, announcing that Chris Read 'lacks the character to face pressure'.

First, Flintoff's batting. For much of the time, he looked like someone trying too hard, almost watching himself. Like a poacher turned game-keeper, wearing his best clothes, uncomfortably respectable, touching his forelock. It was painful to watch. I had the sense that for him batting was on this tour a matter of playing a part, rather than simply playing. At Perth, soon after he'd come in to bat, a fast bowler bowled a delivery just short of a length and just outside his off-stump. Flintoff carved at the ball, it caught the outside edge and flew first bounce to the fielder placed just for this ploy, perhaps twenty yards in from the third-man boundary. Flintoff stood stock still, looked back and suddenly jerked as if to run. I felt that he hadn't noticed the fielder there, otherwise there would have been an easy single. What was his state of mind? How could he not have noticed, especially as this was, by now, a regular – and sensible – ploy by Australia? He seemed in a dream.

My guess, from a distance, is that all this was part of the onus of captaincy, that for this immensely gifted and likeable cricketer, it was a constraint, an oppression. His way out of this straitjacket was – sensibly – to revert to the bludgeon in the second innings at Perth.

Image number two. England had been dismissed for 159 on day one at Melbourne, in difficult batting conditions (though they had succumbed from 101 for 2, having got through the most trying period). In the field, with Flintoff bowling with fire, and despite two questionable decisions in Matthew Hayden's favour against Matthew Hoggard, England had fought back. Before lunch on the second day, the score was 84 for 5. Harmison had just got Michael Clarke with a beauty, seaming and bouncing awkwardly from a perfect line and length.

At this juncture, in came the uneasy, uncertain, but undoubtedly dangerous Andrew Symonds. It happened to be the day when England's bowling plans, pinned up in the dressing room, had been snitched and revealed on radio; they included, in bold type, the words 'bouncer essential' for Symonds. Yet the on-side field for Symonds from the beginning was two men in the deep for the hook, and a mid-on. No one at short leg, or even at square leg, for hasty defence or a mistimed shot. Every time a short ball was bowled, the batsman simply nudged it down on the leg-side and rotated the strike. Symonds made no attempt to hook or pull. The field was not changed. Not long after, against Panesar, singles were to be had all over the ground. Symonds was thus given an easy passage through his initial nerviness. Along with Hayden, he went on to play a tremendous match-winning innings.

I was reminded of 2005, when the scenario had been reversed. For this was exactly how Australian captain Ricky Ponting had responded when Flintoff himself came in to bat. How critical we then were of Ponting for allowing Flintoff to get going without being put under pressure! And how could Flintoff himself not remember? On each occasion, the message was negative and passive, conveying to the batsman – and to his own bowlers – the message that the captain didn't believe his bowlers could get a dangerous player out unless the latter behaved impetuously. In each case it relied on the batsman doing something stupid. How easy it is to fall into a fixed mind-set, to follow slavishly a rigid plan.

This is what my third image leads me to: the idea of an *idée fixe*. I was reminded of how close I was to being stuck in such a state of mind, back in 1978–9.

For that Ashes tour of Australia, we had five fast bowlers – Bob Willis, Ian Botham, John Lever, Mike Hendrick and Chris Old. The first Test was at Brisbane, which we won, omitting Lever and Hendrick of the five. The next was at Perth, and before this we played Western Australia on the same ground. The pitch was not only fast and bouncy, but grassy, and the ball moved off the seam. Despite scoring a total of only 270 runs in our two innings, we won by 140 runs. Hendrick took 5 for 11, and 3 for 23.

Nevertheless, at this point I was inclined to leave him out for the upcoming Test. But after the match John Inverarity, captain of Western Australia, said to me in a matter-of-fact way that Hendrick was easily the best of our bowlers in that match (the other seamers being Botham and Lever). It was only then that I could begin to see what my eyes should have told me. I don't think it was favouritism (I was a great admirer of Hendrick, as of the others). But I did have a blinkered view, some prejudgement, prejudice, based partly on the idea that Lever and Old were the front runners, the bowlers in occupation (Willis and Botham were automatic selections). Hendrick was newer to the team. He was an extremely accurate, English-type bowler. We, or I, had the pre-formed idea that he would be unlikely to be so dangerous in drier, sunnier Australian conditions. So it took an independent view, an opposition view, for me to trust my own eyes. Hendrick was duly selected, not only for this Perth Test but for the remaining five of the series, and played a vital part in our 5–1 win.

To return to 2006–7: England's on-tour selectors seemed to me to have some such distorting glasses when viewing their choices between Chris Read and Jones as wicket-keeper, and between Ashley Giles and Panesar as the preferred slow-left-arm bowler. I felt incensed at the dropping of Read, especially at the publicly insensitive comments on his demotion. Not that I didn't admire Jones, too. He was a fighter who made the best of his ability. He had been a more than useful batsman for England. But as a keeper he was not of the highest class. He caught the ball with tight hands, lacking the ease with which Read took the ball, the sense he gave of having time to spare. When Read caught a difficult catch, standing back, he made it look as if he could have gone another few inches if he'd needed to; when Jones went for a similar catch, one sensed an element of desperation, as if he were at the limit of his range. And standing up to the stumps there was no comparison; one looked makeshift, the other to the manner born. I could see no good reason for the selection of Jones for the first Test. Read had done well against Pakistan, and had scored more runs than Jones had been doing for some time. His batting failures in India, in totally different conditions, and in a totally different kind of competition, were, to my mind, irrelevant. I felt similarly about the dropping of Panesar too, though I could see the problem his presence posed for the batting line-up.

Finally, the fourth image, clearly related to the third one. In his 2007 memoir, the manager Duncan Fletcher stated that Read 'lacked the character to face pressure'. I think managers/coaches have a hard job in deciding how much to say to the media. They can easily be misquoted, or quoted out of context. They can say something that will come back to haunt them, something thought or felt in the heat of the moment, or in one part of the mind, that they wouldn't really believe in a more mature, or more rounded, state of mind. We all have such thoughts and feelings, and it is all too easy to spill them out. Even *not* addressing an issue can get one into trouble.

In press conferences, Fletcher's way was to spill less than almost anyone else. He was a master of saying nothing. In his public appearances, he conveyed such a dullness, perhaps almost depression (even when winning) that it's difficult to envisage him arousing a team's positive emotions. But this is not a bad way of doing things; or at least it is one way. So why – and from where – did this potentially damaging comment about Read come from, that he 'lacked character'? What would such a remark do for Read's confidence? Was there something about Read that annoyed Fletcher; that got under his skin?

Wicket-keepers can be a funny breed, with strange superstitions and mannerisms, like Alan Knott – in my opinion the greatest of them all. Certainly, Read was a quiet presence on the field, unobtrusive. He didn't feel comfortable orchestrating a lot of noise around the batsman. There was nothing of the exhibitionist about him. But he could lead people, as he showed in captaining Nottinghamshire from 2008 to 2017, including leading them to the County Championship in 2010. He was a superb 'keeper, and a more than useful batsman.

Surely the aim of the coach is to integrate and permit differences? And the strange situation seemed to continue beyond the Australia tour, Read remaining constantly under sceptical scrutiny, despite his immaculate and classy keeping in the last two Tests of that series. I was interested to hear Ian Healy, holder of the world record for wicket-keeping dismissals in Test cricket, when commentating at Sydney, compare him with Knott, as did Rodney Marsh. Isn't that good enough, at least for the time being?

9

GIANTS

How good was Ian Botham as a fast-bowling all-rounder? How did he compare with his contemporaries in international cricket – Richard Hadlee, Imran Khan and Kapil Dev? And with the three other fine England cricketers before and after him – Tony Greig, Andrew Flintoff and Ben Stokes?

Like all the others in my list except Greig, Botham was primarily a bowler. I was lucky to captain him in his early prime, between 1977 and

1981. In those first glorious years, with his pace, sharp swing, attacking instincts and combative presence in the batsman's face, Botham was the most brilliant bowler of the four England players, and at that time at least the equal of Hadlee, Khan and Kapil.

Botham the bowler, like Botham the batsman, almost always erred, if that's the right word, on the side of attack, regularly wanting more close catchers, whether in the slips or at short leg.

Over the 1980s, however, his magnificent bowling declined somewhat, his physique, strength and elasticity diminishing, through injury to his back and perhaps over-work. As well as suffering from wear and tear, he also paid a price for not looking after himself. He hated training, and put pressure on his body with his hundreds of miles of road-walking, heroically spearheading the raising of £13 million for research into children's leukaemia.

Thus, while Imran and Hadlee improved their effectiveness and flair as their careers developed, Botham did not manage to do so. In personality, he was extrovert, generous and a touch grandiose, without the obsessional qualities that helped Richard Hadlee improve, with both bat and ball, well into his thirties. Botham lacked prudence, meanness, calculation. A quick learner in his young days – Tom Cartwright, player/coach at Somerset, described him as 'one of the most receptive people I've ever worked with' – but he did not have to work long hours away from the middle, and was unwilling to do so in the second half of his career.

Imran Khan was at first an in-swing bowler who was barely above medium pace. He discovered almost by chance that he could bowl fast. Later he also learned the art of reverse swing from Sarfraz Nawaz. Slim but powerful, with a great leap into his bowling action, Imran became a memorable, excitingly athletic fast bowler and an attractive stroke-playing batsman. Both he and Hadlee became much better batsmen once helmets became available.

Imran Khan

Kapil Dev, too, was a remarkable cricketer, the first to reach 4,000 runs and 400 wickets in Test cricket. Like Botham, he had a terrific start to his career and with his fine, high action, was skilful at swinging the ball away from the bat at speed. His body likewise suffered from the strain, and he had to undergo knee surgery in 1984.

Over a whole career, I would place Hadlee at the top of the pile as a bowler. He was waspish in pace, without huge effort. He swung the ball away. He was extremely accurate. Graham Gooch once described New Zealand's bowling as 'world class at one end, "Ilford third eleven" at the other'.

Among the other England cricketers, Flintoff and Stokes both had Botham's heavy ball, and his full-hearted energy, but neither had his ability to swing the ball away, nor his at times outrageous willingness to try anything.

In 2005, Flintoff developed reverse swing to a high level, but he was never quite the supreme attacking bowler as his predecessor. And Stokes looks to me as though he may turn himself into a predominantly batting all-rounder, someone whose bowling may become secondary, offering England a useful enforcing option, often as fourth seamer.

Kapil Dev

Greig (like his fellow-South African, Jacques Kallis) was always primarily a batsman. He swung the ball away, but at a gentler pace than the others. (Unlike them, he also learned to bowl off-cutters well enough to offer a further option in this other style when conditions suited.)

Being an all-rounder is of course a great bonus for a cricketer. You're always in the game. Having two skills gives you licence at least in the lesser one. Alan Knott, for instance, used to say that he would never have got away with the eccentricity of his batting style had batting not been his second string. He would have been expected to bat like a 'proper' batsman – if not classical, then at least po-faced. You can't turn up at a Palace garden party doing cartwheels.

In many ways, this licence serves these fast-bowling all-rounders well. If they are to bowl long spells in match after match, they mustn't tire themselves out playing too many six-hour innings. And the freedom encouraged in this aggressive attitude to batting may be vital to their performance.

All these fine cricketers have been clean, hard-hitting strikers of the ball, often going all-out for their shots. Of the seven (leaving aside Greig)

I think the best batsman may turn out to have been Stokes (twenty-six years old as I write this). His basic technique is correct. He plays straight, well forward or well back; he pulls, hooks and cuts with power and control, and his balance is excellent. And he hits the ball very hard.

Stokes appears to me to have long been working hard at his batting technique with the aim of turning himself into a complete batsman, rather than an exciting and brilliant hitter. In my view, he has shown, particularly in his wonderful hundred at the Oval against South Africa in 2017 – probably his best-ever innings for England so far – that he is already well embarked on this transition. This was an innings of range and versatility. For a long time during the first day, he was facing fine bowling in conditions that helped them. The ball swung, bounced and moved off the seam. The fact that his defensive technique stood comparison with that of Alastair Cook, who in fact scored more quickly than he did during that period of play, speaks highly of Stokes the batsman. On the second day, his innings blossomed with classically orthodox shots to all parts of the ground.

More generally, Stokes is open to self-criticism and humble about his own shortcomings. He studies the computer after he's out. When during the tour of India in 2016 the England players were given the option of rest and recuperation in Dubai for a few days before the first Test, he stayed in Mumbai, working out regularly in the gym. Against spin bowlers, Stokes quickly realized that his main challenge lay in staying in and building an innings, especially on 'holding' pitches; that is, on dusty surfaces where the ball does not 'come on' to the bat. In the sub-continent, particularly, the most difficult time is the first half-hour, and you have to be able to rely on soft hands and correct play to see you through until things begin, hopefully, to feel easier.

In attitude and technique, he is already more of a complete batsman than either Botham or Flintoff managed to be. Stokes is now (2018) up with Cook and Joe Root as one of England's best batsmen. No one has as many gears as he does.

Making the transition from hitter to batsman is not without its risks. One may become too cautious, losing the spontaneity and flair that the all-rounder licence permits, or one may fall between two stools. If you get it wrong, you may turn out to have promoted yourself to your level of incompetence. But I see no hint of this sort of internal conflict in Stokes.

Whereas Flintoff showed little sign of making a serious attempt to alter his batting technique or approach, Ian Botham would, I think, have liked to do so. In the early to mid-1980s, I for one believed that he might make this transition. Indeed, I seem to recall England teams in which he went in at five or six, ahead of specialist batsmen like Derek Randall, presumably with just this aspiration in mind. But I don't think Botham ever quite overcame technical flaws in the way Stokes appears to be doing. He tended to play 'inside out', that is, from leg to off, in his driving and hitting, and he continued to plant his front leg too close to the line of the ball, especially when defending against spinners.

All seven cricketers were, or are, excellent fielders, Botham, Stokes and Greig brilliant, especially in the slip/gulley region.

Having said all this, I am old enough to have seen and played against the man who was, I think, the greatest of them all – Garry Sobers. His batting was utterly stylish and free, correct and dominating together. He was a fine left-arm fast-medium bowler, swinging the ball in to right-handed batsmen. He was a wonderful fielder. As if that were not enough, he also bowled left-arm spin in two modes, with flair and skill. He was, as his supporters named him, the 'King', the 'Four in one'.

PART 3

HEROES

10

WHAT MAKES A HERO?

I have mentioned my choice, as a seven-year-old and beyond, of Jack Robertson ahead of Denis Compton as my number one hero. It is an interesting question what sorts of considerations enter into such early choices, and indeed continue to influence those that we make later in life.

I reported three possible reasons for my Robertson-choice. First, did he remind me of my father? Second, was his prodigious 331 not out in 1949 iconic for me, aged seven? And third, did this choice indicate some unconscious sense of my own likely scale and type of achievement? Or perhaps these factors came together, each buttressing the others.

With regard to the first: a boy's father often is his first hero. I remember being convinced that mine was the best car-driver in the world. We acquired our Ford 8, registration number US 7563, in 1949, the same year as I acquired Jack Robertson as my hero. On rare occasions we got taken to school in the car; these were red-letter days for me. I remember well the car loaded up for our holidays in August on the south coast, first at Rustington near Worthing, then, from 1948 to 1959, at Bognor. There was a long, slow haul up Berry Hill in the South Downs, my sisters and I cheering when we reached the top. The expedition (as I remember it) took most of the day, though it was only about seventy miles. My father would drive. We would stop for lunch, not without painful indecisions and irritations when the suggestion for stopping at what must have been a perfect place came too late for my father to negotiate, or the 'perfect' place turned out to be full of horse flies or cow-shit or rabbits blinded by myxomatosis, and we would remount the car and labour on. The same car later had a hole in the floor just ahead of the passenger seat, through which this small passenger could see the road racing backwards, and a tendency for the doors to fly open when we went round corners. My father's solution, not a satisfactory one to my mother, was to tie the door handles to the steering wheel with string, so that at least they wouldn't open very far.

In fact the car was itself a hero, especially on those rare occasions when the best driver in the world would put his foot on the accelerator, and, probably downhill, overtake another car. More cheering. When we later sold the car, I witnessed from my bedroom in the front of the house US 7563 being driven away forever. I cried.

But to revert to the origins of this child's cricketing hero. I certainly think Jack Robertson was a professional version of my father, also an opening batsman. And I have a clear memory of my excitement at his triple century, which I would emulate in my own games against myself, or rather Middlesex's against Yorkshire, which took place when I threw a tennis ball against the kitchen wall, usually missing the kitchen window, so that it landed on the strip of grass that I cut and rolled assiduously. I then awarded myself runs whenever I hit the ball into gaps between the putative fielders in the small garden. Robertson scored further triple centuries in London, W5.

I'm rather less inclined to believe the third possibility, that I could in some way have both known, and even constructed, my future self. Might it not equally well have been the other way round: that my choice played a part in how I turned out? Had Compton scored 331 at the key moment, might I have turned out like him? If only!

We naturally put people onto pedestals. I know what that is like from the other end. I remember one small boy writing to me in the late 1970s that when I got a good score he was very happy, but when I got a low one he was utterly miserable all day. Unhappy lad! Shortly after being appointed captain of England, I was touched to be addressed as 'my captain' by a man in Greenwich High Street. But being the recipient of such projections and potentially being 'owned' by people who know one only from a distance can also be a burden, both of expectation, and of profound disillusion and sometimes even hatred when you or what you stand for disappoints.

But my understanding, through ordinary observation as well as psychoanalysis, that we all exaggerate and diminish the good in people who impress us or are important to us, has not stopped me too being excited by other role models as I grew up, even as I grow old. A few have radiated a sort of glow for me. I write later in this section about Viv Richards – the greatest demolisher of good bowlers that I saw, but also a man with powerful presence on and off the field. I include Tom Cartwright, a true craftsman as cricketer and person, who in his honesty and devotion reminded me of Caleb Garth, the land-agent in George Eliot's *Middlemarch*. Garth himself was partly modelled on her own father, also a land-agent. I include too the great fast bowlers, Michael Holding, that athlete of the cricket field, and Dennis Lillee, the best bowler I played against (and a man of whom his team-mates once said he moved from being WOT – the world's oldest teenager – to FOT – fucking old tart – with no intervening gap). Finally, there is Bishan Bedi, the most graceful slow bowler I have seen.

But gradually, as with everyone in this list, heroes merge into friends, people I admire for very different kinds of qualities.

Friendship is not, though, the same as hero-worship. The former may or may not be based on idealization; the latter has to have some element of it. Psychoanalysts and psychotherapists have to deal with something similar. Freud drily concluded that when his patients fell in love with him, it was not due to his personal charms. To a sceptical mind, falling in love might be described as the extreme over-valuation of one woman over all others.

Children, who need their parents in order to survive and flourish, may grow up blaming themselves to save their parents as figures worthy of their love, and to save themselves from disillusionment.

But where would we be without falling in love, a background that provides some at least of the heat that keeps relationships going. We are not, thankfully, passionless computers, calculating the virtues of our husbands and wives, our heroes, lovers and friends. We need not be like those British characters in E. M. Forster's *A Passage to India*, who are said to 'weigh out their emotions like potatoes, so many to the pound'. We can't fully admire a man (or woman) who insists on a prenuptial agreement before consenting to marriage.

And with heroes come villains. The most obvious thing to do to someone on a pedestal is to knock him off it (though I do remember how those Yorkshiremen who put Geoffrey Boycott there would forgive him almost anything before turfing him off, even temporarily).

The other side of the coin, that which we can't allow in ourselves, or in our heroes, we find hooks for in other people. As an occasional cricket-hero myself in the eyes of people who subscribe to a myth about me (on top of my actual good and bad qualities), I am well aware how vulnerable one is to this kind of reversal. I remember, for instance, being pushed into a patch of rose bushes at Burton upon Trent in 1973, when John Emburey played his first game for Middlesex (and was aptly described, by *Daily Telegraph* writer Michael Carey, as the 'emburyonic Titmus'), by an ardent female Middlesex supporter called Margaret. But what it was I might have done wrong there escapes me.

Dale Sivell, who worked for Middlesex and helped me with sorting out mail that arrived when I was captaining England, told me after some time that she protected me from the worst missives by throwing them away.

One feature of the Ashes is its peculiar, almost mythical capacity to see cricketers as figureheads of virtue or a sort of vice.

11

'IN MY OPINION'

When at the crease the charisma was palpable, and I have known fine bowlers intimidated by him. What is it? Where does it reside?

In 2016 I was in Dubai for two or three days, observing the second-ever Day–Night Test match. I went to the commentary box to meet my colleague from the World Cricket Committee, ex-Pakistan player, Rameez Raja. I hadn't known Viv was in town, let alone in the box.

As I walked in, I could hear his unique voice: Viv was there no doubt to support the currently struggling West Indian team, as well, perhaps, as cricket in the UAE. He was in flow at the microphone.

A single phrase and you know it's him. He speaks fast, almost nervously. While verbally expressing uncertainty and the possibility of opinions different from his, he speaks with conviction. Of left-hand batsman Darren Bravo, batting in the middle, he comments: 'He moved more confidently towards that ball. I should still like to see a bigger stride with his right foot, but here he seemed to mean it more. I like it. (Pause.) In my opinion.'

'In my opinion' – qualifying the view he has just expressed. And even with the qualification, one would be nervous about opposing it (or rather him). There is something of an emperor about him.

I am standing behind him. Viv looks round, between comments, smiles warmly, shakes my hand, indicates he will be free in a few minutes. His shiny black suit could be that of a senator; or perhaps of a Mafioso. He is a handsome man, but it is his presence more than a conventional handsomeness that strikes one.

The best portrait at Lord's is the one of Vivian Richards, by Brendan Kelly. It captures something of what I'm trying to put into words: the forceful gaze, the imperious look, his fine Roman nose. His face, broader than when he played, seems big like his body, like his muscles, perhaps I should say – the skin interestingly creased. His head is now brilliantly bald, as imposing as when he used to be wearing that small, maroon, West Indies cap (a junior schoolboy's cap on a large sixth-former) to face the fastest bowlers, scorning a helmet. His head has a smooth lump at the back, above the neck. He has the neck of a bull.

After his stint at the microphone, he is extremely friendly. I'm touched. I want him to like me. I am almost surprised he remembers me, that he wants to talk to *me*. But I don't feel relaxed. I don't easily take in what he is saying. I have to listen hard. He is, as my colleague John Stephenson, also present, said afterwards, a true alpha male. One can't imagine a woman not being fascinated. As a man (am I one?), older, in every sense paler, I am charmed, but also a tad intimidated, even by his friendliness. Not quite mesmerized.

And by what he is saying. He asks me first what I think of the current state of the game. I murmur something about it being good. He voices agreement. Then he tells me that we need to teach younger players about the values of Test cricket. Our game of cricket, in his opinion, has more to it than T20. More to it than hitting a six and a four. We have to instil in them the values of Test cricket. Of learning the game in its longer form. The fellows who do best in T20 know the game already when they start – they learned that first, through four- and five-day cricket. They know we have to learn a technique. In his opinion.

I feel he speaks to me as if we are on a par, as if I too, with my history of moderate and cautious technique, and modest achievement at the highest level, might have an important opinion. As if, despite his having been one of the greatest attacking batsmen of all time, he was allowing me the same sort of grounds as he had for an opinion no doubt similar to his. It was as if he were saying to me: 'You and I had to learn the hard way what is involved in Test cricket. It is not something one can walk into, relying on youthful flair. Don't you agree?' You and I, he implied as he went on, have to persuade the younger players to wait for their riches. It's good that players can make big money for T20, but let them wait. In baseball or American football, they start as amateurs in the college teams. Only later do they know what's what.

I can only agree. I try to summon up some authority, mentioning how there are players, like David Warner, the Australian opener, who have graduated in the other direction, from the short game into being a top Test batsman, but I feel like a schoolboy myself. At seventy-four! And I love the man, too. I imagine he is one of those who don't suffer fools easily, who don't forgive easily. But he treats me like an equal, and this is authentic, I'm sure. He smiles, tells me how pleased he is to see me again, wishes me well. He has to do some work. He leaves the box. The box is the poorer for it. A force of nature.

Masculinity is not what it used to be, not simple any more. Being a man is not just (not even?) being someone who makes women swoon and men admire, pulling lesser men into the wish to be like him, willing to try to do anything for him, probably in fear of him.

No. Today the model for a man includes considerateness, humility, receptivity, kindliness. A real man is one who takes on his full (or perhaps nearly full) share of the child-rearing and the domestic chores. Who is considerate in bed, and elsewhere. Who has doubts about his manliness. I'm not saying that Viv is a throwback. There is no superiority, he is generous to us mere mortals. But he has something of those older qualities.

The previous time I met Viv to talk to, a year or two before, he had spoken with admiration of my old Middlesex and England team-mate, Mike Gatting. Hit full in the face by a bouncer from Malcolm Marshall, he went home with a broken nose, the bruising spread over his eyes and into his cheeks. Three weeks later he was back facing the same intimidating attack. 'That's what I call courage,' Viv said. He recognizes guts, and the qualities of good professionals, of mere mortals.

He himself hardly ever got hit. I once saw Dennis Lillee hit him on the cheek-bone, hooking. Viv had got through his shot too quickly and the ball hit his right cheek. Following through, Dennis looked for a moment like a boy who had at last made his mark, eager for his moment of triumph. It was too soon for concern. But instead of collapsing on the floor, being helped off to hospital to have a smashed cheek-bone prised out towards its pristine shape, Viv merely shook his head slightly, as if disturbed by an irritating Western Australian fly, and resumed his posture, frail cap tugged down over dominant head. Lillee, almost crestfallen, trudged back to his mark. I reminded Viv of this moment. Sometimes, he said, you have to make it look as if it doesn't hurt. But what I really should have said was: he must be made of sterner stuff all through! Anyone else's bones would have shattered. It wasn't that it hurt (though obviously it must have, and he was courageous); it was more a matter of 'what manner of man is this?' Even flesh, blood and bones impervious? What a man!

12

'MICHAEL BOY'

The first epithet that comes to mind for Bishan Singh Bedi's bowling is 'beautiful'. More than with any other slow bowler, this is the word that stays.

He prepared to bowl with a routine of stretches; he was remarkably supple for a man who was not slim. I presume he practised yoga. His fingers were wonderfully supple, too, and part of his theatricality was his fizzing the ball from one hand to the other before starting his run-up. He was also striking in his choice of patkas, often pink or bright blue. When Bedi came on to bowl, the crowd would sit up.

He was not an elegant mover with the bat, or in the field. In both departments he could be clumsy. Like Colin Cowdrey among batsmen, and Allan Jones among fast bowlers, Bedi was one of those athletes whose athleticism was expressed almost exclusively in the thing he did best. His bowling was all grace.

Unlike his contemporaries Bhagwat Chandrasekhar or Derek Underwood, his run-up was not long. A few easy rhythmic steps, perfectly balanced, and he moved smoothly into the delivery stride. There was no sense of striving, nothing rushed or snatched, no hiccups, just an easy flow. He bowled at the slower end of the spin bowler's range, though not dead slow. Like most great bowlers, his variation was subtle. Of all the slow bowlers I batted against, none required you to commit yourself later than Bedi did. With tiny, last-second adjustments of wrist and hand angle, he could bowl successive balls that looked identical, perhaps as if each would land on a length just outside off-stump; but with the first he would cock his wrist more, deliver the ball slightly higher – it would spin sharply, stay wider of off-stump, and be shorter than one anticipated. The next ball, ever so slightly undercut and bowled a little quicker, would pitch further up and come in towards middle and leg stumps. To the first ball you were likely to play inside the line, and away from the body; to the second, outside the line, and round your front leg, so that there was a risk of an inside edge onto the pad. The error of judgement induced in the batsman could be as much as a yard in length and a foot in width.

So firm and balanced were his action and rhythm, Bedi could make these changes at the last moment, in the moment before delivery, according to what he sensed the batsman was trying to do.

Bedi was a gentlemanly cricketer. If you hit him through the covers for four he would say well played (for some reason he would say to me, 'Well played, Michael Boy'). When David Hughes of Lancashire hit him for three straight sixes in a Gillette Cup Final, Bedi applauded each one. By contrast, being a purist, he didn't approve of the lap or the sweep; he felt these were unworthy shots, cruder, cross-batted. Alan Knott must have driven him insane, for he could, and sometimes did, sweep anything. Bedi enjoyed getting people out in classical ways, caught off the outside edge pushing forward, or off the inside edge and pad to the arm ball: he liked to defeat the batsman in the flight and have him stumped or caught off a skier. He was never a journeyman; never one who willingly sacrificed classicism for mere efficiency.

Having watched the England players being mesmerized by him in India in 1972–3, and written about them not using their feet, I batted against him at Northampton for Middlesex a few months later. The outcome? Brearley st. Sharp b. Bedi, 18 (though I did get 57 against him in the second innings!). Bedi took 550 wickets in six seasons of first-class cricket for Northants.

He liked to bowl in an attacking vein, with several fielders round the bat (and he was blessed when playing for India by the assistance not only of the remarkable Eknath Solkar, one of the great short-leg fielders – and that in the days before helmets – but also of Ajit Wadekar and Abid Ali). He did not readily bowl defensively – flat and directed to middle-and-leg – though he could also do this.

He was part of another sub-team within the team: the spin trio or quartet. His allies here were Chandrasekhar, Srinivasaraghavan Venkataraghavan, and Erapalli Prasanna. The last two were off-spinners but very different from each other. Venkat was accurate, orthodox; Prasanna was a minor genius of flight and guile. Venkat was tall, and flighted the ball less; he was not a big spinner of the ball. Prasanna was rounder, shorter, more like a mirror image of Bedi (though without his grace) in deceiving the batsman in the air. Chandra was the unique one, who had suffered from polio as a boy, and bowled quick leg-breaks, googlies and top-spinners with his withered arm. He could even bowl a bouncer. Especially on Indian pitches, this quartet was a formidable combination, and offered the captain something for every challenge. They were all, however, indifferent batsmen, so India often had a long tail. This was feature of the old school of Indian cricket – with its reliance on sheer skill and subtlety, and something of a scorn for utilitarian things like squeezing out extra runs from the tail, or saving a few runs by athleticism in the field.

Besides being a gentlemanly cricketer, Bedi was also a terrific competitor. Tony Lewis, who captained the MCC in India in 1972–3, said of him that he was a Dennis Lillee among slow bowlers. On the one hand, if he liked you he would be extremely friendly. I greeted him with a *Namaste* (the Indian greeting with hands together) when I came in to bat at Lord's, and he enjoyed that. He remembers us discussing on the field in the same Test whether what I suffered from when a Ghavri bouncer hit my visor was a hump, a bump or a lump.

But if he took against you, he could be a fierce antagonist. He was put out by the Vaseline incident during the MCC's 1976–7 tour of India. Tony Greig was captain. The team's physiotherapist, Bernard Thomas, came up with a ploy to deflect sweat away from the bowlers' eyes, which involved putting a strip of Vaseline-covered gauze around the brow. Bedi felt outraged at what he thought was cheating. I doubt if he ever forgave Greig.

Bedi is an outspoken man. He is not diplomatic. He can be choleric. Recently, he has not minced his words about Muttiah Muralitharan and Shoaib Akhtar, whom he has compared to a shot-putter and a javelin-thrower respectively. He is worried for future generations of spin bowlers, worried that they will copy these actions. He feels they were not only illegal, but threatened the purity of cricket.

He has no faith in cricket's administrators, believing that cricket was better-led imperially, when England and Australia had a veto, and the whole international game was more or less run by Gubby Allen and Don Bradman; now, he says, the Asian countries make everything murky. He regards T20 cricket as rubbish. I would not like to find myself in outright opposition to him on an issue that mattered to us both.

He could act in demonstrative and trenchant ways. In the final Test of India's tour to the West Indies in 1976, on an uneven pitch in

Jamaica, Bedi declared India's first innings on 306 for 6; two batsmen had retired hurt, and Vishwanath had been injured too. In the second innings, India were all out for 97 with only five batsmen dismissed (five were recorded as absent hurt), leaving West Indies with only 13 runs to win. He believed that the umpires had been too weak to put a stop to intimidatory and dangerous bowling.

At the same time, he was and is a generous man. During a Cavaliers match in Karachi in 1982, he saw in the Dawn newspaper an appeal for blood of a rare group for a young boy who was in a critical condition. Bedi rang up and said if they wouldn't mind Indian blood he was happy to give his, which was of the same group. The press got hold of the story, and Bedi had, he told me, the entire Pakistan nation at his feet, all on account of this pint of actually and symbolically life-affirming blood. He was subsequently embarrassed to go into shops because people refused to let him pay for anything, and he was plied with gifts. Benazir Bhutto sent him two carpets and a tea-set; and they became friends.

In 1987, Pakistan toured India. The fifth Test was on what Bedi called a minefield at Bangalore. On the evening of the third day's play, when India needed 122 runs to win with six wickets standing (one of them Gavaskar's), there was a function, which Bedi, who was writing on the match, attended. Pakistan's spinners, slow left-arm Iqbal Qasim and off-spinner Tauseef Ahmed, asked Bedi how to bowl on this particular pitch. Bedi told them the basics of bowling on a spinner's pitch: that 'you don't need to bowl people out, the pitch would do that for you'. 'If Iqbal was cover-driven the ball should end up at slip, if Tauseef was cover-driven he should be bowled or caught off the inside edge,' he said. Next morning Qasim took four wickets, and Tauseef two. Gavaskar was eighth out for 96, Pakistan won the match by 16 runs, and their first series in India. Bishan says he spoke to them for ten minutes, far less time than the countless hours he'd spent talking to Maninder Singh, India's slow left-armer, who took ten wickets in the match but ended up on the losing side. Bedi was labelled a traitor in the Indian press.

In his retirement, Bedi writes and speaks on cricket, but his main job is running a cricket school in Delhi for youngsters, some of whom he and his wife will take in if they can't afford the cost of lodging. This is symptomatic of his generosity and his love of cricket.

13

FROM WOT TO FOT

Dennis Lillee was the best bowler I played against. He was the perfect fast bowler: genuinely quick, hostile and accurate. He also naturally swung the ball away, which of course is so much more lethal when done at his kind of pace. He had a magnificent physique. As with Allan Donald more recently, he was so well proportioned that you didn't realize until you came close that he was six feet tall. He had a perfect run-up and classical action, his left arm high and bent at elbow and wrist. His bowling arm was high and strong. In his run-up, he accelerated menacingly (with occasional speed wobble); he had a full follow-through. He would always prefer to attack rather than defend. Courageous and persistent, he would come back with the same energy at the end of the day as at the beginning. He was also shrewd, a master of bowling on pitches that got slower and the bounce became lower, as well, of course, as when there was bounce and movement. He was a captain's dream.

Don Bennett, for many years Middlesex coach, described a Lillee master-class at Lord's one day during the great man's prime, when he happily showed aspects of his art to the young cricketers present. In the middle at the Nursery ground, he bowled an over in which he nominated each ball – 'out-swinger to hit off-stump', 'out-swinger to hit middle stump', 'in-swinger to hit leg stump' – Don said he bowled an over at good pace in which each ball did exactly what he intended. It must have been like Daniel Barenboim showing how Beethoven should be played.

Rod Marsh, by the way, told me that Dennis didn't bowl an in-swinger, and he should know. Yet Don was convinced. I asked Dennis himself, and he wrote back as follows:

I did the clinic (that Don referred to) and remember it well. Can't remember the year which will be significant as it will determine my age at the time. Rod is correct in saying I didn't bowl an inswinger. When I played I could be a smart-arse and say 'why should I bother when I don't need one?'. But I would have loved to have one. I always practised hard at that ball but could only get it to go occasionally. Rod was probably suffering on those occasions! Though I couldn't bowl an inswinger to the right-hander I used the width of the bowling crease to create an angle in, but also bowled an outswinger from wide on the crease to try to confuse the batsman, with good success. But after I finished playing I managed to learn how, so Don was absolutely right about the clinic, as it all clicked on that occasion.

If this story shows Lillee's diligence, technique and control, here is one about his intensity, conviction and commitment. In a one-day match in 1976 between Western Australia and Queensland, at that time the two most powerful state sides, WA had been bowled out for 77. Rod Marsh, their captain, who tells this story partly against himself, partly to show the kind of man (and player) his friend Dennis Lillee was, began to give a team talk to his disconsolate players. 'Let's at least put up a show for our home crowd,' he said, 'and get a few of them out.' Lillee burst in angrily: 'Put up a show? We're going to win.' He charged out onto the ground, bowled Viv Richards for 0 in his first over, got Greg Chappell caught behind for 2, ending up with 4 wickets for 21. Queensland were all out for 62.

I opened the batting against him in the Centenary Test, at Melbourne, in 1977. We had won the toss on a green wicket, put Australia in, and bowled them out for 138. Rick McCosker broke his jaw trying to hook Bob Willis. We had an hour or so to bat at the end of the first day. Lillee bowled immaculately. He had seven men on the off-side, six of them in the slips; a short square leg, and a fine leg. There was hardly a ball that one could easily let go outside the off-stump, nor anything nearer to one's legs than on middle stump. He was also swinging the ball away, and bowling very fast. Wonderful stuff. Lillee went on to take 6 for 26 as we were bowled out for 95.

In the second innings, the pitch was quieter, the grass drier. After an initial opening burst Lillee knew he was unlikely to get batsmen caught in the slips; the ball was hardly swinging, the bounce was lower, and edges carried less far. So, increasingly, Lillee bowled to hit the stumps (or the pads), with the occasional cutter (he bowled an off-cutter, and when in carnival mood, a leg-break and a googly).

The match ended with a win for Australia by 45 runs, exactly the same result as in the first match, 100 years before. Lillee took eleven wickets. Derek Randall was Man of the Match. When handed the microphone after being given the award on the outfield (not something that usually happened in those days), Randall said something like: 'Thank you all very much for coming' – except he said 'cooming' – 'and thank you, Dennis, for t'bump on the 'ead. If you'd hit me anywhere else it might've 'urt.'

This reminds me of watching the World Series game on television a couple of years later, when Lillee hit Richards on the jaw with a bouncer. Extraordinarily, Viv simply shook his head and went on batting.

Batting against Lillee, especially in Australia, could be a fearsome experience, at least for ordinary (non-Richards) mortals. The crowd would be psyched up, shouting 'Kill, kill, kill' in time with each step of his run-up, mounting to the crescendo of the delivery. Lillee was not averse to geeing them up.

Perhaps Lillee's menace peaked in the notorious 1974–5 series, when he was partnered by Jeff Thomson. There were some lively and uneven pitches, and both bowlers were probably at their fastest and best. Thomson had not yet had his damaging shoulder injury (which happened in 1976), while Lillee had courageously fought his way back to fitness from the serious back injury; when he returned from the 1973 tour of West Indies, three small fractures were discovered in his vertebrae. He had decided against an operation to fuse the bones, which would have enabled him to have a decent lifestyle, but would not have allowed him to bowl fast again. Instead he was encased in plaster for six weeks, and went through drastic and laborious rehabilitation for months afterwards.

Lillee and Thomson were wonderfully matched, not only in both being fast, skilful and lethal, but in their contrasting styles. Lillee was an orthodox and (as I've said) accurate bowler. Batsmen facing him could at least line the ball up; there was nothing obscure or eccentric in his action. Thommo was different. He bowled with a great athletic sling, bringing his right arm like a catapult from near his right ankle. The ball was thus hidden from view for some of the final arm-swing. What's more, the bowler himself didn't always know where the ball was going, which meant that the batsman had no idea whatever.

The 1974–5 Ashes Test matches were the first overseas series to be televised in the UK, the day's highlights being shown just after 7 o'clock on BBC. My old friend and opening partner at Middlesex, Mike Smith, used to tell us how he would pour himself a stiff gin and tonic, turn on the television, and hide behind the sofa watching these X-certificate highlights, ice shaking in the glass. One ball, I think bowled by Thomson, who got such steep and vicious bounce, summed up the Brisbane Test for me, and no doubt produced more than usual perturbation in the ice in Smith's gin. This ball flew from just short of a length to Keith Fletcher, brushed his glove on its way to striking St George (on the MCC cap badge) full-on, and rebounded from there in front of square on the off-side, where it was almost caught by Ross Edwards diving forward from cover-point. I'm not sure who was more disappointed, Thommo or Fletcher.

There was a particularly courageous show of bravado during that series. Tony Greig reckoned that Lillee bowled worse when he was trying to hit you rather than get you out, so he deliberately provoked him, laughing at his bouncers, and histrionically signalling his own boundaries like an umpire. I would never have had that kind of nerve. Nor would I have shared John Edrich's attitude; apparently he preferred to face Lillee and Thomson rather than leg-spinner Terry Jennings.

Dennis Lillee had a vivid presence on the field. He could be irritating, even a bit delinquent. He once (the only time I saw it) encouraged the crowd to have a go at one of our players – who happened to be me. I had thrown at one stump to try to run him out in a one-day match at Sydney in 1980, and Dennis ironically (and extravagantly) clapped me when I missed.

One way we have of dealing with those who frighten us is to use humour to lessen the threat; thus in 1978 we quickly named the 'slippery' (Don Bradman's word for him) Rodney Hogg 'Quintin', 'Road', and 'Hedge'; thus reducing him to less terrifying kinds of hogs. I did call my daughter 'Lara Lillee', but that was after I stopped playing.

And I once named a soft-toy lizard given to me by a nun in Queensland 'Dennis'; I regret getting a cheap laugh on TV in Australia when I answered the inevitable question about why the lizard with a remark about 'small head and big mouth'. It was my big mouth.

Dennis could also be genuinely and collegially funny. I remember him shaking his hand as he picked up a defensive push from me in his follow-through, as if I'd stung him by the ferocity of my drive. I enjoyed that.

At Perth in 1979 he notoriously used the aluminium bat against us. He had flagged up his intentions before the match. It seemed a bit of a stunt; or possibly a marketing pitch; either way, it was a case of DKL being provocative. Coming in to bat shortly before the second new ball, he hit a couple of shots, which made a curious and unattractive clanging sound. But more relevantly, the metal bat scarred the new ball, and I complained. Rightly, the umpires ordered him to change his bat. Dennis was reluctant, to say the least. It took captain Greg Chappell, striding out in his upright and dignified way with an armful of (wooden) bats, to get him to climb down, but Lillee made his point even more blatantly by throwing his piece of aluminium thirty yards away towards the boundary. He even did that stylishly, like a discus-thrower!

(There is a postscript to this story. I had forgotten that before Chappell's arrival on the field, Lillee had gone to the Australian dressing room. Recently Marsh told me that he was watching the whole episode with amusement. When Lillee was about to return to the middle with his wooden bat, Marsh, sitting by the door of the dressing-room, stirred the pot. 'Are you going to let them tell you what bat to use?' he asked quietly. Lillee, re-incensed, rushed back to his bag, retrieved the aluminium bat and returned to the fray for the final confrontation.)

Geoff Boycott, who did not share Greig's approach to batting against Lillee, was angry with me for firing him up. We were soon 41 for 4 in our second innings, three of them, including Boycott (lbw Lillee 0), to Dennis.

Lillee was a legend among cricketers. The same Mike Smith who hid behind his sofa nicknamed Lawrence Williams, the Glamorgan fast-medium bowler, who had a passing resemblance to DKL, but with all dimensions including pace considerably reduced, the Lily of the Valleys.

Dennis himself thinks his results might have been even better overall had he bowled more like Richard Hadlee, concentrating on line and length; but he could never resist the lure of the interpersonal battle with the batsman, which led to his more varied approach, inviting strokes, risking bouncers and yorkers. That is where what was sometimes wrongly called 'sledging' came from, he says; the sheer eyeball to eyeball confrontation in the heat of battle. He acknowledges that sometimes he might have got a bit too personal.

In 1981, Dennis was not quite the bowler he'd been, having had a serious viral infection early in the tour. He and I had another little disagreement over his disappearances after each spell of bowling to have a short break and change shirts. I was technically in the right, but I think in retrospect that it was a bit hard on an ageing fast bowler recovering from pneumonia!

In that series, Lillee was on the whole less dangerous than Terry Alderman, and, sometimes, than Hogg and Geoff Lawson. One felt he was hanging in, using all his resources of shrewdness to keep going at the top level. He came up against some rough treatment from Ian Botham, who notoriously hooked him for three sixes with his eyes shut at Old Trafford, and mauled him, along with others, in his famous, more bucolic, innings at Headingley. It must have been tempting at times for captain Kim Hughes to give Alderman first choice of ends, but I think that would have been a hard call, especially given the tensions that we later learned were at play between the old guard (Lillee and his great companion and ally Marsh) on the one hand, and the young, talented but probably naïve Hughes.

David Constant was one of the umpires at Old Trafford in 1981. He had a chirpy sort of South of the Thames humour. Towards the end of the match, I was fielding at silly mid-off to Lillee when John Emburey was bowling. My shadow was on the pitch, but I was (as required) staying still. Lillee stood back and complained. Constant, twenty-two yards away at the bowler's stumps, said sardonically: 'You've always got something to complain about, Dennis. Why don't you just get on with the game?' Dennis took it well. 'I *am* popular,' he muttered, and indeed got on with the game.

Australian cricketers pride themselves on their toughness. They *are* tough. They play hard, but usually straight. I was always impressed by the story told me by Alan Knott, that Ian Chappell, one of the toughest, was twice in a Test match in Melbourne given out caught behind down the leg-side (by Knott) when he hadn't hit the ball, once off the bowling of Tony Greig, who was not above a bit of triumphalism on such occasions. Each time, Chappell walked off in such a way that no one would have known he had been given out incorrectly. His remark to me at Adelaide when I was batting, 'You do the batting, Mike, we'll do the appealing, and leave the umpiring to the umpires' reflected a standard by which he himself, and most Australian cricketers, including Lillee, lived. I have always admired it.

Tough and straight. But what I have also come to realize is that there is a softer side, if one is allowed to mention this about iconic Australians like Lillee, Marsh and the Chappell brothers, all of whom I regard as friends. Dennis himself is warm and generous. In 1988, when both sides from the Centenary Test gathered together in Australia for a veterans' series, he took the trouble to get the aluminium bat signed by all the England and Australia players (he reminded me that when I signed it I wrote that I wished him all the best with sales), and gave it to my twelve-year-old son, Mischa. He also wrote a generous postscript to my book on the 1981 series.

When in 2008 I was about to become President of the MCC, Dennis sent me a charming letter out of the blue, suggesting that my experiences facing belligerent fast bowlers would no doubt stand me in good stead for dealing with anything the 'egg and bacon brigade' might throw at me at an AGM, and wishing me all the best in my year. When I went to Perth for a few days during and before the last Test there in 2010, he told me he was sorry we hadn't known each other better when we played against each other, a limitation probably caused more by me than by him, since I used to feel uneasy about too much friendliness when it was interspersed with attempts to knock my head off (though of course this didn't apply to my England colleagues whom I'd happily face in county cricket, so there was no logic to it). I regret it too.

He is a modest man. 'Should I mention this?' he asked his wife, Helen, when I asked him at dinner during the Test match in Perth in 2010 what had produced such a remarkable change in Mitchell Johnson's bowling earlier the same day, when he took six wickets in England's first innings for 38, in effect winning the match for Australia. She nodded, so he told me.

After an unsuccessful first Test at Brisbane, Johnson had been dropped for the next one, at Adelaide. He went back to Perth, where Lillee spent several days in the nets with him. Lillee gave him an acronym, as a reminder, a key to hold in mind – TUFF. The talk would have been simpler than the following, but in summary it went, I learned, along these lines:

'T is for Target: as soon as you get back to your mark, throughout the run-up and delivery, look at the target. U is for standing up as you run in and bowl, be strong and bouncy; walk tall. First F is for front arm. As you load up (that is, as you get into your action proper in the delivery stride), keep the front arm strong and hard, raising it above your head rather than pulling away towards the right-hand batsman's leg-side (which tends to open your chest and cause you to drop your bowling arm, thus losing accuracy, swing and pace). The second F is for follow-through.'

The transformation was remarkable, and indeed Mitchell paused, stood tall, didn't try to bowl too fast, followed through, and found both the swing and the control that had eluded him for weeks. (Clearly he should have taken Dennis around with him for the remainder of that series!)

This story fits Dennis's theory of coaching. Too often, he says, people say the obvious: that a bowler doesn't get his wrist behind the ball, for instance. Good coaching goes beyond this, he says, partly by seeing and saying *why* it's not right – which is often the result of what goes wrong elsewhere in the action – and partly by *showing* the difference.

Dennis Lillee has done a lot for cricket. Since retirement, he has set up fast-bowling camps in India, contributing to the building of a tradition of fast bowling in a part of the world that was at one time a no-go area for this particular skill (with the notable exception, from the end of the 1970s, of the remarkable Kapil Dev).

He has been an outstanding President of WACA, playing a large role by his presence, personality, good sense and approachability in turning a huge deficit (around 14 million dollars, I believe) into a profit of around 4 million in five years, though typically he is quick to mention the teamwork involved, the contributions of David Williams, the Chairman, and of Tony Dodemaide and Graeme Wood, past and present Chief Executives.

Now still a fine figure of a man, striking of looks and direct of gaze, Dennis Lillee gives the impression of being a person who has enjoyed his life, and continues to do so. He has never become a caricature of himself (a risk for people who are seen as 'characters' in sport). He remains a real Aussie, one who can afford to show his softer and more generous side more amply now that he doesn't have to live out the burden of 'If Lillee don't get yer, Thommo will'. It has been a privilege to know him and indeed to have batted against him, however ineptly.

14

WHISPERING DEATH

In 2013, I met Michael Holding at the Oval, on the first afternoon of the fifth Test against Australia. I wanted to talk to him about fast bowling, and its decline in Test cricket; about his own feat on a low flat pitch on the same ground thirty-seven years before, when he took fourteen wickets against England, twelve of them bowled or lbw. I asked him about the rise of the West Indian team for twenty years from 1976, based as it was on a succession of magnificent and varied fast bowlers, able to maintain an onslaught on opposition batsmen; and how and why the decline came, so quickly and steeply, since the mid-1990s.

Having recently watched the film *Fire in Babylon*, the story of the early days of that West Indian emergence into cricketing superpower, I was struck by how tame fast bowing is nowadays. The dearth is quite a contrast with the 1970s and '80s. Then batsmen faced Dennis Lillee and Jeff Thomson, as West Indies themselves did, succumbing to a 5–1 defeat in 1975–6, and, as all other international batsmen had to do, there was the remarkable succession of West Indian fast bowlers – Andy Roberts, Michael himself, Wayne Daniel, followed by Colin Croft, Joel Garner, Malcolm Marshall, and ending with Courtney Walsh and Curtly Ambrose. And we shoudn't ignore many others from the same era, including Bob Willis, Ian Botham, Imran Khan, Mike Procter, Richard Hadlee, Wasim Akram and Waqar Younis.

In the current Ashes series, there had been excellent fast-medium bowling, most strikingly from Jimmy Anderson and Ryan Harris, but where were the men who bowl at 90 mph and over? Where was the sheer pace and hostility of those earlier years? Eight or nine fast bowlers played, and against most of them, for almost all the time, you wouldn't fear injury. A dimension was lacking.

Technology bore out this impression. Benedict Bermange, the Sky Sports statistician, let me have details of maximum, minimum and average speeds for all bowlers in that 2013 series. The figures were remarkably similar – all averaged around 84 mph, with fastest deliveries usually around 87. All were grouped within a small range.

And it's not of course just the element of danger; there is also the sheer excitement both in facing such bowling (until the shell-shock starts to turn some otherwise fine batsmen into quivering wrecks) and in watching them. The athleticism of a Holding or a Thommo, combined with the ability to swing the ball at pace of a Roberts, Marshall or a Lillee, was aesthetically superb. And to see a great batsman, Viv Richards, say, or Greg Chappell, take on the fast bowlers with audacity and skill, was the icing on the cake.

I remember playing for Middlesex against Somerset at Lord's, when Wayne Daniel bowled flat out at Richards, who went for him – the contest was electrifying. It was alarming even to be fielding in the slips.

Ironically, our Oval meeting happened just after a spell of old-fashioned hostile fast bowling from Stuart Broad; for a few overs, there were short-pitched balls, even two short legs. Top-class batsmen were made to jump around, to play the ball down from the splice. Michael Clarke was almost bowled (and/or hit wicket) when he tried to guard his stumps against a ball spinning back towards them from his shoulder, and centurion Shane Watson was hit just where helmet and back of the head met. There was a physical as well as technical challenge. But that spell stood out as a rarity in recent Test cricket.

For this match, the England selectors underlined the modern attitude by picking as third seamer Chris Woakes rather than either of the quicker and more hostile options, Steve Finn or Chris Tremlett. England have often preferred the control presumed to be offered by a medium-fast bowler, whilst at other times ignoring medium-paced bowlers as not quick enough.

The first reason for this homogenizing trend was, according to Michael, caution. The current mind-set seemed to be based on taking wickets by restriction. Hence, too, the tendency so often to have only one or two slips, and no short legs. Contrast the fields set for Holding and Roberts themselves, or for that matter, for Willis and Botham. As Michael said:

> People complained that Finn would go at four runs an over, but they didn't ask how quickly he took his wickets. That's what I would want to know. You might get an average player out by means of this restrictive approach, but the best players find ways to score, they take the singles and the twos, and suddenly they are on top. You have to get twenty wickets to win a Test match.

Players do play a lot of cricket these days. They are looked after, but the strain on the body is considerable. You can't coast in Test matches, the way you might sometimes do in county matches.

The implication is: modern fast bowlers settle for lower speeds and for accuracy, learning to look after themselves by this restraint.

Today, he continued, there is over-reliance on computer cricket. I think he meant that calculation trumps flair: not that planning and shrewdness are irrelevant; clearly not. For he also said what a great thinker about the game Roberts was, someone who had not only all the skills but also the ability and shrewdness to plan how to bowl against different types of batsmen. Holding's view was that the 'scientific' approach – including the number of people in support teams, all of whom feel they have to contribute, and must therefore run the risk of confusing players – results in a lessening of independence and perhaps also of spontaneity in players and captains.

He did not think the restriction on bouncers (only two allowed per over) had been a factor. He rarely bowled more than two; the definition of a bouncer is that the ball passes the batsman above shoulder height; and he and his colleagues aimed at the gloves and ribs, not the head.

Another factor was to be found in the pitches. In parts of the world, many pitches have (he said) become slower and flatter. Drainage, especially in the UK, may have affected the height of the water table, contributing to pitches being less firm and resilient than in the past. Perhaps, he said, groundsmen have to learn the skill of applying water, and knowing when to stop. The current pitch at the Oval was, he thought, too dry for the start of a match, as it was for the previous Ashes Test at the Oval, in 2009, when it took spin too early in the game. Mind you, he added, it may be a matter of 'doctoring the pitches' to suit England, a practice that he was against, believing that the aim should be to prepare pitches that are good for Test cricket as a whole, for the expression of all skills of the game, and that this is not a matter for the home boards but for the experts – the groundsmen.

So what were the causes of West Indies' bursting into supremacy when Holding was (in my view) the fastest bowler in the world? One element, he thought, was the fact that cricket was the one thing that represented the people of the Caribbean as a whole. 'Usain Bolt is a source of pride for all West Indians; but he competes for Jamaica. Only cricket' (and I would add, the University of the West Indies) 'gives people the sense of pride on behalf of the whole culture.' As Learie Constantine said to C. L. R. James in the early 1930s.

The arrival of Independence in the early 1960s more or less coincided with Frank Worrell becoming the first black captain (1960). All this reinforced the proper pride that West Indies cricket expressed and developed. It took fifteen or so years for the process to come to the fruition that first became crystal clear in 1976.

Another factor, clearly stated in the film, and confirmed by Michael, was the sheer toughness of Australia under Ian Chappell. 'Off the field they were friendly; I would have a drink with them after play. But on the field they were ruthless. And some of the Australian public said things they shouldn't have said, after a few drinks and so on. The players never did.' Clearly those insulting and sometimes racist comments fuelled their opponents' determination, as did the racism of colonialism in the Caribbean, and similar attitudes in England, which were more blatant in those days.

Michael saw Tony Greig, 'with a smirk on his face', give his notorious TV interview in the early part of the 1976 season in England. In those days the touring sides didn't play on Sundays, and the (West Indies) team, who were at Hove, watched the interview live. Greig announced that he would 'make West Indies "grovel"'. After a pause, Michael said: 'He thought then he'd better not suggest he would do it all on his own, so he added something like "with the help of others such as Brian Close"'.

But apart from the unconscious superiority of the 'grovel' remark, Greig had a theory too; one 'not unlike that of current strategists'. Wear them down, grit it out, pick people who would take a blow, who had undoubted courage. And set defensive fields. The assumption was that the West Indies didn't have the persistence or discipline to stick it out. How wrong could one be!

At that time, Holding and his team-mates didn't know Greig at all well. Later, they came to respect and like him. His comment stoked up the Fire in Babylon.

Another factor, Holding said, was Clive Lloyd's captaincy; he was totally fair, and would never pick sides on the basis of island affiliation; he was a father-figure who would not show someone up on the field.

And then, a year later, in 1977, Dennis Waite, the Australian trainer, joined the West Indies squad for World Series Cricket. The players insisted on having him as trainer subsequently. He made them very fit, and this dedication was intrinsic to their ambition for, and achievement of, success.

One other factor, which surprised Michael: when, in World Series Cricket, the West Indies lost badly to Australia, Kerry Packer came into their dressing room.

'We thought he had come to crow. But no, he had come to tell us we weren't playing up to the mark; he wanted a proper contest, above all. He threatened to send some players home.'

And Michael's own bowling feat, here at the Oval? I mentioned the fact that the other fast bowlers hardly took any wickets; Roberts one, Wayne Daniel none, Vanburn Holder three; Bob Willis one, Mike Selvey none. Michael smiled. 'I was the only one young enough and naïve enough to run in and bowl fast on that pitch!' he said. 'And the series was settled.' He had to pitch the ball up; there was no bounce at all to be had. I asked him if (as I seemed to remember) he got reverse swing in those conditions. He said, 'Yes, that's how I bowled Greig twice in the match! But all we knew then was that at a certain point the ball would tend to swing the opposite way to the newer ball, so we just switched it round in the hand.'

I learned that, after the 3–0 win against England that year, Holding almost gave up cricket. Following his fourteen wickets at the Oval, the government gave him a scholarship to university. He had a shoulder injury too. But the main thing was that he could see no future, as a career, in cricket, given the wages paid at that time. He didn't want to be a county player, however much he earned (indeed, he was offered a good sum by Sussex, at Greig's instigation). A few months later, Lloyd rang him up to invite him to join World Series Cricket. Without this, Holding might never have been seen again on the international cricket field.

For any readers who have not seen Michael Holding bowl, do look him up on the Web. Called 'Whispering Death' for the smoothness and lightness of his run-up, not to mention the sheer speed of his bowling, he was a beautiful sight. He had been a 400 metres hurdler, and it showed. Now he expresses his elegance through his voice and his presence, as part of the Sky commentary team.

But what, I asked him, caused the decline in West Indies cricket from the mid-1990s onwards?

Not American TV. First and foremost, it was lack of discipline. Curtly Ambrose, for instance, stopped playing because he couldn't bear the indiscipline of the younger bowlers. Second, lack of adaptation. They didn't learn, they didn't make use of the technology [which as he had said before can get out of hand, but which was moving other sides on]. And, third: When things started to go wrong, the administrators never intervened in a good way; too many were in it for the prestige, so as to be able to say they were Members of the Board.

In his view, the new Caribbean Premier League, which had been inaugurated two months earlier, and was as we spoke about to reach the Finals stage, had been a total success. 'Why could not the board have arranged something of this kind? Why could it not have found, as the Caribbean Premier League had done, nineteen sponsors?' Asked to contribute to the development, he at first declined, not wanting to be associated just with T20 cricket. But when he was told the aims would be to find Test players as much as short-game players, and that his link would start in January 2014, he had agreed to play a part.

Who knows, maybe this will be the beginning of a revival, and we'll see a new batch of Holdings, Roberts and Marshalls gracing Test cricket once again.

15

CALEB GARTH:
THE CRAFTSMAN

'Poetry without the aid of the poets'
Middlemarch, George Eliot

'His virtual divinities were good practical schemes, accurate work and faithful completion of undertakings; his prince of darkness was a slack workman.' This is Caleb Garth, in George Eliot's *Middlemarch*.

But it might as well have been Tom Cartwright, cricketer with the name of an ancient trade, for whom, as for Garth, 'bad work' (like a young man's fancy handwriting that wasn't readily legible) 'dispelled all his mildness.'

When I first played against top cricketers, in the early 1960s, there were several such men on the circuit. As bowlers, or bowling all-rounders, they were utterly consistent and accurate, and they all revelled in hard work. Captains relied on them to keep it tight on good pitches, to bowl sides out when conditions favoured them. Their names were uttered with awe and respect among opponents.

Of Tom Cartwright, even so fine a batsman as Tom Graveney said, 'I hated batting against him. I could never see where I was going to score a run.' All bowled very straight. If you missed, they hit. All bowled with split fields.

To name a few: Derek Shackleton, who took a hundred wickets in twenty consecutive seasons for Hampshire, never had a hair out of place, never bowled a bad ball. His team-mates allowed him one half-volley a season. He trod lightly on the ground, almost floating through his action, a caresser of the ball (in that way, rather like Mike Hendrick a decade or two later, though Hendrick was faster and taller).

Then there were quicker, more physically threatening bowlers, some of whom had a mean streak, all accurate, straight, persistent: Les Jackson of Derbyshire, Jack Flavell and Len Coldwell of Worcestershire, Brian Statham (Lancashire), Alan Moss (Middlesex). Most of them conveyed a dislike of the batsman, sometimes even a scorn. They gave you nothing. Their excellence bought wickets for their bowling partners.

Among the spinners there were Fred Titmus of Middlesex and Ray Illingworth of Yorkshire, both mean, both keen on getting wickets by starving you of runs. Perhaps the epitome was Don Shepherd of Glamorgan, a brisk off-spinner who also swung the ball away. Don dominated Welsh cricket. Like Cartwright, he had an acerbic streak, set in and balanced by a warmth of personality.

Shepherd never played a Test match; Cartwright played only five, Shackleton seven. They were felt by selectors to be not quick enough (or in Shepherd's case, perhaps too quick), or not quite penetrative enough, for Test cricket on Test pitches. This may well have been an error of judgement.

One consequence was that these cricketers became stalwarts of the county game. I think of them as yeomen cricketers. I didn't know Shackleton at all well; I can hardly remember facing him. I became friendly with Shepherd, whom I visited once – I think greatly to his surprise – in his family's small provision shop at Port Eynon, on the Gower peninsula. I always struggled against him, too, often getting pads and bat caught up together. Especially on slow Welsh pitches, it was extremely hard to score off his bowling.

But I came to know Tom best. We toured South Africa together in 1964–5. The day before we left was election day, and he and I happened to be standing by the Grace Gates at Lord's when Quintin Hogg's electioneering car drove by, its loudspeaker projecting magnified Conservative rhetoric. Cheerfully, we both shook our fists at the car, grinning at each other. That was a link. In South Africa itself we went our own ways, but we had our eyes opened to, and also sought out – to see for ourselves – something of the appalling nature of apartheid.

Like Caleb Garth, Tom had integrity. His work ethic, his values, were of a piece. To start with the bowling. He came in off a short-ish run, one or two steps, then, head down – the horse bowing to, and straining at, the plough – he accelerated easily into a jump and a high action, with a strong follow-through. He bowled from close to the stumps. He was quicker than he looked to a casual spectator, putting a lot of effort into each ball; the ball hit the bat hard and higher than one might anticipate. He was fully and personally *present* in his bowling (unlike the more ethereal Shackleton). Tom lived what might have been his mantra: what you put in you get out.

His regular field was: two slips, a gulley, cover and mid-off on the off-side; mid-on, short square leg, backward square leg, and either mid-wicket or a second short leg on the leg-side. He rarely had a fine leg or a third man – he would never give the batsman anything to cut, nor anything wide enough to enable him to free his arms and hands. Edges would not race away to third man or fine leg; they might be squeezed out for a couple in these general directions.

Cartwright rightly objected to being called a negative bowler. He liked to keep the field tight, along these lines. The wicket-keeper would often stand up to the stumps, increasing the batsman's feeling of claustrophobia.

He had endurance. He believed in the 'faithful completion of his undertakings'. In one spell in August 1967, in seven consecutive three-day matches, he bowled 383 overs and took 61 wickets. 'Bowling is bloody hard work, but medium-pacers should thrive on hard work,' he said.

Tom had a sense of the way life could fall apart if one lost one's discipline, realism and honest effort. I captained the MCC tour of Kenya and Tanzania in 1974. Tom was our star bowler. In the three-day match against East Africa, we were contemplating a declaration in our second innings. I was inclined to declare early, thus giving us a long time to bowl the opposition out, but also a chance of another route to victory if they were to get close, and could be persuaded to take risks. Tom would have none of that. 'If you want us to get bloody frazzled in the sun all day, declare now!' he said. He wanted us to give them no chance, so that he could keep his attacking fields all the time. But I was struck by the 'frazzled' – maybe the bombs that devastated Coventry when he was five, forcing the family into their own air-raid shelter overnight, killing hundreds in the neighbourhood, were more devastating to this little boy than he knew. For some people, disaster-scenarios unconsciously firm up their resolve; I remember the head of Northgate Clinic, an in-patient unit for adolescents, imagining a scenario in which the whole place was flooded. I learned from this how easily things fall apart, how alert one must be not to fall back into complacency.

Tom had an alternative image too, one of purity, an image at least glimpsed in cricket. Purity from ugliness, from hypocrisy and from dishonesty.

If I go onto a ground in the morning, an hour before a game, it's the loveliest of times . . . There may be a mower still ticking, and the groundsman marking the ends, but there's a silence as well. You can stand and think and listen . . . I used to love to go out to open the batting at the start of a match and to see the white lines, the 22 yards of beautiful strip. No ball marks, no foot marks. All the preparation. It's something very special.

And at the end of Stephen Chalke's book Cartwright says: 'Cricket is not like any other sport. It has a purity, and that purity is being taken away. It's so important that people who love cricket stand up and fight for it.'

Cartwright did not suffer fools gladly. His 'mildness' was, like Caleb Garth's, dispelled by bad work, or fancy ideas. He knew his own value. In that same match, I gave Richard Hutton's brother John, who had a turn of speed, the end with the wind behind him when opening the bowling, requiring Tom to bowl into the breeze. After a few overs, he scowled at me: 'If you want me to float up a few out-swingers, then I'll carry on here. If you want me to really bowl' – implicitly, if I want him to win the match for us – 'put me on at the other end.' I did; he took 5 for 30 off 18 overs, and MCC won by 237 runs.

In later years, he was in charge of Wales Under-16s, as well as Director of Coaching for Wales. Mark Wallace, who became Glamorgan's wicket-keeper and played in a record 230 consecutive County Championship games between 2001 and 2015, found the rough edge of Tom's tongue once, when he scored a flighty thirty or so for the junior team. Tom told him he had to decide: did he want to become a proper batsman or was he going to chance it? Tom was not mild. And he believed that sometimes we need a shock if we are to register our need to work at something and change. We should not rely on chancing it.

Stephen Chalke recalls telling Tom a story about a young cricketer playing a club match some years ago. He threw his bat through the pavilion window when given out, and the club tried to lodge a complaint. But they were told he was already on a last warning and would face a lengthy ban. 'He's a future England cricketer. Do you want to set him back like this?' They withdrew their complaint, he progressed to the England side, where he handled himself badly and never fulfilled his potential. Tom replied immediately. 'They wouldn't have been setting him back. It was letting him off that cost him a long international career.'

He recalls a severe telling-off that he received from Eddie Branson, the schoolteacher who inspired him and encouraged his cricket as a boy. Tom respected the firmness of male authority figures, and became such a man himself. His father, who worked for Riley the car manufacturer, 'taught us to know the difference between right and wrong, between truth and lies. And to treat other people in the way you'd like other people to treat you,' he said. Tom's brother-in-law John said of Tom's father: 'You knew where you were with him. He was straight down the middle.'

Like Tom, and like his bowling, Tom Cartwright hated cant. He mocked pretensions and snobbery. His work ethic was leavened by his sardonic Coventry humour, by a grin, honed in the car workshop (he fitted junction boxes in the wiring of the engines of Humber Super Snipes). When he moved to Somerset from Warwickshire in 1976, he found the forelock-touching and the stolidity limiting; he longed for the cut and thrust of urban argument and debate, on politics, sport, the meaning of life, that he had been brought up on in the Midlands.

Some who didn't know him well, or who were flaky or showy themselves, found him curmudgeonly, sarcastic, troubling. But those who got beyond this loved him. He had total integrity. He saw things from the side of the underdog. He ruffled feathers but with passion. He was an enthusiast. His Puritan work ethic was tempered by understanding of the weaknesses of all human beings, by his love of the game and his devotion to those he coached and came across.

It was tempered too by an openness to the new, and to the uniqueness of the individual and of his culture. Garth allowed his son to study, though for him academic life was second to work, or 'business'. He gave room to his daughter's values and emotions. Cartwright said: 'The art of coaching is to prepare people so that they can teach themselves. [And of course you can take a horse to water, but you can't make it drink.] If you impose on people, they don't make decisions for themselves.' He also said: 'You can't impose a system that's the same in Yorkshire as it is in Essex or in Wales . . . Each area has a different history and different social and economic conditions.' And for Trinidad, where he was asked to write up some sort of coaching structure for them, he commented in his report: 'Whatever you do, I hope you pursue a structure within a West Indian way of playing cricket.' His view was that if you were to stifle natural inclination, you'd lose something precious.

Stephen Chalke read Tom a piece he had written about Hampshire batsman Alan Rayment, who ran ballroom dancing classes in a hotel next to the old County Ground in Southampton, on Northlands Road. Rayment observed his fellow-cricketers through the eyes of a dancing instructor, ending with an answer to the question as to which other cricketers might follow in the footsteps of Mark Ramprakash and Darren Gough in *Strictly Come Dancing*. 'David Gower would be the very best,' Rayment said. 'He has the beautiful coordination, the grace, timing, nonchalance, sophistication, and he wouldn't be embarrassed. He would be the tops.'

Stephen commented to me:

Tom was fascinated, immediately likening Alan's observations to the way the best cricket coaches used to work. 'They saw the uniqueness of the individual and developed it; too often nowadays,' he said, 'they tried to make the person fit the template.'

And one should never lose the delight in playing. Of his school-teacher Eddie Branson, Cartwright said:

> He'd say to a fourteen-year-old, 'For goodness' sake, James, smile a bit. It's got to be fun too.' He [Eddie] wasn't an expert, he was an enthusiast. And I'd rather have an enthusiast working with kids any day. The expert can crush enthusiasm, turning people off wanting to play.

There are many crafts associated with cricket – bat and ball making, groundsmanship, umpiring, scoring. There are also batting, fielding, wicket-keeping and bowling. Caleb Garth again:

> You must be sure of two things: you must love your work, and not be always looking over the edge of it, wanting your play to begin.
>
> And the other is – you mustn't be ashamed of your work and think it would be more honourable to you to be doing something else . . . no matter what a man is, I wouldn't give tuppence for him, whether he was the Prime Minister or the rick-thatcher, if he didn't do well what he undertook to do.

Stephen reminded me of Bill Shankly's remark: 'If I was employed to clean Huddersfield market place and toilets, they'd be the cleanest in the whole country. You've got to have pride in what you do.'

As Dennis Silk said, on the occasion of Bob Barber's seventieth birthday cricketing party at Broadha'penny Down, in 2007: 'Tom Cartwright is one of the great unsung heroes of English cricket.'

PART 4

CRICKET AND RACE

16

CRISES IN CRICKET

The essence of cricket remains unchanged – contests between bat and ball, with two main protagonists in a team context. But what spectators see and look for in top-level cricket has been transformed during my cricketing lifetime.

Technology has entered the international game, with ball-tracking devices based on sophisticated weapons technology. Cricketers may now legitimately challenge umpires' decisions. There has been corruption in the form of match-fixing or spot-fixing, which has resulted in the institution of anti-corruption units by ICC and by boards of control in individual countries.

One-day, limited-overs cricket, about which Len Hutton mused, 'Fancy that, batting without worrying about getting out!', arrived in England in the form of the Gillette Cup in 1963. The forty-overs-a-side John Player League followed, in 1969. In 2003, professional T20 cricket began in the UK. In 2008, the Indian Premier League erupted onto TV screens, with dancing cheerleaders, fireworks and extremely loud music. The proliferation of, and money on offer in, T20 domestic leagues all over the world now constitute the biggest threat to international cricket, and in particular to Test cricket.

But cricket's most divisive conflicts have centred on two issues: first, back in 1977, World Series Cricket announced its imminent hijack of many of the best players. This was Australian tycoon Kerry

Packer's so-called 'circus', a scheme grounded on his resentment at being cold-shouldered in attempts to acquire TV rights for Test cricket in Australia for his Channel Nine.

Second was cricket's response to apartheid, most starkly exemplified in the D'Oliveira affair of 1968 and its aftermath.

News of the imminent World Series broke on an astonished and often outraged cricket world immediately after the Centenary Test at Melbourne in 1977. I played in that match, but had no inkling of a secret plan involving many of those involved. By contracting the majority of the world's top players, and scheduling matches during series arranged by the official boards, this venture was a threat to established cricket, and was felt by many to be a betrayal. But in the High Court in London, on the grounds that to prevent those who had signed from also playing in top-class officially administered cricket would be a restraint of trade, Packer won the case against the Test and County Cricket Board. Eventually, after two years, the Australian Cricket Board succumbed, giving the contract to televise international cricket to Channel Nine, and the enterprise was quickly wound up.

I was approached by Packer later in 1977. He hoped I would bring to World Series Cricket the whole England side. This was not a difficult decision for me; I did not like the idea of a revolution, nor did I like the idea of cricket being controlled by an individual, outside the whole cricketing structure. I was also uncomfortable with the degree of commercialism involved.

But at the same time, I understood its appeal. Test cricketers were paid little; we who played in that Centenary Test joked that we were the worst-paid people among the 250,000 who came to watch – and though this was probably not strictly true, it wasn't far from being so. There was an assumption among administrators that they didn't have to move with the times. Paternalistically, they smugly accepted that cricketers were to be paid like wage-earning subordinate employees: one member of the Middlesex Committee, assuming that I was not (really) one of this substrate, commented to me when I joined Middlesex as captain in 1971: 'Of course you must have a private income'.

I could also see the benefits of some of Packer's experiments – day–night cricket in coloured clothing, improved marketing, restrictions on the number of fielders on the boundary in one-day games, even a degree of razzmatazz. I felt no personal animosity to those who signed up to it.

Though much of its cricket was of a high standard, this was not its main significance. World Series cricket's impact was to push the game into the modern world, making it more marketable, more commercial. My guess is that the long-term consequences have been more good than bad. WSC built on already established one-day cricket. It made possible good career prospects for international cricketers worldwide, and to some extent, money filtered down to less prominent players, too. WSC was a forerunner of the Indian Premier League in appealing to many who had not been interested in older, more sedate forms of the game.

To my mind, the current threat to Test cricket arises not from T20 cricket per se, but from its speedy burgeoning throughout the year, and the damaging impact, already felt to some extent, on Test cricket's appeal.

But what I will concentrate on in this and subsequent chapters of part 4 is cricket's relations to apartheid and racism. David Sheppard described it as the biggest challenge to face cricket in its history.

In September 1968, Basil D'Oliveira, a so-called 'coloured' from Cape Town, South Africa, was eventually picked by the MCC for the prospective tour of South Africa. He replaced Tom Cartwright, who had pulled out. The South African Government, claiming this to be a political decision that bowed to the demands of the anti-apartheid movement, called off the tour. Soon after, Peter Hain, a South African exile who had, when aged fifteen, spoken at the funeral of John Harris

– the white freedom fighter or terrorist, depending on your point of view, hanged for murder in Johannesburg on 1 April 1965 – led a campaign to 'Stop the 70 Tour': South Africa's rugby team were touring the UK in 1969–70.

The combination of direct action, peaceful protest and impassioned argument led many sporting bodies and governments to stop or discourage representative sporting contacts with (white) South Africa.

Amazingly, two decades later, an agreement brokered between the recently released Nelson Mandela and F. W. de Klerk, Prime Minister of the Nationalist Government, meant the end of apartheid. Stopping contact and competition between sportsmen and women from other countries with teams and individuals from South Africa had been I think a significant factor in this new readiness of white South Africa for radical change. There was also a worldwide readiness for compromise: the release of Mandela and the dismantling of apartheid came more or less simultaneously with the fall of the Berlin Wall.

In the cricket world in England, there was much unease about the ban. Players who relied on overseas coaching and playing contracts during the English winter months were disappointed and in some cases aggrieved that they, along with other sportsmen, were having to bear the brunt of the protest. Actors, musicians, businessmen could ply their trades in South Africa, but not sportsmen – unless they were prepared to incur disapproval and penalties from their home boards. There were several illegal tours there, during the 1970s and '80s.

I follow this introduction to Part 4 with a portrait of Doug Insole, who became a close friend. Until he died, aged ninety-one, in 2017, he had been the last person directly involved in the selection process of 1968. As Chairman of Selectors, he had presided over the whole selectorial process – the controversial non-selection of D'Oliveira for the MCC tour of South Africa, followed by his also controversial inclusion as a replacement a month later, which led to the refusal by the South African Government to accept the revised team, and the subsequent cancellation of the tour by MCC. I later write about Basil D'Oliveira himself, before going on to bring a new piece of evidence about what might have happened at that fateful selection meeting. If true, this would alter the generally accepted version of what went on there. I also write about David Sheppard and his part in protesting against the way the MCC had conducted itself during this difficult period.

I then cover the public protest made in 2003 by Zimbabwean cricketers Andy Flower and Henry Olonga against the 'death of democracy in Zimbabwe'. Finally, I reflect on an earlier protest campaign, run from 1958 to 1960 by C. L. R. James, editor of the Trinidad paper *The Nation*, calling for Frank Worrell to be made the first black man to be appointed as first-choice captain of the West Indies (George Headley had captained but only for an isolated match).

I believe that the outrage about, and outcome of, the D'Oliveira affair played a (small but significant) part in the eventual dismantling of apartheid.

17

'BATTING LIKE A GORILLA'

I first got to know Doug Insole in the early 1970s, through the annual county captains' meetings at Lord's, which he chaired. He often emphasized the spirit of the game. He used to tell the Essex players, 'Winning trophies is good, but it's not the be-all and end-all of cricket.' He became a father-figure to many, especially at Essex, where he held long-term the roles of President and Chairman of the Club. Despite his rank, and his age, he would take on mundane jobs at Essex matches, manning the car park, for instance.

We became firm friends during and after the tour of Australia in 1978–9. Doug was the best manager I had any dealings with. He loved the game and the players, without in any way being indulgent (except in his generous provision of fruit to the team room – he could demolish an orange in seconds).

Doug, who in his paid working life was the public relations officer for the building firm, Wimpey, saw his managerial role as wider than that of simply dealing with official matters, or chatting with the Australian Board. He was *our* manager, and he was both kind and firm. On one occasion in Perth, he rightly told me off when I lost my temper. He talked long and hard to one player whose personal life was in a mess. He was aware of another's loneliness and did his tactful best to help him. When he distributed pool money at the end of the tour he offered to give each person his share in a currency of his choice – Australian dollars, pounds sterling, or possibly American dollars, he assumed. When one player decided that the most promising investment currency was Jordanian dirhams, and he would like to be paid in that, Doug was highly amused and also clear that this would be a step too far.

Here's an example of his impact on the field. By the beginning of our second innings in the fourth Test at Sydney, Derek Randall had twice been out for nought, hooking, including in the first innings of that match. Doug tackled him: 'You've got to get the pace of the pitch before you start hooking.' Derek responded, 'But it's my nature, I need to hit a few fours, feel the ball on the bat.' Doug would have none of it. 'In that case,' he said, 'you'd better rethink your nature. You've got to get in first. What's more, you've got to bat sessions, bat to tea, to the close of play.' Randall then played one of the innings of his life, a never-fluent 150, which turned an almost certain defeat into a position from which we won by 111 runs.

Insole's cricket career involved playing for Cambridge and Essex, and then captaining the county for nine years through the 1950s. He was noted for being a 'bottom-hand' batsman, an on-side player, not the side most associated with the classic amateurs of his time. His nine Test appearances were spread over eight years. In the hard-fought third

Test at Durban in 1957, he scored 110 not out while off-spinner Hughie Tayfield took 8 for 69 in 37 overs. (Barry Richards watched this match, aged twelve; he described Insole as 'batting like a gorilla'.)

Like that earlier hero of mine, Jack Robertson (31,914 runs at 37.50), Doug's final career record was more or less exactly the same as mine (his was 25,241 at 37.61, mine 25,186 at 37.81).

He was also a fine footballer, who played right wing for Corinthian Casuals in the Amateur Cup Final at Wembley in 1956.

He enjoyed telling the story of his last appearance for Essex. On 27 July 1969, the first season of the John Player League, Essex were in second place with nine wins out of ten. Doug, aged forty-three, was asked that morning to travel to Yeovil as an SOS. He hadn't played for Essex for six years. On the train journey back, the carriage was full of people returning from the seaside. He put his cricket bag down in the corridor, and someone said, 'My son is very tired, would you mind if he sits on your bag?' And he peed all over the bag. But this was only the icing on the cake. In the match itself, after a dodgy start in which Essex declined to 19 for 3, batsmen Brian Ward and Keith Boyce, reckoning that off-spinner Brian Langford was the danger man, decided to play him out. Doug, a fine attacking player of off-spin, had to sit watching Langford's unique achievement: eight overs, eight maidens, 0 for 0. When Doug did eventually get to the crease, he was run out for a duck by a direct hit from the boundary. And Essex lost by two wickets.

Some of his stories went back, of course, to team-mates from the 1940s and '50s. He was fond of both great English batsmen, Len Hutton and Denis Compton, who didn't have much in common. Doug was touched that, a few weeks before Len died, in 1990, the two of them spent a whole afternoon at Lord's together, absorbed in their conversation. My guess is that he made that meeting possible himself.

Doug and his partner Norma had a great capacity for enjoying life. On the day before he died, he was enthusiastic about the cricket and athletics to be shown on the box that evening (which they watched). A few weeks earlier, they went by train to Liverpool Street, pottered around in the bookshop, and had a happy lunch at a café in the station.

In 2016 I went to his birthday party, at Chelmsford, on a freezing cold Saturday in April. People were there from his playing days – Ken Preston and Brian Taylor – up to more recent times. I can't remember a party at which I laughed as much. How wonderful, for your ninetieth, to be the occasion of memorable affection and hilarity!

Doug was an amusing companion and speaker. His speeches started tentatively, but expanded with his warmth and humour. His vulnerability (expressed partly by his slight stammer), his pride and his humility both, his total lack of pretentiousness or snobbery in a class-conscious world, made him widely loved. He was a warm guest and host, always making people feel comfortable, always interested in others' lives.

18

'NICE BONKING PACE'

Basil was born in Cape Town, of Indian-Portuguese ancestry. He was thus, in apartheid South Africa, designated a Cape Coloured. In 1960 John Arlott, the cricket and wine writer, helped to arrange for Middleton, in the Lancashire League, to take him on as their professional. In 1964 he joined Worcestershire, and became a British citizen. He was cagey about his age, telling the county that he had been born in 1934, so he would have been, on that reckoning, thirty-one when he first played for England. His birth certificate apparently revealed that he was in fact born in 1931, which made him thirty-four when he won his first England cap, and forty-seven when he retired from first-class cricket in 1979. Only in 1972 did the Wisden Almanack change his official date of birth from 1934 to 1931.

English cricket was highly alert in 1968 to the forthcoming tour of South Africa scheduled for 1968–9. Australia were also due to tour England in 1968. Basil had had a moderate tour against the West Indies the winter before, but was picked for the first Test, at Old Trafford, which Australia won by 159 runs. He bowled economically, but took only two wickets. Having top-scored with 87 not out in England's second innings, he was surprisingly dropped for the next Test. The argument must have been that his bowling was not penetrative enough for a third seamer in Test cricket. Barry Knight, the Essex all-rounder, who was more of a bowler, was preferred for the second and third Tests. Meanwhile, D'Oliveira lost form in county cricket. But when opener Roger Prideaux withdrew from the team for the fifth Test, and there were fitness doubts about Tom Cartwright (who, like Knight, was a better bowler than D'Oliveira), D'Oliveira was called up as cover for them. He scored 158.

His omission from the touring party announced a few days later was received with astonishment in many quarters. Doug Insole, Chair of Selectors, insisted that the decision was based on purely cricketing considerations. Presumably, D'Oliveira was considered to be neither one of England's best six or seven batsmen, nor good enough as a bowler to count as an all-rounder. The bad reports he had for drinking in the Caribbean the previous winter did not help.

But there was a further twist to the story. Cartwright withdrew, for a mixture of reasons: a shoulder injury; but also because he could not stomach touring a country where the Nationalist Party conference stood up and cheered when they heard that D'Oliveira had not been selected. His replacement was named as Basil D'Oliveira.

Immediately, South Africa's Prime Minister, B. J. Vorster, accused England of bringing politics into sport, and announced that the team was not welcome. Next day, the MCC called off the tour.

I myself had been on the MCC tour of South Africa in 1964–5, together with Cartwright, and had become aware of the appalling *nature of apartheid. When I learned in early September 1968 that there was a group of MCC members who were troubled by the MCC's role in this whole saga, I joined with alacrity. Other members included film lecturer Charles Barr, David Sheppard, actor and cricket lover Peter Howell, and Surrey cricketer Mike Edwards. This group called for a Special Meeting, which was held on 5 December 1968, at which David proposed and I seconded the vote of no confidence in the MCC committee.*

The death of Basil D'Oliveira is not only sad in itself, but a reminder of a watermark not only for cricket and its dealings with apartheid, but also for consciousness about racism in our own society and ourselves.

D'Oliveira himself became a symbol for non-whites (as they were called) in South Africa, and for racial minorities in this country. As C. L. R. James wrote about cricket in the West Indies during the colonial era: 'The cricket field was a stage on which selected individuals played representative roles charged with social significance.' Being thrust into this role, with the extra strain it imposed, was not, I suspect, something that D'Oliveira himself relished. Not only was there the pressure to prove in Test cricket that the coloured South African was the equal of any white player; he also had to deal with the demands and sometimes the scorn from people on both sides.

But he was willing to bear the 'representative role', to be 'of social significance'. He desperately wanted to be selected for the tour of South Africa in 1968–9, to enhance the proper pride of his compatriots. He turned down offers of large sums of money from the South African Government to make himself unavailable for the tour, and later on, in the early 1980s, to coach on behalf of the South African Government. But he refused to be drawn into politics more directly. He left that to others.

As a cricketer he was an exceptional player of fast bowling. He once described Wes Hall and Charlie Griffith, bowlers who terrified batsmen in the early 1960s, as men who 'bowled at a nice bonking pace'. He was quick to pounce on the short ball, with short-armed pull shots and hooks. At the same time, he missed no opportunity to get onto the front foot. He often dominated bowlers of all sorts. My own image of him is of someone who stood absolutely still in receiving the ball, his head and eyes level. He gave an air of calm authority.

He was more than useful as a bowler, with his medium-paced out-swingers. Ray Illingworth, who captained England between 1969 and 1973, would often turn to D'Oliveira at moments of frustration, to break partnerships or keep an end tight, and he often produced both desired results.

He had his disappointments too, notably during the tour of the West Indies in 1967–8, when he himself said, 'I had too much to drink, I lived too well.' In the Caribbean, he was already under pressure from all sides, from militant black groups accusing him of selling out, from friends and activists demanding that he be a flag-carrier for the anti-apartheid movement, and from those who tried to bribe him to opt out of the whole story in order to let cricketing contacts carry on as usual.

One of the things that seemed so wrong about his not being selected for the tour of South Africa, immediately after scoring 158 against Australia in the final Test at the Oval in 1968, was that this innings was a triumph of composure and determination under extreme scrutiny and pressure.

So what was the social significance of what became known as the D'Oliveira affair? First, of course, there was the tangible political out-come; from 1969 South Africa was isolated from international sport, not only in cricket. More broadly, it was one stage in the ongoing fight for awareness of the prevalence of racism in our society, and in ourselves.

The overt political stance against apartheid became possible because of a shift in emphasis, a shift in perception. First, many people were made more radical, more aware of the ramifying impact of racism, and in particular of our (English) collusion in it when we actively participated against white teams from a country whose whole structure was based on apartheid.

Second, the issue itself became more prominent. Even those who argued for continuing contacts had to deal with the counter-arguments. It was on agendas. It could not be shuffled off as unimportant. Through the 1970s for instance, though a majority of professional cricketers in this country were opposed to measures restricting contact between English cricketers and South Africa, their views were challenged.

The arguments *for* continuing contact were not risible. It was hard on sportsmen to bear the brunt of the bans, while others were not precluded from productive, profitable and no doubt often enjoyable dealings with that country. Without question, there was in the ban on international sport a limitation on people's freedom. It is conceivable (though in my view unlikely) that persisting with the status quo might have nudged South African opinion towards a more liberal attitude – the view of many in the cricket establishment in England at the time. Second, there were no doubt many in the white South African Establishment who would have preferred to have a more open system within their sport – so banning the country was hard on them personally. And – another question that was sometimes asked – how could we be sure that the outcomes of isolation would be better in the long run?

We could not be sure. But as Alan Paton, the South African novelist and author of *Cry, the Beloved Country*, said to me in Pietermaritzburg in 1965, there comes a time when inevitable uncertainties about the future have to be set aside, and we have to decide for ourselves: does it feel right or wrong to have dealings, including sporting dealings, with a country permeated by this kind of all-embracing injustice? My view, which was itself sharpened by all the argument and debate during the D'Oliveira affair, was that I was not, and that English cricket should not be, willing to continue to participate in such a situation.

Basil D'Oliveira retained his dignity throughout the ordeal of being at the centre of the storm. It was a storm that helped change the atmosphere of cricket and of our society more generally. And it was a real storm, arousing strong passions, including coldness and fury.

In December 1968, the MCC won the vote and the battle, but lost the war. The most significant message, shared by many people of a wide range of political positions, was that racism must be opposed, and that English cricket had taken too easy an option, as I had done a few years before, in touring South Africa for MCC in 1964–5.

Apart from the Paton argument, there was always the chance that isolating South Africa *would* have the required effect (though none of us imagined it might work so quickly). I think in fact this turned out to be the case. The uproar about D'Oliveira, and the radicalization this episode intensified, flowed into the campaign for the much wider exclusion of South Africa from world sport, of which, in retrospect, Graeme Pollock, the hugely gifted South African batsman, deprived of Test cricket for much of his prime, generously said (quoted by Peter Oborne): 'Peter Hain and his guys got it absolutely right that the way to bring about change in South Africa was through sport.'

The issue of racism does not, forty or fifty years on, go away. But nowadays it, or suspicion of it, is harder to get away with, and that is a good thing. Just after D'Oliveira's death, in November 2011, John Terry, England's football captain, was accused of racist remarks during a match. He denied that he or his comments, made in the heat of the moment, were racist. But by now the size of the reaction was a measure of the increased awareness. When Sepp Blatter, President of FIFA, minimized the problem by suggesting that racial discrimination on the field could be settled by a handshake, the outrage led to his having to apologize.

Of course hyper-sensitivity, a victim mentality, over-simplification and political correctness may become onerous and call for opposition. But the issue of racism is a deep and insidious blight in most if not all societies. We are right to get worked up about dismissing too carelessly the hurt caused. We should not turn a blind eye to flippant or casual racism. We correctly prioritize the damage of racist attitudes, and hold others and ourselves to account for assumptions of superiority or entitlement.

Sport, perhaps most notably football, has played an important role in lessening racism in British society.

It takes people a long time to become aware of the damage that deep-seated disrespect causes, to institutions as well as to individuals. Over recent years, the most pressing issue facing cricket has been corruption. Here too we resisted such awareness. ICC's Anti-corruption Unit was accused by players and ex-players of lacking teeth; its former Chair, Lord Condon, suggested that players were not being sufficiently forceful in reporting abuses they knew about or suspected. Probably the truth is that we all come to recognize the full impact of an evil too slowly.

D'Oliveira himself had a highly successful career after the storm (as well as before it), as player and as coach. And when South Africa re-joined the world of cricket from the 1990s, he was recognized in his home country as a pioneer. Appropriately, it is now for the Basil D'Oliveira Trophy that England and South Africa play Test series.

19

'WE PICKED HIM'

We all suffer in the course of our lives, and Doug Insole showed great resilience after several family tragedies. In 1955, his brother Geoff died of tuberculosis at the age of twenty-two. In 1979 the light plane his daughter Susan was travelling in disappeared over the Gulf of Alaska; no wreckage was ever found. Three years later, his wife Barbara died from motor-neurone disease.

Insole had also confronted difficult issues during his time as selector and administrator. In 1967, when he was Chairman, Geoff Boycott was dropped for 'batting in a selfish manner' when making 246 against India – Boycott never forgave him. In 1977 Insole was Chairman of the Test and County Cricket Board when it banned the players who had signed for Packer's World Series Cricket. The TCCB was challenged in the High Court on grounds of restraint of trade, and lost the legal battle.

But the aftermath of the D'Oliveira affair of 1968 was, as with Susan's disappearance, something that Doug could never lay to rest. I'm told that for some time after this he was on valium. In 2004, Peter Oborne wrote: 'Today he refers to the D'Oliveira episode as the worst few months of his life. This proud man broke down and wept when talking about the affair in front of one witness.'

Insole was Chair of Selectors. As noted earlier, D'Oliveira came in as a replacement for the last Test against Australia in August of that year, and scored 158, an innings (as Peter Oborne put it) 'scored under conditions of unspeakable personal difficulty, against an attack comprising Prime Minister Johannes Vorster and South African Apartheid at its most savage and corrupt, supported by the weight of the British Establishment'. A few days later, on 28 August, the team for South Africa was announced. D'Oliveira was omitted. He was in fact chosen as a reserve, but this fact was not disclosed.

A few weeks later, D'Oliveira was named as the replacement for Tom Cartwright, with predictable consequences.

The initial selectorial decision, as presented, was of course not only Insole's. It was shared. There were five selectors – Insole, Peter May, Alec Bedser and Don Kenyon, along with captain, Colin Cowdrey. In addition, at least three senior MCC officials were present at the meeting. But a lot of the opprobrium fell on Insole's head, and he was the one left to bear the brunt of suspicions of a bungled process, even of insincerity and betrayal, ever since.

Between the two decisions – non-selection and, finally, selection as replacement – he wrote a private note to D'Oliveira, in which, according to the latter, he 'expressed his understanding for the disappointment which he knew I would be feeling'.

I agree with Oborne when he says, 'it would be unfair to doubt Insole's integrity as a man or a selector'.

Doug was a discreet man, who never said in public all that he knew (during the last year of the war, he had after all worked at Arkley, the army station that intercepted the messages that Bletchley Park decoded). Just as umpire Steve Bucknor, who, when asked to change a key decision (he'd just given Tendulkar out in a crucial Test against Pakistan at Calcutta) because it had led to violence and might provoke a riot, refused to accede, Insole saw the selectors' role as a straightforward one: to pick the best team. 'Look, let's forget about South Africa,' he said, 'let's pick a team to go to Australia.' The selectors' job was to come to a specific, honest decision, and avoid being ruffled or swayed by considerations extraneous to that task.

I always wondered if Insole himself had argued for D'Oliveira's selection, or indeed whether the selectors themselves had supported it, but had been overruled. But in public and, as far as I knew, in private, Insole justified the selection on cricketing grounds: 'We've got rather better than him in the side,' he said.

I was able of course to follow the arguments about whether D'Oliveira was one of the best seven batsmen, and whether he could be considered as a front-line bowler, but nevertheless the decision did not seem to me to make sense from a cricketing point of view. It was (many of us believed) unprecedented and almost unbelievable that someone who had just scored a big hundred in the final Test, especially against Australia, should be deemed not part of the best sixteen or seventeen for a winter tour announced the day after that Test ended.

Oborne alludes to Basil's 'wild behaviour during the West Indies tour'. Insole told Oborne that 'This *was* a factor. There was no doubt that if the management of that previous tour had been 110 per cent behind him, it would have made an enormous difference.' He added that Cowdrey 'made it factually clear that on balance he wanted Basil out of it'.

'Insole went on to stress', Oborne writes, 'that there was no anti-D'Oliveira feeling at the meeting. "We were all supporters of Basil. We had supported him and picked him before." And while the selectors' meeting did not choose Basil for the team, he was chosen as a reserve.'

This was always Doug Insole's account. However, years later he apparently came out with a different version. At the MCC's Carol Service in 2016, he quietly told a member of the MCC and of the Cricket Society, who in turn told me in 2018, six months after Doug's death, what I had suspected might have been the case.

The gist was that Insole told him: 'We picked him but it was reversed.' I asked what this meant. Insole apparently explained – D'Oliveira *was* in the squad initially selected; but the decision was rescinded by 5 p.m. on 28 August (the selection meeting having lasted for six hours, from 8 p.m. on Tuesday 27th to 2 a.m. on the 28th).

In those days, England touring teams were officially picked by the MCC, and wore its colours. The MCC had a veto over particular selections, in particular if a player chosen by the selectors might bring it or cricket into disrepute. Oborne writes that before the selection meeting, the MCC had already informed the selectors that Barry Knight, who had replaced D'Oliveira for the second Test of that summer at Lord's, was 'not suitable to represent MCC abroad. Knight suffered from acute domestic problems' (Insole's words, quoted by Oborne) – though this could only have been part of the reason. Surely not even the most blinkered cricket aficionados of that time would have thought acute domestic problems to be *in themselves* grounds for 'unsuitability'.

According to this information, then, it was the MCC who vetoed D'Oliveira. If so, I am unclear whether the veto was stated decisively during the selectors' meeting (night of 27–28 August), by the officials of the club who were present, and merely rubber-stamped by the full MCC Committee at their meeting in the afternoon of the next day, or whether the Committee itself had a debate about the issue and made a definitive decision. According to Oborne, no one spoke out against it.

The MCC's papers and Minutes say little about the processes that went into the outcomes that I've just reported. In the Minutes of the Committee meeting of 28 August, there is a curious paragraph stating that the voting at the meeting would not be revealed. It is not clear to me whether this meant voting at the Selection Meeting the night before, or at the Committee Meeting itself. Either way it seems strange that this should be mentioned, as it would I am sure have been (as now) unthinkable that voting in either forum would have been made public. Does the presence of this comment, which draws attention to the issue of voting, imply some special significance in the fact that votes were needed and possibly contentious?

If this Carol Service version is correct, the suspicion that many of us had that there was something fishy about the context of selection, about the mode of selection, and about the communication (and obfuscation of communication) of it, was, in the end, even more justified than we knew at the time or since.

We already realized that several of the senior MCC officials involved knew, and had known for a long time, from more sources than one, that any team including D'Oliveira would not be allowed to tour South Africa. In spite of what Sir Alec Douglas-Home told David Sheppard and me at the Committee meeting in September 1968, soundings *had* been made (hypothetical questions asked) of the South African authorities, and a clear answer – that a side including him would not be welcome – had been received.

In March, for instance, Arthur Coy, an official of SACA,

decided to send a secret message, through trusted channels, back to Lord's with a warning that South Africa would call the tour off if the MCC picked D'Oliveira. There could not have been a better qualified man for the job. The tenth Lord Cobham . . . was a cricketing grandee. He had a South African mother, and extensive business interests in the Republic. He [had] captained Worcestershire. Later he went on to be the President of the MCC . . . At the end of February Cobham had dinner with Coy, with a follow-up meeting the following morning. On 4 March Coy wrote an account of their conversation in a letter to Jack Cheetham, who was on his visit to London at the time . . . It is a document of importance, because it illuminates the identity of interest, prejudice and approach between white South Africa and the British establishment in the 1960s.

Coy told Cheetham that Cobham would 'do almost anything to see that the tour is on'.

Oborne supposes that this 'almost anything' would involve offering D'Oliveira 'a scheme that would make him unavailable' Moreover, Cobham expressed his wish to meet Vorster, and did meet him several days later.

[Vorster] told him the truth: that the tour would be cancelled if D'Oliveira was chosen. It was obvious that Vorster intended this information to be passed back to the MCC. Cobham was happy to help . . . E. W. Swanton, Gubby Allen's official biographer, asserts that 'Cobham passed on the information to Lord's in an unusual way . . . not to any officer of the Club, but to a senior member of the Committee . . . The receiver passed it on to the Secretary, Billy Griffith, and he in turn gave the information therein to the President, Arthur Gilligan, and the Treasurer, Gubby [Allen].' Swanton then describes how the three decided to keep the information to themselves.

And more recently, a blatant statement to the same effect had been made on the very day that D'Oliveira scored his 158, when a director of Rothmans, Tienie Oosthuizen, who had previously offered D'Oliveira a large bribe to make himself unavailable for the tour, and who had been monitoring the fateful innings closely in the Prime Minister's Office in Pretoria, phoned Geoffrey Howard, the Secretary of Surrey. He told him he was phoning from the Prime Minister's Office; he was unable to get hold of Billy Griffith, MCC Secretary. 'Will you take a message to the selectors,' he demanded. 'Tell them that if today's centurion is picked, the tour will be off.' According to Oborne, Howard did pass on the message to Insole, who said later that 'there were lots of stories flying about during the Oval Test, and that he had ignored them all'.

I don't think we will ever know for certain whether the selectors did, initially, officially select D'Oliveira and then have their decision over-turned, either that evening or the next day. For the latter to have been the case, everyone involved – not only the selection committee and the MCC committee members – must have maintained an unusual degree of solidarity in sticking to the official story over four decades.

And even if the reality was that during the selection meeting Allen had said 'you can't have him', why would Kenyon have told people later that he was the only one to stick up for Basil? Unless, as seems also unlikely, he meant that he was the only one to *continue* to stand up for him.

According to my informant, the veto occurred 'when it was realized that there would be problems over that selection'. It is difficult to believe that there was anyone who had not known for some time that there would indeed be problems over his selection. It seems naïve for anyone to have advanced such as the reason. And if the 'problems' were the problem, then how come D'Oliveira's inclusion as a reserve was permitted? I think that in the end, whatever happened at the meetings of 27 and 28 August, the decision was a fudge, with motives other than simple cricketing ones entering into the outcome. My suspicion is that some did not like apartheid but wanted at all costs to maintain sporting contact (whether for selfish reasons or from genuine belief that contact was for the good); others may have been sympathetic to South Africa's system.

As for Insole, if it is true that D'Oliveira was initially picked, he had, indeed, ignored all the 'stories flying about', and had presided over a selection committee that did its best to pick the best team, without allowing its collective mind to be tangled by political considerations. Assuming that what he said at the Carol Service was true, he then heroically kept quiet about the fact that his selection committee, despite only lukewarm support for D'Oliveira from Kenyon, and (presumably) opposition to him from Bedser and May, as well as lack of support from the captain, nevertheless did pick D'Oliveira – only to have their choice rescinded.

I still believe that cricket failed the biggest test that confronted it.

One thing seems clear: at some point, Cowdrey's influence must have been key (even if he himself might have oscillated). Cartwright told Chalke that Cowdrey phoned him after he had pulled out, pressing him to start the trip so that, when he withdrew, they could pull in somebody who was coaching out there, perhaps Don Wilson, to replace him. This suggests that he was doing all he could to stop Basil being selected.

There are two further anecdotes that have some implications at least about the beliefs and characters of some of the central protagonists in that drama of 1968. One event occurred between 1987 and 1993, the period when Lieutenant Colonel John Stephenson was Secretary of the MCC. I heard the story from Duncan Fearnley, Chairman of Worcestershire CCC from 1986 to 1998. Fearnley had played for the club over seven seasons in the 1960s. Later he became a bat-manufacturer, making hand-made, top-quality bats. He knew D'Oliveira well. They were neighbours in Worcester, and Fearnley's time as Chairman overlapped with D'Oliveira's as coach and later 'ambassador' for the club.

Worcestershire were at Lord's playing Middlesex. Duncan was in the Committee Room one evening, not long before close of play. Gubby Allen, for years Treasurer of the MCC, was in his usual seat by the window. Suddenly Basil burst in, stormed across the room and confronted Allen, poking him in the chest with his finger. 'You stuffed me, you [swear words redacted] . . .' and stormed out. There was, of course, a deathly silence. Next day, whilst sipping his glass of Tío Pepe before lunch, Allen beat a hasty retreat when someone mentioned that D'Oliveira was in the Pavilion, making his way through the Long Room towards the Committee Room.

Fearnley thought D'Oliveira got something off his chest (and probably into where he thought it belonged, in Allen's chest). It was plain to everyone present that the allegation of having been 'stuffed' referred to his view of who had been responsible for his non-selection.

I'm not sure about which of the protagonists the story is most revealing. Certainly, there is little doubt that the wrong that had been seething in D'Oliveira's pectoral cavity related to 1968, and his view of how his non-selection had come about. Clearly it also indicates one reason for the unease in some quarters about his liability to become fiercely angry when he'd been drinking.

Further, Fearnley suggested I phone Ray Illingworth, who admired and respected D'Oliveira. Illingworth had been one of the finest of England captains – tough, shrewd, frank and loyal. Fearnley wondered if D'Oliveira might have talked further to Illingworth.

'No, I didn't know about that and Basil never spoke about it to me,' Illingworth told me. 'I had made myself unavailable for the tour of South Africa; I had a job lined up, and hadn't been playing for England.' But for the tour of Australia in 1970–1, which England won 2–0 under Illingworth's captaincy, he told the selectors that if D'Oliveira wasn't selected he himself wouldn't go. 'I'd promised him,' he said. (The promise was made, I learned from Oborne, when, after the fourth Test against the Rest of the World in August 1970, the selectors wanted to leave D'Oliveira out for the fifth in order to blood the much younger Dennis Amiss. Illingworth agreed to go along with the decision provided the selectors guaranteed D'Oliveira his place on the subsequent tour of Australia. He also took him to one side to tell him, in no uncertain terms, that he'd better behave.)

'And [vice-captain] Colin Cowdrey,' Illingworth continued, 'didn't want him to go because of the trouble he'd had with him in the West Indies in 1967. Mostly, Basil was fine in Australia. I did get on well with him. He was a very good batsman, and he was a far better bowler than people thought. When I played against him early on, it was hard to get runs off him, particularly when you'd just come in. And he wasn't only a defensive bowler; with a breeze from fine leg helping his out-swing he got good players out.'

I commented that there was a bias in many people against medium-paced bowlers, with which he agreed. 'I liked Basil,' he said. 'Mind, I did get Basil's finger jabbed in my chest more than once. And he did wreck his room on one occasion after he'd had a few. We got it paid for out of team funds we had from appearances and so on. I gave him a severe rollicking, and kept him on the phone for a long time.'

So even three years after the West Indies tour, Cowdrey was still dubious about D'Oliveira. I think Illingworth would have been much better able both to enlist and confront someone with this sort of vulnerability. His remarks also suggest a different depth of commitment to a man whose cricket you value, and offer a different valuation of D'Oliveira's usefulness as a bowler. (His 551 first-class wickets were achieved at a remarkably low average cost of 27.45, incidentally.) Clearly too Allen wasn't the only one to receive D'Oliveira's jabbing finger when he'd been drinking.

Certainly, for almost fifty years, Doug Insole, with his strong sense of 'cabinet' responsibility, took the flak for the selectors' decision.

We may never know exactly what happened in those meetings. In one version, he may have protected the senior officers of the MCC, many or all of whom were keen to keep cricketing contacts alive through mutual tours between England and South Africa, with its apartheid laws and policy that affected every area of life, including sport.

Insole resisted numerous attempts to persuade him to 'open up about it all'. He put his sense of duty and confidentiality ahead of self-justification.

20

'HALF A GOOD NIGHT'

David and I first met in 1968, over the D'Oliveira affair. The Special General Meeting occurred on 5 December. David proposed, and I seconded, the case for a vote of no confidence in the MCC committee. Several weeks before, three of our group had been called in to meet the committee. Alec Douglas-Home, ex-Prime Minister, and currently the Shadow Foreign Secretary, made a point that he had flown down from Scotland especially to meet us, and to persuade us to call off our plan to have a Special Meeting. He spoke to us as if we were schoolboys who understood nothing of politics. He said it was naïve to suppose you could ask hypothetical questions of a foreign government (in other words, asking whether a team that

included Basil D'Oliveira would be acceptable, and explicitly requiring the South African Government to admit any players eligible for
England who might be selected). David's response to what we both
experienced as superiority and contempt was characteristic; polite but
firm. He would not be rattled by bullying. We would not call off our
Special Meeting.

At the meeting itself, in his excellent, measured yet passionate
speech, David stated that enquiries *had* in fact been made, in January
1968, in an official letter sent by the MCC in January 1968 asking of the
(white) South African Cricket Association whether any team selected
from players qualified to represent England would be acceptable.
No reply was forthcoming (according to the Committee Minutes for
meetings held on 21 February and 21 March), despite the Secretary
pressing a prominent member of the SACA Board for an answer on his
visit to South Africa in December and January.

Only years later was it revealed that, as David had in fact known at
the time, an emissary had reported to some MCC office holders that
the answer to this hypothetical question *had* been given and was in
the negative. This was clear at least to some of those in the selection
meeting of 27–8 August, in which D'Oliveira was not selected.

The MCC Minutes reveal that it was Douglas-Home himself who
persuaded the committee not to press for an answer to the letter. At
the March meeting, he reported on his own recent conversations with
South African Government officials and members of the South African
Cricket Association. He advised the committee that 'arrangements for
the tour should be made on the assumption that when the time came
for the tour, the team would be acceptable'. (By now, D'Oliveira's own
loss of form in West Indies must have been well-known. Many must
have hoped that the problem would simply go away.)

Sheppard recognized in his speech that the MCC were and had
been faced with a very difficult situation. His main argument was that
the MCC had not followed through on their admirable attempt to

find out what the South African attitude to the possible selection of D'Oliveira was and would be. This failure to stick with the policy led, in his words, to 'the tangles of August and September when the name of English cricket was discredited in the eyes of so many'. Instead of following a firm policy, the (MCC) Committee 'chose to stumble from one selection or non-selection to another, and hoped that it would be "all right on the night"'.

He added that, eighteen months before in an article for *Punch* on 22 February 1967, he himself had written: 'It is unthinkable that everything should wait until July, 1968, when the team would normally be selected. We shall then be at the height of a Test series against Australia, and it would be quite unfair on both D'Oliveira and the selectors to wait until then. The matter must be settled before the 1968 series starts.'

This was far-seeing and in my opinion absolutely right. 'MCC's policy left the selectors in a situation where English cricket appeared to be bending to a racialist wind. I do not say', Sheppard added, 'that the selectors actually did bend to South African pressure. I carefully say "*appeared to be* bending".'

Several years before, when I played cricket at Fenner's, in Cambridge, Cyril Coote, our groundsman and mentor, admired Sheppard above all the fine post-war Cambridge batsmen, including Peter May and Ted Dexter, for the correctness of his play, the elegance of his cover drives, and his great concentration – all qualities that reflected the dignity and integrity of his personality in general. Coote often recalled David's straight drive off the bowling of Sonny Ramadhin during his double century against the West Indies in 1950, which hit the clock on the pavilion roof. Robin Marlar, who played with David for Cambridge and Sussex, went so far as to suggest that, despite being only 'lightly touched by genius', he was the best English batsman not only at Cambridge, but of his era.

David played twenty-two Test matches (which would of course

have been many more had he made different life choices). He scored two centuries against Australia, captained England twice, and is the only man to have played for England as an ordained priest.

He was known to be a tough captain. There is a story of a ploy that the Cambridge team under his captaincy tried. It may well be apocryphal, and was not confirmed by any of those I spoke to about him. The story was that when standing up to the stumps the wicket-keeper would take the ball down the leg-side, turn sharply round as if he'd missed it; at the same time, slip and short leg would run towards fine leg, apparently opening up the possibility of byes. The striker would set off for a run and be smartly run out.

Another episode was vouchsafed by David himself; against Gloucestershire at Cheltenham in 1953, he ordered his bowlers to bowl wide of the leg stump so as to preclude ordinary cricket strokes by the batsmen, just as Len Hutton had instructed Trevor Bailey to do a month before at Headingley, in order to save a Test against Australia. David apologized to the Gloucestershire captain a month later.

I mention this ruthlessness as a captain because David might have struck some as being too nice to be tough; he wasn't. He also knew that to occupy a space you have to have boundaries, you have to be willing to say no to others.

And surviving members of the Sussex team from 1953, the year of David's captaincy of the county, viewed him as the best they had played under. He took time to hear their personal problems, and at the end of the summer wrote them each a letter, thanking them for their work.

David went beyond that, too; he also had the rarer capacity to remain civil and friendly with those he deeply disagreed with. If he condemned, it was the sin but not the sinner. He was not doctrinaire. When the D'Oliveira issue threatened to lead to rifts with some cricketing friends, David invited several of them to talk through their differences together, and (though not with Peter May, who responded that they had nothing to talk to each other about) old friendships were often revived. Sheppard and Insole, for example, became closer after the controversy.

In the 1980s, when South Africa was still under apartheid, David had the further courage to go there to see for himself the achievements of the Cricket Board in developing cricket in the townships. He was willing to stand out not only against apartheid, and against the MCC, but also against those who were more fundamentalist than he was in their rejection of all contacts with the country.

David could have had a brilliant life as a full-time cricketer, no doubt captaining England long term, and going on to a successful worldly career (perhaps in law, which he read at Cambridge). Alternatively, he might have had a comfortable time in the Church, working in public schools or universities, or being a priest in well-heeled middle-class parishes. Instead he chose to commit himself to working in the inner city. From 1958 he was in charge of the Mayflower Centre at Canning Town, in the East End of London, where I visited him. When he became Bishop of Woolwich in 1969, living just off the Old Kent Road, he was reminded by the all-male diocesan staff meetings, where seniority was scrupulously observed, of the time when he first played for Sussex. 'If we went to the cinema, we entered in strict order of who received their county cap first.' From 1975 to 1996, he was Bishop of Liverpool. In 1983, he wrote *Bias to the Poor*.

I don't think this shift was achieved without soul-searching. I had heard David preach when I was an undergraduate in the early 1960s, when he was, I think, more evangelical than later, devoted to the idea of preaching with passion as one individual to other individuals. I remember feeling a mixture of awe and unease at his fervour.

In his early days he was liable to embarrass cricketing colleagues by earnest attempts to convert them, believing in what some would call an inspired, others 'priggish', way that they had been placed by God in the team so that he, David, could lead them to the truth. One player asked, 'Why did he pick me to convert?' and answered his own question: 'Because he thought I went to public school.'

He had to recognize in himself and in others tendencies to supe-riority, to middle- or upper-middle-class assumptions, including the idea that Ministry in the Church is a clear-cut matter of teaching one's flock, rather than also learning from them. He had to learn that lis-tening was a form of giving, and he came to appreciate the need to be open to leadership qualities from within deprived communities. He realized that many 'ordinary' people were often more able to come alive and feel free in company or groups, than in one-to-ones. He saw the need for both sides of the argument between those stressing per-sonal commitment to God and the individual soul, and those stressing the need for changes to the structures of society so that more indi-vidual souls have a chance. As time went on, his emphasis became weighted on the side of 'the poor'.

David also came to enjoy ordinary things and ordinary people. After he had officiated at the Walthamstow wedding of the Essex coach, Frank Rist, some of the guests, encountering him for the first time, commented: 'He's a good bloke, that Dave.'

When he was a member of the House of Lords, he had a flat near us in Chalk Farm, northwest London, but no television. On rare free evenings he would come over to watch programmes in a popular series – the series might have been *It Ain't Half Hot, Mum*, or possibly *Brookside* (which was set in Liverpool); his daughter Jenny suggested it was perhaps *Boys from the Blackstuff*.

As Bishop of Liverpool, he and the Roman Catholic Archbishop, Derek Worlock, worked together on behalf of all the communities. They made big steps towards reconciliation between the two branches of Christianity. David's theological beliefs and convictions became allied to a passionate concern to reunite his Church with those who are disadvantaged and discriminated against.

He had a nice sense of humour. He pictured Mervyn Stockwood, the flamboyant Bishop of Southwark, who enjoyed fine wines, dinners and social life, as: 'At the end of the evening, wearing a silk purple cassock, saying as he fingered the decorated pectoral cross given to him by the Patriarch of Romania, "I'm only the servant of a poor carpenter."' And he quotes writer Caryl Brahms saying to Stockwood when at the Bishop's House for dinner: 'If you, a bishop, were to convert me, a Jewess, that would be nothing. But if I were to convert you, that would be really something!'

David was a kind and deeply thoughtful person, who helped people see what they had in common. He inspired love, and brought out the best in others. He was generous. He also knew how to accept the generosity of others. He knew that, if he and his wife Grace were to be in a state to help others, they had to look after themselves, giving themselves time out. They both greatly valued retreats. By chance, I've just come across something written by Grace, which could, I think, equally have been said by David: 'Learning to receive became as important as learning to give without counting the cost.'

I have come to know the recent Archbishop of Canterbury, Rowan Williams. There is an old Italian proverb which says, 'If you want to know that a fish is bad, look at its head.' The Church of England can't be all bad, with good, fine people like David and Rowan leading it.

He and Grace were immensely courageous and cheerful in the face of his terminal cancer. When I asked him on the phone a few weeks before he died how he'd been, he said, 'Quite good, I had half a good night.' I suspect that in his position most of us would have emphasized the other half of that good night.

21

BIBLE AND PASSION

Another member of the group of MCC members who called for a Special General Meeting of the MCC to protest against the Club's handling of the D'Oliveira affair was the actor Peter Howell. Peter was born in 1919. I spoke at his ninetieth birthday party. He died in 2015.

Peter was a devoted romantic about sport, and especially cricket. One of his uncles, who died in the First World War, is said to have opened the batting with Jack Hobbs. His daughters regarded his passion as a sort of benign insanity. If a sporting event came up, Peter would cancel any family meeting, however long it was since he'd seen the person concerned.

He was a handsome, striking man, with a hooked nose and fine cheek-bones, a noble face. When I knew him he had a shock of white hair that was never tidy. He was one of those people who could look utterly informal, even crumpled, in a tie and jacket.

Educated at Winchester College and Oxford, his accent accorded with his origins. But his beliefs and passions were all on the side of the underdog. He hated school, though loving the chance it gave him to play cricket. He was a lifelong supporter of and activist for the Labour Party. He served for years on the committee of Equity, the actors' union. He was active in his work to create the Watermans Arts Centre in Brentford, facing Kew Gardens across the River Thames.

Peter was always troubled by others' cynicism, by Thatcherism and other celebrations of, or exhortations to, selfishness and to over-reliance on competition and the market. He campaigned for social justice all his life, and found apartheid particularly abhorrent. It was appropriate that we first met, in 1968, on that basis.

Like many intellectuals, Peter was a theorist, but here too he regretfully admitted from time to time that the beauty of a theory (in sport or politics) could be trumped by fact, however sordid and disappointing this could be. At such moments his face would drop, as an illusion had to be modified or given up, before resolutely recovering itself. A romantic at heart, he regretfully knew that pragmatism has to have its say; he listened to its humdrum voice, and gave it grudgingly its due, but what he really wanted was the beauty, elegance and potentially civilizing qualities in sport, as in life, to predominate.

From 1968 onwards, we would talk from time to time, often at Lord's. I also saw him act on the London stage, including in *Conduct Unbecoming*, set in India during the Raj, in which, characteristically, he played a liberal, decent British officer, who did not relish pig-sticking.

We played squash together. Peter was twenty-three years older than me, and I could beat him. But he ran and ran, maintaining that this was huge fun. It was about the same time that I could at last beat my father at squash, which only happened when I was nearly thirty. With my father I was anxious that my new-won superiority would result in a Pyrrhic victory, with my red-faced antagonist slumped on the floor. It was much the same with Peter, though he gave the impression of enjoying it more than my father did. Peter was a generous man and a good loser. I think he might have found winning more difficult to enjoy than losing.

As a boy, he went to the MCC's Easter classes, where his coach Bill Bowes, the Yorkshire and England fast bowler, and later cricket correspondent for the *Yorkshire Evening News*, was said to have predicted that he would play for England one day. He was a stylish player in every way, and clearly a talented leg-spin bowler. But apparently he was always nervous, even terrified. While as an actor his nerves helped, in cricket they hindered, and when it came to the big match he was liable to disappoint.

Leg-spinning is the most likely aspiration of the cricketing romantic, since it is so hard to do, and so pleasing when you get it right. There is an aesthetic, almost artistic delight at a perfectly pitched and spinning leg-break, drifting in towards the batsman, then passing the edge and hitting the top of the off-stump, or of a googly completely bamboozling the batsman. I remember both of us swooning over the sheer flair and style of Pakistan's wonderful leg-spinner, Abdul Qadir. Leg-spinning is an art at which the odd rank bad ball is expected and forgiven.

Another shared hero was Bishan Singh Bedi, India's most graceful bowler. Here is how Bedi's biographer Suresh Menon describes him: 'Bedi was an artist and will not be remembered for his wickets alone. He was a throwback to the Golden Age, a reminder of the essentially romantic nature of cricket, where sometimes beauty overrode effectiveness, but, at its best, was essential to it.'

(One might contrast the more pragmatic, even curmudgeonly, effectiveness of the attitude of that other type of spinner, Raymond Illingworth. I once commented to Raymond that, when Middlesex played Essex, Ray East [Essex's slow-left-arm bowler], would quickly dismiss Wayne Daniel [our fast bowler from Barbados]. Wayne would hit him for a huge six, but then there'd be an even slower ball, a terrific wind-up from the batsman, and that was it – bowled, stumped, or caught. 'One for six,' I said. Raymond's deadpan comment was: 'Why give him six?')

When Peter was a child, his mother would say to his sister, 'Find Peter and tell him I want *The Times*' – for Peter would be lying on his stomach for hours reading the cricket scores and thereby hogging the paper. On the village green in Devonshire when staying with his grandmother, he sat watching cricket for so long he got sunburned. He persuaded his elders to take him to Lord's, and his poor sister Gill had to tag along, sitting in Q Stand from childhood to her eighties, when Lord's at last opened its pavilion up to women and she could discover that it wasn't quite so big as it had seemed during all those decades.

Peter studied law at Oxford, which he had taken up to please his solicitor father, but left it early to join up for the war effort. Regarded by his family as the most unpractical of men, he was assigned to a Radio and Technical Communication department and sent to North Africa. There he got dysentery, and was in hospital when his whole battalion was wiped out. His experiences of racism and classism in the Army intensified his socialist beliefs and his commitment to making hierarchies flatter and inequalities less blatant.

Peter ended his life in a home for actors. He was probably as happy there as his condition allowed, but the dementia of his last years meant that he was often self-disparaging and despairing about his failing memory, and anxious about what would happen next. It was an eccentric place, a sort of benign, upper-middle-class locus of Beckettian logic. Indeed, one of his fellow-actors there was the famous Beckett actor, Billie Whitelaw, who died shortly before Peter.

On one of his daughter Camilla's last visits to his bedside, she went to take out of his hand the Labour Party Manifesto that he was clutching while falling asleep. 'No,' he said, holding on firmly. As his children said, that was 'his Bible and his passion'.

Peter was always immensely charming, articulate, honest and passionate. He was fascinated by ideas, and particularly by ideas of fair play. He was always curious, involved and interested in what other people were doing; for example, in our children, who knew him only slightly but were very fond of him. He had a devoted family. His wife Susan, who was equally passionate about their shared social and political principles, and about her work as a primary school teacher, who travelled to Punjab in India to visit families of her small pupils, died from cancer in 1992. They had three daughters, a son, and several grandchildren.

22

THE ZIMBABWE AFFAIR

Andy Flower was Zimbabwe's best-ever cricketer, a wicket-keeper batsman. He was one of the new country's leading sportsmen. When Henry Olonga, born in 1976 in Lusaka, Zambia, made his debut aged eighteen, in 1995, he was the first black cricketer to play for Zimbabwe.

Just before Zimbabwe's match against Namibia at Harare in the World Cup of 2003, co-hosted by South Africa, Zimbabwe and Kenya, the two men made a public protest against the Mugabe regime and its policies, wearing black armbands on the field of play. They made a statement soon after, 'mourning the death of democracy in [their] beloved Zimbabwe'. This was dangerous and discordant behaviour. The outcome was that both had to emigrate, settling in the UK and giving up a comfortable and congenial lifestyle as national heroes.

Andy Flower doesn't stand out in a crowd. He was not recognized at the Birmingham restaurant where we met. He had short blond hair, with a vestigial 1950s James Dean quiff in the front – his only gesture of outward distinctiveness, unless you counted the tell-tale wicket-keeper's scabs and plasters on both arms below the elbow. He was, and is, a quiet, unassuming man, son of an accountant. Preparing to follow in his father's footsteps, he had as a school-leaver worked for a year with Anglo-American in Harare.

Flower was the leading Zimbabwean cricketer. By the time of his protest, he had played for his country for eleven years, starting in 1992, three years before Zimbabwe got Test status. Apart from Len Hutton, England's first professional captain, he and Olonga were in 2003 the only people to have been offered honorary membership of the MCC while still professional cricketers.

For him personally there could hardly have been a worse time for the protest, the consequences of which were unpredictable. His English wife was due to have their third child a few days before the World Cup. She was unable to fly (and thus get away to the safety of the UK) either in the last weeks of her pregnancy, or immediately after the baby's birth. He was keen to be there for the birth, and both of them naturally wanted an atmosphere of peace and quiet for their early days with the new baby, Danielle.

Yet the World Cup was the one occasion when their protest against the murderous gang led by Robert Mugabe would gain worldwide attention. The reasons why the time was right included England's continuing uncertainty whether to play *their* match in Harare on grounds of morality as well as of safety. It was, he felt, now or never. Later his wife came round to his point of view, and agreed that they had been right to do it when they did.

His decision to ask Olonga to join him was based on the latter's iconic standing in Zimbabwe as the first black to have played international cricket for the country, on his personal charisma, and also on his being 'the fine man he is – he has no edge'. Moreover, Flower said, Henry was a committed Christian.

Olonga agreed without hesitation. Their aim was to wake a few Zimbabweans up from their apathy, thereby playing some small part in the fight for human rights in their country.

They wore black armbands, and prepared a joint statement.

Prior to this, they spoke to the team's security men, trustworthy because they had previously worked for the shadow Justice Minister,

who was a friend of Flower's. The advice was that they themselves were too high profile to be arrested by the state security, at least during the World Cup. But as they expected, there would be physical risk. Thugs hanging around the fringes of the ruling cliques might look to make a mark by a hijacking or car-jacking – increasingly commonplace in Zimbabwe in those days. Their emails were likely to be bugged, and their phones tapped – Flower thought that did indeed happen. They should keep their eyes open and their cars locked; they should watch out at crossroads, and keep a watchful eye on what was to be seen in their rear mirrors. If anyone looked at them strangely in the street, they should look them in the eye, directly. They were advised not to stay in their homes for a few days. They employed twenty-four-hour guards. On returning home, he and his wife moved bedroom into one that had a shared bathroom as the only divide from the children. 'It's easier for Zimbabweans than for the English,' he said; 'we were used to this from the civil war.'

I asked Andy about the attitude of the rest of the team. At first, he replied, the two of them felt that the greatest impact would be created by a protest including the whole team. Some players, including Andy's brother, Grant, wanted to join. But on reflection they realized that the fact that eleven of the fifteen players were white would allow the government to dismiss them as colonialist racists. They therefore told their team-mates that they were free to do whatever they decided, but the pair would prefer it if they did not join them. Another factor was that they were keen not to distract the players more than necessary from their cricket. They had no wish to detract from a successful performance, which would justify the hard work done in attaining Zimbabwe's role as secondary hosts to South Africa; nor did they wish to invite the extra charge of fomenting trouble within the team.

Following their plan, they showed their clear statement of protest to the team manager at 9.15 on the morning of Zimbabwe's first match of the World Cup, against Namibia.

The statement was as follows:

It is a great honour for us to take the field today to play for Zimbabwe in the World Cup. We feel privileged and proud to have been able to represent our country. We are however deeply distressed about what is taking place in Zimbabwe in the midst of the World Cup and do not feel that we can take the field without indicating our feelings in a dignified manner and in keeping with the spirit of cricket.

We cannot in good conscience take to the field and ignore the fact that millions of our compatriots are starving, unemployed and oppressed. We are aware that hundreds of thousands of Zimbabweans may even die in the coming months through a combination of starvation, poverty and AIDS. We are aware that many people have been unjustly imprisoned and tortured simply for expressing their opinions about what is happening in the country. We have heard a torrent of racist hate speech directed at minority groups. We are aware that thousands of Zimbabweans are routinely denied their right to freedom of expression. We are aware that people have been murdered, raped, beaten and had their homes destroyed because of their beliefs and that many of those responsible have not been prosecuted. We are also aware that many patriotic Zimbabweans oppose us even playing in the World Cup because of what is happening.

It is impossible to ignore what is happening in Zimbabwe. Although we are just professional cricketers, we do have a conscience and feelings. We believe that if we remain silent that will be taken as a sign that either we do not care or we condone what is happening in Zimbabwe. We believe that it is important to stand up for what is right.

We have struggled to think of an action that would be appropriate and that would not demean the game we love so much. We have decided that we should act alone without other members of the team being involved because our decision is deeply personal and we did not want to use our senior status to unfairly influence more junior members of the squad. We would like to stress that we greatly respect the ICC and are grateful for all the hard work it has done in bringing the World Cup to Zimbabwe. In all the circumstances we have decided that we will each wear a black armband for the duration of the World Cup. In doing so we are mourning the death of democracy in our beloved Zimbabwe. In doing so we are making a silent plea to those responsible to stop the abuse of human rights in Zimbabwe. In doing so we pray that our small action may help to restore sanity and dignity to our Nation.

They expected the team manager to refuse permission, at which point they would hand the protest to representatives of the world's press, gathered in Harare, ready to argue that their contract did not allow permission to make public statements to be unreasonably refused. In fact the manager's response was to consult the chief executive. When the latter did later refuse permission, the match had already started and the protest had been made public. The chief executive demanded whether they had considered the repercussions of their action. Olonga replied: 'Have *you* considered the repercussions of our *not* acting?'

As I did, Andy admired Nasser Hussain's captaincy of England, both in holding things together in the recent tour of Australia, and in questioning the appropriateness of England playing in Zimbabwe. Ronnie Irani, a team-mate of Nasser's at Essex, and a member of the England squad, had recently phoned Flower on Nasser's behalf from Australia, asking his advice on the issue. Flower had hoped that the England players might have followed their lead, playing in Harare but with black armbands. (I too had wanted them to take this line of solidarity.) He felt the most telling gesture would have been for them not to come at all – but for explicitly moral reasons. As it was, the central issues became clouded by what he felt were spurious considerations of player safety. In England sporting contacts with Zimbabwe understandably lost prominence in comparison with the huge dissensions over the Iraq war.

Nevertheless, cricket writer Scyld Berry, who was ghosting Nasser at the time, describes the latter's unfeigned anguish on the issue. According to Berry, the team's majority verdict was not to go to Harare, and it was reached on mainly ethical grounds. Hussain said, he reports: 'We couldn't have lived with ourselves if we had played that game and spectators, or people outside the ground, had been arrested and beaten up.' Berry comments: 'Fruitless, perhaps. Yet it was one of England's finest performances.'

The moral/ethical issue was, and is, a hard one: where should one draw the line? In apartheid South Africa, racial politics infiltrated every form of life, including sport. In Mugabe's Zimbabwe it was not so clear-cut. But there were powerful arguments for not playing sport with that country, and/or for making a brave protest.

Flower and Olonga expected to be hit financially, and brought before a court or a tribunal. (In the event, neither player was, I believe, paid for the World Cup.) Olonga was omitted from the next matches, not allowed even to be twelfth man. Both men were forbidden to wear the armbands, so next time it was black sweat bands. In response to this, for the third match, Flower was forbidden to wear anything not-white (ironical in the circumstances). So he wore white sweat bands. Different symbols, same message.

The two men received massive support, both from outside the country and, more importantly, from within. They knew that there would only be a small minority angered by their gesture, the henchmen of the Zanu-PF party which was 'plundering the country'.

The team itself proved to be a microcosm of the country at large. When the selectors were about to drop Flower for 'not trying', other players threatened to pull out, and he was reinstated. While some of the squad were vigorously supportive and interested, others attempted to go on as if nothing had happened.

Flower was irritated by and scornful of the hypocrisy of his government; they had celebrated the exclusion of South Africa from world sport twenty and more years before, but now argued that politics and sport shouldn't mix. He said that the administration of cricket was closely tied up with the government.

Moreover, the government newspaper reported that Flower took this action 'because of his family's possession of tracts of land due for repossession' – a blatant but typical lie.

But he had kept his house, and much of his heart, in Harare. As for the more distant future, he had an open mind. In five years' time there might, he thought, be a different leader in their country, an end to the horrible atmosphere. In the meantime, there was the pleasure and challenge of cricket with Essex, and a three-year contract due to start later in the year with South Australia.

As we know now, Flower followed his playing career (he retired in

2006) with a spell as England's assistant coach, and then, in 2009, he became head coach. He continues to work for the England and Wales Cricket Board.

Olonga's future was less clear and less to be relied on. As a cricketer, Olonga was kicked out of his cricket club, and had to retire from first-class cricket, his career effectively over. More seriously, the action led to a warrant for his arrest on charges of treason, which could carry the death penalty in Zimbabwe. He faced death threats and had to go into hiding. If rain hadn't given Zimbabwe points in their match against Pakistan, thus enabling them to progress to the next round of matches in South Africa, he might never have got out of Zimbabwe, and might have faced trial, imprisonment and worse. But he managed to find safe passage to England, where, however, he had no automatic right to stay. In that first summer he had a work permit to play for a club, commentated for Channel 4, and looked for opportunities in music. Olonga has a fine tenor voice. His usual forfeit at the team meetings (often for being a teetotaller) was to sing – an unusually cheering alternative to the usual crudities of such male-bonding occasions.

Later, after his Zimbabwean passport expired in 2006, he could not leave England for nine years until finally getting his citizenship. Then, in 2015, Olonga settled down in Adelaide with his Australian wife and their two daughters, where he now performs as an opera singer. Quite a life, so far!

After the protest, the world looked a different place for these two previously privileged, even cosseted, sports stars. Having spoken their minds, however, despite having to look over their shoulders, both players felt immediate relief. Their dramatic and courageous action focused their minds. It was an interesting experience to have left their comfort zones, and to have been released into a different realm. Olonga said he felt fully alive.

Truthfulness can indeed be food for the spirit.

23

COMETH THE HOUR

From 1976 to 1991, when Viv Richards, Gordon Greenidge, Jeffrey Dujon and Malcolm Marshall retired, West Indies dominated world cricket. From 1991 to 1995, they did not lose a Test series, but more series were close-run. Since 1995 their form has declined, especially in the longer game.

That amazing twenty-year period was the culmination of earlier efforts over many decades, efforts of various kinds. West Indies had always produced extremely talented players, from Learie Constantine and his father, Lebrun, George Headley (known as the black Bradman), the three 'W's' – Clyde Walcott, Everton Weekes, and Frank Worrell – spinners Sonny Ramadhin and Alf Valentine, Garry Sobers and many others.

But only after they were led by a black man, Worrell, from 1961, and became a predominantly black side, did they evolve into the best team in the world.

Worrell was chosen as captain for the 1961 tour of Australia, after a long campaign for him, a black man, to be appointed. He was described by his wicket-keeper, Deryck Murray, as the best captain he ever played with or against. He was wise, shrewd and calm.

The campaign was led by C. L. R. James as Editor of the Trinidad newspaper, *The Nation*, from 1958. James had previously been a friend of and adviser to Learie Constantine, when the latter played for Nelson in the Lancashire league, and when he wrote about cricket.

I played only two Test matches against the West Indies, my first two, aged thirty-four, in 1976. In the first, at Nottingham, West Indies, led by Clive Lloyd, selected four fast bowlers and no spinners, though they reverted to Raphick Jumadeen, a steady slow-left-arm bowler, for the second Test at Lord's. While I was batting in the first innings, Jumadeen bowled three overs, of which I faced not a single ball, Brian Close shielding me from the full force of his threat while I relaxed against Andy Roberts or Michael Holding at the other end. I think this was the last time for years that the West Indies picked a front-line spinner, at least when playing elsewhere than in Trinidad or the sub-continent.

Lloyd's greatest achievement was to bring together players from many parts of the West Indies into a coherent side. He never favoured or ignored a player on the basis of where he came from. Over the next two decades, West Indies produced a remarkable number of fine fast bowlers, starting with the 'father' to this latest generation, Roberts.

They had, too, a wonderful group of mainly attacking batsmen. All these cricketers developed their skills and technique by playing full seasons in English county cricket. They never sledged. As Viv Richards once said, 'We let our cricket do the talking.'

West Indies took this quaint British game and made it their own, playing in their own inimitable style. As James said in a film made for the BBC, but never as far as I know shown: 'Caliban – by which I mean myself, or Frank Worrell – has to find out qualities, has to venture into fields, that Caesar never knew.'

The fast bowlers were extraordinary. In earlier decades, it used to be said of the north of England: 'Shout down a coal pit and up comes a fast bowler.' The Caribbean version was: 'Shake a palm tree and a fast bowler drops out.' I remember the story told about Ezra Moseley, one of their minor, but genuinely quick, bowlers. He was working as a waiter in a Barbados south coast hotel where England's cricketers were staying. Someone suggested that he would be a useful net bowler for them to practise against. He is alleged to have bowled faster than any English bowler while carrying a tray of drinks in his left hand.

Wayne Daniel, also from Barbados, toured England in 1974 at the age of eighteen, for West Indies schoolboys. Middlesex signed him up, though he was not able to play for us until 1977. In the first match of that season, on a slow pitch against Kent at Lord's, Clive Radley and I were, as usual, standing in the slips. After each ball of his first over, we rubbed our hands in glee, and moved a foot or two deeper. Wayne was rapidly nicknamed (by our opening batsman, Mike Smith) 'the Black Diamond', and 'Rent and Rates', his presence making a difference not only to our results but to our win bonuses. One year we seemed less able than usual to persuade him to bowl short balls; it was August before we discovered the reason – he was determined to win the *Sun* newspaper's 'demon fast bowler' award, which was given to the number of batsmen clean bowled in a season. Wayne was strong and genuinely fast. Such was the quality of his rivals for the international team that he played in only ten Tests in his entire career. Yet his average was virtually the same as Roberts's – 25 runs scored off him per wicket – and his strike rate was a wicket each 48 balls as opposed to Roberts' one per 55.

A quiet and graceful man, who used to swear by the virtues of an acne cream to soothe his sometimes painful Achilles' heel, Wayne could be persuaded once every year or two to tell his story about the fictional Bajan fast bowler, 'Hammy'. Hammy had a day off, and decided to go down into the country. While there, he saw cricketers knocking up before a village game. Taking the trouble to put on his darkest shades to hide his identity, he couldn't resist staying to have a look. One of the local players saw this fit-looking young man and asked him if he would help make up the numbers; his team was one short. Hammy agreed, with some reluctance, and was lent kit. In the field, his team was being hit all over the ground. Eventually the captain approached him, asking if he bowled. 'Yes, a bit,' said Hammy modestly. With Hammy coming in off his short run, the fluent young player drove him, and cut him for boundaries. Then hooked him for six. (Wayne played the strokes, with all the flamboyance and style of the most elaborate Bajan batsman.) This challenged Hammy's pride, so he went off a longer and longer run. The batsman now hooked him for fours, and clipped him off his legs. At last Hammy started his run-up in earnest, from the sight-screen. He bowled another bouncer; the batsman went for a hook, missed and was hit on the head (no helmets). He quickly got up, and was ready for the next ball. At this moment, one of Hammy's friends had by chance arrived by car, and was likewise drawn to see what was going on in this rural game. He sees Hammy pawing the ground in front of the sight-screen. Shielding his eyes against the sun with his hand, he shouts, 'Hey, Hammy man, what you doing down in the country?' The batsman, aghast, utters a tremulous 'Hammy?' and promptly faints.

The story took perhaps twenty minutes to tell, with many imper-sonations. Wayne loved it, depending as it does on the self-mockery involved in questioning how much the impact of a Test player rests on mere reputation. It's a democratic story, playing on the strength and pride of cricketers in the Caribbean.

I am reminded of CLR's story of his maternal grandfather, Joshua Rudder, being called in when retired to repair a cane-crushing engine, which had broken down at the crucial crop time. He asked to go in alone. Within two minutes he was out, and the big wheels started to revolve again. James writes:

> The usually exuberant Josh grew silent for once and refused to say. He never told them. He never told anybody. The obstinate old man wouldn't even tell me. But when I asked him that day, 'Why (and perhaps: how?) did you do it?' he said, 'They were white men with all their big degrees, and it was their business to fix it. I had to fix it for them. Why should I tell them?'

Shannon (the team of black lower-middle classes in Trinidad, that of the Constantines and the St Hills) were similarly proud without being arrogant. How much integrity was needed, how much maturity and confidence, to find oneself as a cricketer in this class- and race-ridden milieu! How much judgement to know where and how to stand out, to find a way of walking tall in an unjust world! Remember that 'with the emerging popularity of cricket arose *illusions of social unity* which suggested the game transcended normal divisions of colour, class and status, even though it quite clearly preserved careful social distances within its organizational structures' and was a 'major bulwark against social and political change'.

The achievement was to avoid not only kow-towing, but also behaving with a violence or stupidity that might have set back the cause of the elements of fair play so admired on the cricket field itself.

What happened within the boundary would profoundly shape what happened beyond the boundary.

Progress towards inclusion and fair play had been slow. Back in the 1890s, Trinidad, a racially mixed island, with many Indians, Portuguese and Chinese, pioneered the gradual opening up of cricket to non-whites, allowing the fast bowlers, 'Float' Woods and Archie Cumberbatch, who had their roots in Barbados, and batsman Lebrun Constantine (Learie's father) to play in matches against visiting English teams. These same bowlers were not, however, permitted to play in inter-island matches.

One of the values of cricket is that it is not easy to keep good players excluded indefinitely. Skill will out, scores tell a truth. In West Indies, small integrations led to recognition of the qualities, personal and technical, of the trailblazers, which in turn promoted the extension of recognition to other non-white players.

Moreover, even in the early years of the twentieth century there were also voices for inclusion among the local whites and from visiting MCC grandees (including Plum Warner), just as there *was*, occasionally at least, support for education, enfranchisement and human rights. In Jamaica, for example, there was a prominent advocate of Fabian socialism in no less a figure than Sydney Olivier, Governor of that island between 1907 and 1913, having previously been its Colonial Secretary.

Though the idea of a West Indies Federation has failed, it has survived in the two key instruments of mobility, cricket and education, evident in the University of West Indies and the West Indies cricket team, both of which have weathered challenges from a recrudescent insularity.

I find it remarkable that people whose ancestors were enslaved and then released into a world of prejudice, arrogance and power, with many of these arrangements extending into cricket, should be so patient, so keen to learn, so open to the values that they found in this quintessential game of the empire: cricket. It seems to me that West Indians have been able to be humble (in the sense of knowing there was a lot to learn) without being abject, and proud without being arrogant. They have been prepared to celebrate the glass as half full rather than simply rage against its being half empty. They were willing also to wait.

As Clem Seecharan says, cricket could not be a non-political activity in such a context. This reminds me of the slogan of those arguing for a boycott of South African sport in the late 1960s and '70s: 'no normal sport in an abnormal society'. Or as Seecharan, again, put it: 'cricket was more than a game . . . the game was a weapon of liberation'.

As portrayed in the 2010 film *Fire in Babylon*, their great teams were motivated by the long history of racialism. They were proud, but remarkably free of arrogance or triumphalism.

Cometh the hour, cometh the man

In *Beyond a Boundary*, James writes: 'Once in a blue moon, i.e. once in a lifetime, a writer is handed on a plate a gift from heaven. I was handed mine in 1958.' James was invited to be the editor of *The Nation* (the organ of Dr Eric Williams' People's National Movement), and the secretary of the West Indian Federal Labour Party.

'Immediately I was immersed up to the eyes in "The case for West Indian Self-Government", and a little later, in the most furious cricket campaign I have ever known, to break the discrimination of sixty years and have a black man, in this case Frank Worrell, appointed captain of a West Indies team.'

One might sum up the whole of James's book in these terms: 'Something is required and someone steps in. This someone thereby breaks new ground,' he says. Their arrival is not a matter of pure chance. James again: 'You wouldn't call Shakespeare or Michelangelo an accident.' This is as true of C. L. R. himself as it is of W. G. Grace, whom he writes about in the book, and of Worrell.

A place is ready, a need is there. Throughout the book we see this. 'The cricket field' – in Trinidad, for example – 'was a stage on which selected individuals played *representative roles charged with social significance*', James writes. On cricket grounds, Learie Constantine's father, Lebrun, 'met all men as equals'. Such representatives embody the aspirations, wishes and unconscious aims of people whose lives have been blighted, restricted or suppressed.

People looked out for Lebrun, the first black man to play for the West Indies, in 1895, against a touring England team. They knew he was precious and special. In 1900, James said (though more likely it was 1906, when the second team left for a tour of England), 'Cons', though selected, had remained behind:

> He was not a rich man who could pay his own way. He was not a professional for whom everything had to be found. He had not gone because he couldn't afford it. A public subscription was organized on the spot, a fast launch was chartered and caught the boat before it reached the open sea.

He became the first West Indian to score a century in England, at Lord's.

Years later, people watched out for his son Learie, too.

> Wilton St Hill (of Shannon) met me and said: 'You heard? Learie is injured playing football. That fool! What right has a man like Constantine to be playing football, you tell me!' He was terribly angry. All of us were looking to him to do great things.

By the early 1930s, in England, Learie, who was playing for Nelson in the Lancashire league and winning over the people of Nelson (by whom he in his turn was won over), said to James, 'You have it all wrong. You believe all that you read in those books. They are no better than we.' James implied that his 1933 pamphlet, 'The Case for West Indian Self-Government', was inspired by Constantine.

Once, in 1943, when in London to play for a Dominions XI against England, Constantine was evicted from the Imperial Hotel in Russell Square when American guests at the hotel objected to his presence. He fought and won a case against the hotel for racial discrimination. He later became High Commissioner for Trinidad in London. He was the first black person to be elevated to the House of Lords.

W. G. Grace was equally a representative of forces and feelings bigger than himself. James argues that it was through W. G. that 'cricket, the most complete expression of popular life in pre-industrial England, was incorporated into the life of the nation.'

As Seecharan puts it, 'There is no substitute for racial pride, as opposed to racism . . . in countering self-deprecation and inferiority complex, the inevitable legacy of a history of subjugation.'

Since self-deprecation is one consequence of racial and other kinds of trauma, one gift from the cricketing pioneers in West Indies, men like Float Woods or the Constantines, was to help build up the self-respect of their fellows, so that the person in the street walked taller, and the next generation became stronger, more determined, more in touch with *their* proper pride.

And then, after all, there are James himself and Worrell, both men who came at the hour. James writes of the principles involved in Worrell's captaincy. He describes Worrell's priorities: First, 'X was (or was not) a team man'. Second, '"If something was wrong I told them what was right and left it to them." He did not instil into, he drew out of his players.' Worrell clearly had not only a wonderful skill and courage as a cricketer, and a fine cricketing brain, he – in James's words –

expanded my conception of West Indian personality . . . He is one of the few who after a few hours of talk have left me as tired as if I had been put through a wringer. His responses to difficult questions were so unhesitating, so precise, and so took the subject on to unsuspected but relevant areas, that I felt it was I who was undergoing examination.

As James said of Learie Constantine: 'An occasion presented itself and he added a cubit to his stature.'

But the contours of the niche are not ready-made

I agree with James that each innovator needs a context for his creativity. Cometh the hour. When Bertrand Russell enthusiastically exclaimed to his new friend Nehru, 'we are both atheists', Nehru replied, 'Ah yes, but you are a Christian atheist and I am a Hindu atheist.' As Michelangelo famously said: 'I saw the angel in the marble and carved until I set him free.'

But it was *his* vision, *his* angel; it was the form *he* found. Each person has his own style, origins, his own deeper starting-off points, and points of contrast and comparison.

To be a pioneer, to become a representative, one has to be oneself. One has to counter pressures to copy or to be merely orthodox. In the limited field of batting technique, Grace had to move beyond the accepted technique of the day. A new orthodoxy had to be found and invented.

James illustrates this point with Learie Constantine, in his pivotal tussle with the Accrington professional, the old Lancashire and Australia fast bowler, Ted McDonald. There is initial sparring. Constantine is dropped at slip. James writes:

> The spell is broken and things will happen soon. But when it does happen no mortal could have foretold it. Constantine takes a long stride with his left foot across the wicket and, leaning well forward, he glances McDonald from outside the off-stump to long-leg for four.

Constantine did something daring, bold, unorthodox. He took a risky step into the unknown. The ground is prepared, no doubt: but the individual has to have the chutzpah and conviction to occupy it and make it his, the ground of his own being.

As Neville Cardus wrote in his Preface to Learie's first book, *Cricket and I*, a joint effort between Constantine and C. L. R., 'He [Learie] has made a contribution to the style and technique of cricket; at the same time he has told the tale of his people.'

James's own starting points were not only in cricket and his experience of the Trinidad scene, but also in literature. The pyramid on which his mature personality was built consisted of literature, religion and cricket. From the window behind the bowler's arm of his grandmother's house in Tunapuna, he watched the cricket, and could at the same time reach out to the books on the shelves, many of them bought from an itinerant bookseller. Included were *Pilgrim's Progress* and the Bible. Soon he added English novels, criticism, and reflection on society and on social realities.

But James had to overcome his earlier assumptions. He had already had to overcome the demand that he live out a future laid down for him as a clever scholarship winner. He had to overcome his ease and comfort in the civilized atmosphere of his old school, where he also taught for a while. He had to move away from his highly intellectual immersion in literature. He had to rethink sport and its place in what people want, in its relation too to art and drama.

Most of the great batsman's genius comes from his brain. Constantine's classical stroke of playing a ball to fine leg from outside off-stump was 'not due to his marvellous West Indian eyes and marvellous West Indian wrists. It was due to his marvellous West Indian brains.' And the brain-power James refers to is not refined or merely intellectual: it was also 'muscular learning'. Cricket and education jointly were the source of self-discovery and liberation.

Such a person has to 'break new ground'. This involves breaking old prejudices, and arouses retaliation. The innovator has to reconcile himself to subsequent unpopularity.

Only twenty or so years ago, a leading person in the cricket world, in a perverse echo of Constantine's words, said to me in his superior, upper-class drawl: 'The trouble with the modern Jamaican is that he thinks himself the equal of you or me.' The only proper rebuff to this would have been: 'So? What precisely is your point?' I'm ashamed to say that I didn't have the presence of mind to speak so directly. (I don't think he meant it when he said 'you or me'; what he really meant was 'me', i.e. him. And this attitude was not only a matter of colour, it was also a matter of class and religion; the same man made similar anti-Semitic remarks.)

The problem of cross-cultural understanding

Can I, a white Englishman, born and bred in London, understand with any degree of depth the legacy of slavery and colonialism? Can I imaginatively grasp the impact of racism, prejudice and snobbery?

I think the answer is both yes and no. No, in that the depth and ramification of such assumptions over so many generations are hard to conceive for someone relatively free from this kind of traumatic impact. Yes, in that one gets inklings of it in the class and racial attitudes in England, too. We all experience some humiliation, some feeling of being put down, and we are all liable to adopt this kind of superiority.

My grandfather was a Yorkshireman who, like Joshua Rudder, was an installer and repairer of large engines. He too would travel, in his case from his home in the West Riding of Yorkshire all over the north of England, whenever something went wrong with these crucial pieces of mill machinery.

I have spoken of proper pride, and that reminds me of stories of, and a sense of, cricketers in Yorkshire, where for a very long time the similar belief prevailed, that no one but an amateur (that is, a person from a superior social background) could be considered as captain. Lord Hawke famously said, at the Yorkshire Annual General Meeting in 1925:

> 'Pray God, no professional shall ever captain England. I love and admire them all, but we have always had an amateur skipper and when the day comes when we shall have no more amateurs captaining England, it will be a thousand pities.'

It was not until 1960 that Yorkshire first had a professional captain, though England had suffered their thousand pities earlier, in 1952, when Len Hutton (a Yorkshireman) was appointed.

In 1959, I played in a Middlesex II match against Sussex II at Hove. Because I was still at school, and was not paid, I was designated an amateur, and had to change with the captain in a vast room equipped with armchairs and carpets, while the other ten, including the twelfth man (all professionals) changed in a tiny space more or less under the showers. I was taught a stern lesson: I was run out in both innings!

When I became captain of Middlesex in 1971, one of the committee members assumed I had a private income. He meant that for one of us, one of us superior beings, it wouldn't be possible to live in our accustomed style off a professional's wage. (In fact my wage at that time was £1,600 per season, which was exactly what I had been receiving for a year's work as a lecturer at the University of Newcastle upon Tyne.)

So, I could identify with both sides of this pernicious divide and I admired the pride, the proper pride, of the Yorkshire professional. I relished the stories of the senior pros playing cards in the dressing room, and occasionally looking up towards the game in progress. When senior pro Emmott Robinson said, casually, 'Call 'em in, skipper', the (amateur) captain clapped his hands and declared. The captain was at times the puppet of the real powers behind the throne.

Crowned with olive

Slavery and colonialism are akin to the worst forms of intra-family abuse. The underlying similarity is arrogance and superiority, which ramify throughout a context, amounting in some cases to a cumulative trauma. The long-cherished colonial assumption allowed white people to represent black cricketers as all spontaneity and exuberance, but lacking in resolution and solidity, technique and discipline. They were said to fall apart in panic more quickly than whites do (a generalization similar to Tony Greig's in his much later 'we'll make them grovel' remarks). They were viewed as 'children' in comparison with the 'adults'. Of course this meant that it was for many years out of the question for a black man to captain a national team, for children cannot be adults, and children need mature parental leaders.

This picture is of course a grotesque caricature, of both parties and sets of qualities. Exuberance and freedom (qualities that children do have *par excellence*) *may* become irresponsibility and unreliability, may indicate a lack of resolution or technique, but need not. Steadiness and discipline *are* required in leadership, as in batting and bowling, but may become rigidity, inhibition and dulling control. These processes of stereotyping had to be modified before West Indies could in 1961 appoint a black captain for more than a single match (as had happened with George Headley in 1948): Frank Worrell.

The West Indian achievement, in education and in cricket, is a magnificent one. West Indies has produced three Nobel Laureates: Arthur Lewis (in economics) and Derek Walcott and V. S. Naipaul (in literature). Worrell and James rank alongside them.

C. L. R.'s concluding note on Worrell's achievement in Australia in 1960–1 is an inspiring one: 'We have gone far beyond a game . . . Frank Worrell was crowned with the olive . . . I saw all the West Indian ease, humour and easy adaptation to environment . . . I could see

179

his precise and uncompromising evaluations, those it seems are now second nature . . . Clearing their way with bat and ball, West Indians at that moment had made a public entry into the comity of nations.'

PART 5

CHEATING AND CORRUPTION

24

NOT COMMON-OR-GARDEN
CHEATING

In 1996 Hansie Cronje, South Africa's captain, met Indian bookmaker, Mukesh Gupta, who for years had been involved in attempting to bribe cricketers. There began an ongoing sequence of under-performing by Cronje and some of his team, in order to fix matches or parts of matches.

In 2000, Cronje confessed to the King Commission that he had taken bribes, and had enlisted other players to do the same.

In 2001 I wrote a piece about different levels of cheating in sport, specifically in cricket. I made a distinction between 'common-or-garden' cheating, that is, trying to get an unfair or illegal advantage in some episode or passage of play – nudging one's golf ball to a better lie, for example – and on the other hand, egregious cheating, amounting to corruption, that undermines the fundamental authenticity of a game, as when someone 'throws' a game, 'fixing' it or some part of it for personal advantage that lies outside the game itself.

Cronje was guilty of the latter. Comparing his crime to the ball tampering of Australian players Steve Smith, David Warner and Cameron Bancroft in 2018 is like comparing aggravated burglary with minor shoplifting.

In 2001, match-fixing was a relatively new virus in the cricketing world, intimately related to changes in the phenomena of betting, particularly in the subcontinent. My own cricket career, which finished in 1982, took place in another epoch; I was never invited to throw a match, or an innings (I seemed all too able to get out without even trying to). Nor did I ever hear speak of matches between counties or countries being fixed, as Lord Condon (the Head of ICC's then newly formed Anti-Corruption Unit) suggested was happening in the 1990s.

In this respect, my generation of players was innocent; we lived in a Garden of Eden before the fall. People occasionally gesture to the notorious bet placed by Dennis Lillee and Rodney Marsh on England to win the Headingley Test in 1981, bets which won them (I believe) £5,000 each. I'm entirely confident that the laying of this bet had nothing whatever to do with match-fixing. Rather, it was an opportunistic flutter laid by two inveterate tipsters, when the odds offered in a two-horse race (500–1) seemed to them absurd, despite the fact that by this time one of the horses looked lame, out of wind, and a huge distance behind the other horse.

In those days the idea of a player being paid money by a bookmaker to under-perform in any way would have been unthinkable. It would have been laughed out of court (would in fact have got nowhere near a court). Yet by the 1990s and 2000s, the bookmakers and their often criminal agents were tempting players, drawing them in, entrapping them. Some succumbed.

Why this kind of criminality happened just then is a broader sociological issue, but doubtless it was not a matter of chance that these scams coincided with cultures as described in *The Bonfire of the Vanities*, Tom Wolfe's 1987 novel about rampant ambition and greed in New York, and with the later-discovered scandals such as Enron's, and the banking crisis. I surmise that the new modes of wealth creation, some of them dubious, and the new forms of greed and manipulation of markets, themselves a form of gambling, with their paraphernalia of hedging and complexity, provided a back-cloth to spot-fixing.

Like all secret organizations recruiting for illegal activities, Gupta and his ilk drew people in by involving them at first in complicitous activity that was in itself of minor importance. Just as in 2018 we discover that drug dealers have been using children as mules to carry drugs from urban centres to outlying districts all over the country, thus exposing them to blackmail and threats, so the bookmakers and their henchmen first lured cricketers by offering money for relatively 'innocent' information, such as the nature of the pitch, and the fitness of the players in their squads. As Virgil put it in *The Aeneid*, *'facilis descensus Averno'* – easy the descent to hell. There is but a short step into criminality, and in some cases young players have been inveigled into such transactions and behaviours out of fear and a felt lack of mentors who could be trusted.

The revelations implicating Hansie Cronje shook the cricket world. Cronje, an Afrikaner (cricket is more of a British South African game), and a born-again Christian who conducted prayer-meetings with his team, was an unusual cricket captain of South Africa. In that sports-mad country, Cronje's good looks, excellent play as batsman and captain, and apparent decency and honesty, made him an ideal icon for the advertisers.

When he at first denied everything, Ali Bacher, Managing Director of South African cricket, who had worked closely with him for years, backed him – alluding to his 'unquestionable integrity and honesty'.

However, one thing my work as a psychoanalyst, as well as being in analysis myself, has impressed on me is that one can never take (human) appearances for granted; it can sometimes be the case that the larger the front, the larger the behind. Cronje it was who stooped to serial dishonesty, even seducing the most junior players in his team to be his cronies.

Cronje is a disconcerting example of the splits that occur in many people. On the outside, and in many of the contexts of his life, he was a decent, honest, honourable man. But scratch the surface and this alter ego was revealed, this shadow self, corrupt and devious, a person or personality that may well have been as incomprehensible to himself or to his central ego as it was to others.

To some extent, we all wear masks. We present different faces to different people in the world. We dress ourselves up. We put on fronts. As Mark Twain put it, 'Everyone is a moon, and has a dark side which he never shows to anybody.' We may even con ourselves. It is as if there are two or more distinct personalities, each with its own agendas, values and behaviours.

One source of such dissimulation and self-deception arises from being pushed by parents or others to live a role that is foreign to us. One child may react against the role that is demanded of him – to be perfectly behaved – by rebellion and by exaggerating his or her less wholesome side.

Or the rebellious reaction may be against the hypocrisy of the parents, or to their darker side shown only in the privacy of the home. In Marilynne Robinson's novel *Home*, Jack, the black sheep of the family, seems in his persistent and puzzling minor delinquencies to be protesting against the hypocrisy of his religious parent-figures and testing out their love for him.

These constructed selves become rigidly reinforced, and do not fall away at a puff of wind. False selves are both hard to change and instigators of subtle reactions that test out the 'straight' world.

To return to cricket. Examples of 'common-or-garden' cheating would be: claiming a catch when you know the ball has bounced; picking the seam; using illegal substances on the ball. This ordinary cheating occurs within the framework of a game. It is a form of lying, not with words but in action. Those who do this are dishonest in order to gain an unfair advantage within the game by illegal or unethical means.

Cheating of this kind is on a scale with shrewdness, cunning and gamesmanship. There are lines to be drawn here; I'm not saying that subtlety and gamesmanship are dishonest, nor that they are forms of cheating. But all sorts of complexities and grey areas exist, ranging from cheating at one end to putting legitimate pressure on the opposition at the other. Some of the situations that lead to misunderstanding and allegations of cheating are a matter of differing local anthropological customs, or different fashions. In such cases, what one tribe regards as sharp practice, another regards as fair and sensible shrewdness.

One practice that is subject to such vagaries, and can lead to bad feeling where different fashions intersect, is 'walking'. In Yorkshire leagues, or the whole of Australia except for British-style public schools, you would have been regarded as somewhat deranged to have walked when you had nicked the ball to the keeper. In many parts of the south of England, and in most county cricket, up until the late 1970s, you were called a cheat if you did not walk. These are, it seems to me, merely different tribal activities. When either tribe engages in intra-tribal games, there is rarely a problem. The problems begin when the two tribes face each other.

This example reminds me of the Afrikaners in the Boer War, who declined to fight in the gentlemanly British way, marching along in bright red jackets asking to be shot. Instead, they hid under bushes, in camouflage jackets, and did the shooting. Bad form.

What Cronje and others did falls into a different category from these paradigmatic examples of cheating. Match-fixing is a matter not of cheating within a game, but – one might almost say – *cheating the game itself*, the whole fabric of it. What they did undermines and falsifies the whole activity.

Match-fixing has a holistic, ramifying quality to it, which ordinary, deliberate cheating in a particular moment lacks. In throwing a match (or fixing a spot) players cheat everyone – not only their opponents but also their own team, the public, and the game as a whole, as an institution. Opponents are cheated because their victory becomes hollow. Cronje's team-members not in the know, or not in the plot, are cheated if their captain, or their team-mates, are split in their allegiance to the team's success. And the public, who will rapidly become disillusioned if and when they find out that this kind of thing has gone on, are cheated, disabused of their trust in what goes on in front of their eyes. The match-fixer treats everyone, and the game itself, with contempt.

Moreover, it is of the essence of sport that, unlike much music and theatre, the course and outcome are not ordained before the event, however predictable it might be that the favourite will win. The drama of sport lies partly in the way things turn out on the day. There is always the chance of a shock result. The result is not, then, 'fixed' in the other sense; that is, there is no script or score (as in theatre or music): cricket matches are open to the vagaries of form, morale and luck. In normal circumstances we naturally take it as given that both sides are striving to succeed.

There are activities, based on sporting skills, where the sport-element is reduced to a show or an act, to entertainment under the pretence of wholehearted endeavour and competition. Sport proper differs from that which is presented as frank exhibition, as offered by the Harlem Globetrotters, who show a delighted public their basketball tricks in a form of theatre, comedy and athletic showmanship.

Cronje and others attempted to turn cricket matches, or passages of play within them, into the equivalent of some wrestling, but without the latter's blatant play-acting as a form of pantomime. Once spectators begin to suspect the integrity of the game, they will lose interest in it. Fixing throws into doubt the integrity of the whole first-class game. Almost anything becomes suspect. An individual who deliberately cheats the game, however apparently trivially, puts at risk not only his own career, but his profession, and that of his colleagues and successors.

Here is a small example of how mistrust and innuendo, once in, emerges even when the behaviour in question was innocent. India performed badly in England in 2011, against a strong England side. In the last Test at the Oval, with India already 3–0 down, opening bowler R. P. Singh was brought in. He had last played in a first-class match in January, eight months before. His first over included five balls down the leg-side, all at medium pace. Only one ball was on a good length and line. A distinguished commentator made this passing remark: 'Anyone betting on balls down the leg-side in the first over might have made some money' – a clear reference to the spot-fixing scandal of a year before, when Mohammad Amir's first ball of the match had been wide down the leg-side, and was followed by the notorious no-balls bowled by him and by the older and more senior bowler, Mohammad Asif.

All this explains why we need to take corruption very seriously, as a threat against sport, against cricket and against the spirit of cricket. For all these reasons, penalties should have a deterrent element. I support strong action against people engaged in such corruption.

At the same time, we need to make distinctions. There is a big difference between someone who as leader or captain inveigles a junior player to do something illegal, and the junior player dependent upon him. The captain deserves severer condemnation and punishment than the young player. Cronje's actions were more reprehensible than, say, Herschelle Gibbs's.

Similarly, Salman Butt's actions (in 2010) were far worse than those of Amir, a young fellow from a provincial town, playing in a cultural context where unquestioning submission to one's seniors was central to the idea of morality. Moreover, when threatened by a corrupt bookmaker, Amir's fatal mistake was to ask that person on whom he should most have been able to rely, his captain, for help. Instead of being supported, he was put in touch with a second corrupt figure, who threatened him with exposure if he refused to bowl the intentional no-balls. Moreover, Amir was, I believe, minimally interested in financial gain for his part in the 2010 sting. For these reasons he should, I think, have been treated more leniently than he was, and certainly much more leniently than those who inveigled him into it. In the strenuous search for exemplary and deterrent punishment, there has to be room for giving a misguided young player a second chance.

25

BALL TAMPERING:
DISENCHANTMENT

*In 2018, Australia played South Africa in four Test matches. There was
from the beginning ill-feeling and boorishness in some of the exchanges.
In the third Test at Cape Town, when Australia were up against it in
South Africa's second innings, Cameron Bancroft, Australia's twenty-
five-year-old opening batsman, was observed on camera slipping a piece
of yellow tape, later revealed to be sandpaper, down the front of his
trousers. The outcome was the revelation that Steve Smith and David
Warner, captain and vice-captain, had during the lunch interval planned
the use of the sandpaper to rough up one side of the ball. The ensuing
outrage led to bans on all three players.*

The MCC have a slogan or precept: 'the Spirit of Cricket'. Steve Smith himself alluded to the phrase, when he admitted that what they had done was not in that spirit.

But what do we mean by this? Though such a precept may be 'owned' or claimed by one particular group to support its own prejudices and local values, and to scorn people whose culture differs from one's own, it has a good side. It is a useful statement of an ideal. Advocating a good spirit is like speaking up for the truth in vigorous opposition to 'fake news', to the idea that one can believe or state or do whatever one chooses. It offers those who play the game a vision of a better self and a healthy ambience for legitimate rivalry and competition.

Ball tampering has gone on forever. I imagine that few players could say, hand on heart, that they have never contributed to it in any way. The seam of the ball has often been picked to make deviation off the pitch more likely. For reverse swing, the quarter seam, I gather, may be raised, or the non-shiny side of the ball scuffed. Players have used creams or lip-salve to enhance the shine on one side of the ball.

In India in 1976–7, the MCC team of which I was vice-captain (and thus a member of the 'management team') was accused by Indian captain, Bishan Bedi, of cheating. John Lever had had problems with sweat running down into his eyes, and physiotherapist Bernard Thomas had suggested a gauze strip, infused with Vaseline, to be taped to his forehead. Was this cheating, to aid swing? Or was the aim simply to divert the sweat? I have never known the answer to this question. Was I, am I, naïve? I was not involved in the discussions. But nor did I enquire too closely. Did I refrain from enquiry in case the truth might have been unpalatable? I am inclined to think the action was innocent; but certainly I should have made it my business to know; moreover, the plan should have been cleared in advance with the umpires.

So why have the Australians been so singled out? Why has this episode elicited such public outrage in Australia, prompting a bleak and uncompromising statement by the country's Prime Minister, Malcolm Turnbull? Why did it appear as the lead item in the ten o'clock news here in the UK? And why was my Australian friend Kate Fitzpatrick driven to write me an email on the evening after the Cape Town episode, saying she had been

> disenchanted and disheartened by Australian cricket for a long time. But this morning's moronically stupid, entitled, childish, ill-bred, cowardly performance has hammered the lid down for me. Smith, Boof [coach Darren Lehmann] and all the bully boys have to go.

Later she wrote again: 'Smith said they all came up with the idea over lunch. The only thing he could think of in the face of a flogging.'

As Michael Atherton wrote, ball tampering had not hitherto been regarded as a heinous crime. It is regarded by ICC as only a level-two offence (out of four levels). I think the reason for the extreme reactions to Smith and the others lay outside the simple act of using sandpaper to affect the ball.

First, it was planned rather than impulsive.

Second, the fingerprints on the ball were those of the most junior player in the side, a feature which suggested a lack of leadership responsibility; the captain and vice-captain appeared to have made a definite decision to palm off responsibility.

And third, as Kate implied, there had been a constant drip-drip of stories of crude antagonisms and streaks of nastiness, both in the current series in South Africa, and over recent series against India and England. The ball tampering led to a sudden collapse of the team's (and these players') reputation, like that of a camel whose splayed legs suddenly give way when one more straw is piled on its back.

When things go against you (in the field, for example) it is tempting to find any means of rectifying a sense of helplessness. If you have no legitimate tactical or psychological ideas, you may think something illegal will serve. It might even be a bit of a laugh! (I offer this not as an excuse of course, let alone a justification, but as an attempt at explanation.)

All these lines of thought imply, as Kate wrote, an exaggerated sense of entitlement in the Australian team. We can't do it straight, so we'll try something crooked.

A further question arises: how come the players believed that, in this era of close-up cameras – there are twenty-four I believe all round the ground at big matches – they would get away with it? It was, on the face of it, 'moronically stupid'. So what on earth were they thinking?

I have two alternative answers to this.

The first is that this was a further expression of 'entitlement'. Had these players become so arrogant as to no longer believe they could be caught? Was the group's underlying, subliminal attitude: 'We, who are entitled to anything, can get away with anything'?

My second suggestion is based on Freud's idea that some criminality or underhandedness is motivated by the unconscious desire for exposure, for punishment – he wrote about 'criminals from a sense of guilt'. The idea is that it's not so much criminality that leads to guilt as vice versa. Could it be that the Australian team and its managers and coaches felt deep down that they deserved this public excoriation? Probably not, but worth a thought.

The questions apply more widely. We all (or most of us) need to think about why we are inclined to cheat, sometimes in small, sometimes in big ways. As David Richardson of the ICC said when this scandal became public, cricketers and their coaches need to take a hard look at themselves. Maybe this will stimulate action and reflection. And not exclusively in Australia.

One reason is that we so much want to get our own way. We can't bear frustration, especially when we feel helpless.

Moreover, we often feel not only desperate and defeated by our opponents, but also humiliated. Gang warfare is often based on shame and mutual humiliation; we feel, whether justified or not, that the person or team that defeats us is gloating over us, triumphantly boasting and sticking his (or their collective) chest out. We feel that the natural way to retaliate is to hand the shame and the humiliation over (or back) to them, to shove it down their throat, an eye for an eye, a tooth for a tooth. I'm reminded of one party's self-justificatory remark in such a tit-for-tat situation: 'But he retaliated first!'

As for the response in England, there was no doubt an element of schadenfreude, of malicious pleasure at the old rivals going through this public disgrace. We like to think it's them and not us, and we smugly occupy the moral high ground.

What is to be done? It would be naïve to suppose that such behaviours and attitudes can be stopped. We put twenty-two young men into a scenario where rivalries and cultural differences have a long history, and we invite them to be full-hearted in their aggression. It is not easy to enter fully into such a cauldron of potential triumphalism and depression and then be expected to behave as at a vicarage tea-party (though I daresay there are similar attitudes, perhaps less blatant, expressed at some of those).

But we do need to remind ourselves of the Spirit of Cricket.

Postscript

The three players involved were reported to the ICC, which imposed a one-Test ban on Smith and Warner, and a fine on Bancroft. When the Australian Board made further investigations, they penalized the three more substantially. Smith and Warner were banned from international cricket, and from first-class domestic cricket, for a year, Bancroft for nine months. Smith could not captain the side for at least two years. Warner was barred for life from positions of authority in the team.

The chief executive of the Australian Board, James Sutherland, in delivering this judgement, spoke about the penalty as an attempt to balance the seriousness of the offence with the chance of redemption. The banned players will be allowed to play in Grade cricket, or in county cricket (if they get the chance).

The three men were sent home, and on arrival in Australia made painful confessions and statements of remorse on television. All three, plus coach Darren Lehmann, broke down in tears. Lehmann, though exonerated, resigned.

Tears well up from different sources; from guilt, remorse and the wish to make reparation: from shame (from dis-grace); there may too be crocodile tears – hypocritical shows of concern shed while devouring one's prey. It's hard to differentiate the first two. For all three players, there was presumably a mixture. But whether remorse or shame was the greater, the pain was palpable. Some people felt more cynical about Warner's tears and performance. The message that he conveyed was that he was saying to himself one thing: don't answer anything to do with other members of the side and whether they were in on the plan; don't say anything about whether Australia had done similar things in the recent past; just keep coming back to your own culpability. I didn't feel cynical. I thought he did what he was able to do, probably acting on advice.

Once they saw the pain and humiliation for all three in this ordeal, most people viewing the whole situation became less intransigent in their condemnation. If one sees the offence as a rebellion against the father (represented by 'the law'), perhaps we identify with the father in our initial wish to punish – we too are offended, our own sense of proper rules has been flouted. But when we see the pain of these young men, and that of their relatives (Smith's pain at how it had affected his 'old man', and his mother, was particularly acute), when we experience their shame and disgrace, falling from being national heroes to chancers who let down country, families, friends and supporters, and the image of cricket itself, we soften. We even become more maternal in our wish to give them a hug.

There was certainly a big switch from the players' assumptions of entitlement to the extreme vulnerability of their humiliation. They reminded me of figures from nineteenth-century literature, like Sir Leicester Dedlock in *Bleak House*, who become more human and less arrogant through suffering and the development of a sense of guilt. But what an ordeal to go through to get to this point! We would be stony-hearted indeed not to have some sympathy, some thought of 'there but for the grace of God, go I'.

Tom Derose and Ivan Ward, who both work at the Freud Museum, have offered a further insight. They suggest that at the deeper level the humiliation is that of castration. The young men rebelled against the father and his rules; tampering with the ball, they tried to make it magic, to change its qualities, so that instead of impotence in the face of South Africa's dominance, they could become potent on the field. Caught in this act of rubbing the ball up, they are then revealed as naughty boys, and put in their place; as Derose suggests, Smith becomes 'Little Steve', rather like Freud's patient, five-year-old 'Little Hans'. Smith's most uncontrollable sobbing came when he spoke of the pain his act had caused his 'old man'. At that moment, the hand of his father appeared on-screen on his shoulder; the hand of sympathy, but also of authority and disappointment.

Like Sutherland, I too hope the outcome of the whole episode will turn out to have been redemptive. We can't know in advance if the breakdown into anguish and shame will lead to a breakthrough and a deep-seated change of heart, either at a personal level, or for cricket and cricketers more generally.

We are all liable to back-slide. We have to learn to suffer and endure periods of impotence and vulnerability. And we all need, as I say, to remind ourselves of the spirit not only of cricket but of sport and of shared human endeavours.

26

THE STING: LORD'S 2010

On Thursday 26 August 2010, England started their innings in the fourth and last Test against Pakistan at Lord's. The series was still open: England were leading 2–1.

On the Saturday, I wrote a piece for the next day's Observer, featuring what I saw as a strange display of captaincy with regard to the use of the Pakistani fast left-arm bowler, Mohammad Amir, who at eighteen was showing such flair and promise. On the Saturday evening we had several people to dinner, including the Chairman of the Pakistan Board, Ijaz Butt, who left at 1 a.m. after reciting Urdu poetry along with Giles Clarke, Chair of the ECB, an expert in Arabic, Farsi and Urdu.

Butt had mentioned Urdu's lack of a future tense. Next morning the bombshell broke: three players were accused of conspiring to bowl deliberate no-balls at certain specified times. They had fallen for a sting engineered by the News of the World. The three were: Salman Butt (captain), Mohammad Asif (fast bowler) and Mohammad Amir.

I doubt if Ijaz Butt had been told of the scandal about to explode.

Here is my report (slightly altered for style, in tenses, and to explain the context eight years later), published in the Observer on the same morning as the article in the News of the World that revealed the scam.

After a rain-affected first day, when England had been put in to bat, they started the second day, Friday, on 39 for 1.

The Drive to Win – Pakistan's Lack

Cricket is the cruellest game. It is also, by the same token, the kindest. As England's record-breaking eighth-wicket partnership (between Jonathan Trott and Stuart Broad) proceeded serenely on through Friday afternoon and Saturday, Pakistan's mortification and frustration became more and more palpable. Their reasonable prospect of a substantial first-innings lead, and of putting pressure on England on a pitch that might wear, had been replaced by weariness and a sense of inevitability.

There is no future tense in Urdu; the future is in the hands of Allah, it is not for mortal men to speak as if they presume to know what it holds. But Pakistan's players must at least have feared for their future as the stand ground on. Though the pitches at Lord's have tended to get easier, this Test match came later in the summer than usual and the ball was turning more on Saturday than on the day before. Graeme Swann was already having a big impact and would expect to continue to do so.

And Pakistan must have regretted their past. Think of it: at lunch on Friday morning their young tyro Mohammad Amir had bowled 5.3 overs during the session, taking 4 wickets for 10 runs. Having bowled two more overs after lunch he had taken 6 for 12 in the day. Remarkably, England were reduced to 102 for seven. And yet, two overs later, with overall figures of 6 for 37, he was off the field (for only a few minutes, apparently for treatment on his calf), and did not bowl again for almost an hour and a half, by which time the score was 174 for 7; the English horses were galloping away from the stable door.

Amir's absence from the attack reminded me of the Test at Perth in 1978–9, when Rodney Hogg came off after bowling four eight-ball overs with figures of two wickets for no runs. Perhaps Hogg's asthma made bowling difficult, but it would have had to be almost life-threatening to justify removal from the attack at such a moment.

I had no knowledge of the state of Amir's calf muscle on that Friday afternoon, except to observe that when at last he did bowl that afternoon, he was running in with a spring in his step, delivering at his usual 83 to 88 mph.

I cannot imagine Ian Botham or Darren Gough letting anyone else get hold of the ball when they had taken six wickets in nine overs. Individuals and teams experience such achievements rarely in Test-match life, and you need to grab them. As Douglas Jardine said to his fast bowler Harold Larwood, before the Sydney Test in 1933, after winning the Ashes: 'We've got them down, Harold. Now we'll tread on them.' The events of the past two days show how readily it can happen that, if you don't tread on them, they will tread on you. ('I wasted time,' Richard II said in his prison cell; 'And now doth Time waste me.')

Soon enough the boot was indeed on the other foot, and England were the ones doing the treading, not only in the magnificent partnership, but with the ball. (Pakistan ended Saturday on 41 for 4.)

When Amir did bowl, he usually had only two slips, yet he was bowling a probing length at lively speed and moving the ball. He had a deep square leg for Jonathan Trott almost throughout; yet the one area where Trott, who played with magnificent assurance, looked at all vulnerable was outside the off-stump.

Amir was a prodigiously promising cricketer. He was eighteen years old. There was humorous speculation in the Press Box on Saturday that the decision to cut short his bowling spell when he had England for the taking might have been down to the health and safety regulations that now applied to young cricketers. When more recently Parthiv Patel kept wicket for India in England, at the age of seventeen, he ought technically to have brought a letter from his mother giving him permission to keep wicket without a helmet.

While Trott gave the impression of unhurried security, Stuart Broad flowed superbly, and was no mere prop for his senior partner. Again, I think Pakistan played into his hands, by not attacking him enough, especially with Amir, and by giving him too much room outside the off-stump to swing his arms and hands through the ball. Bowlers should bowl much straighter to him. There was some similarity in this regard between Broad and Graham Dilley. Back in 2010, especially on his form in this match, Broad looked as though he might become capable of batting at number eight for England, if not even number seven.

The game of cricket is cruel because one can pay so heavily and in such prolonged ways for mistakes.

Footnote 2018

In writing my article, I had of course no notion of the very different scale of paying for one's mistakes that was about to be enacted on Mohammad Amir. I knew nothing then of his deliberate no-balls, about a betting scam, about the 'Fake Sheikh' (Mazher Mahmood, the News of the World *reporter). Nor of course did anyone know that he would serve time in a prison for juveniles, or that six years later, his rehabilitation would occur on the same ground.*

As I say above, Amir's withdrawal from the attack and the field on Friday struck me as odd at the time. I now assume that this was when the Pakistan team learned of the upcoming revelations, and were trying to decide how to respond. The players directly involved must have been devastated and confused, others may not have known what to believe, and the crisis showed in the sudden decline in their performance on the field. Demoralized, they sank even further on the Sunday, losing the match by an innings and 225 runs.

Butt, Asif and Amir were charged and found guilty. All three were sent to prison.

Mohammad Amir was only seventeen when he first played for Pakistan. From the beginning, there were people hovering around the team, offering money to cheat. During the tour of England in 2010, he was phoned many times by a bookmaker called Ali, who was keen to seduce him into his gambling scams. Amir did three things wrong. First, he showed curiosity and rang this man back, asking questions about what was required. He refused the request, but did not report the contact immediately. Second, the person he did report it to was his captain, Salman Butt, who disgracefully put him onto a corrupt businessman who was his own agent, Mazher Majeed. Majeed told Amir that he was now known to the authorities and was in big trouble, but he could help him out of his difficulties provided he bowled the two no-balls in the Lord's Test. Amir's third foolishness was to do this (extremely inefficiently, his foot going over the line by a massive twelve inches). He was given some money, which he put in a locker and closed the door. Amir said later that he did not want to have anything to do with this money. These no-balls, and one by Mohammad Asif, were the main elements in the scam set up by Mazher Mahmood, the Fake Sheikh, the News of the World 'investigative journalist'.

I happened to have met Gareth Peirce, Amir's defence lawyer, in another context, and she and I, along with her colleague, Sajida Malik, talked several times about Amir's plight and its cricketing context. We spoke after he was charged, in the run-up to the trial, and when he was released from prison, at which point he came with Gareth to thank me for my help. It was a heart-breaking story.

Amir was totally let down by, indeed entrapped by, his own captain, whom he trusted and who was the driving force behind his predicament. The young – indeed, adolescent – man was naïve and wilful, but not malicious or greedy. He was in the end frightened into bowling the no-balls. Butt believed that his own corruption might be deflected if they gave the reporter this opportunity for a betting scoop, so he cruelly implicated the most junior person in his team to do his dirty work. Furthermore, he and Asif made out at the trial that Amir was the main culprit.

In my view, Amir should have been treated much more leniently than those who inveigled him into it. In the strenuous search for exemplary *and deterrent punishment, there has to be room for giving a misguided young player a second chance. I was glad that after serving his prison term and his exclusion from cricket, and from working, he was free to play again.*

In 2016, he returned to the scene of the 'crime', for the first Test of the series at Lord's.

The following is an extract from my piece on that game, written in 2016 for The Times.

The crowd's reception of Mohammad Amir at Lord's made me feel proud. Its understated sense of fair play was both a relief and a reassurance.

Here was a young man who six years ago at the age of eighteen did a shabby thing, knowing it to be wrong, and was rightly held accountable; who spent four months in HM Prison, Feltham, and was disgraced in the cricketing community; who along with others brought Pakistan and its cricket team into disrepute. Now, he had gradually been brought back into the game by the Pakistan Cricket Board, beginning his rehabilitation and his capacity to make amends by warning youngsters about how easily one can be drawn into corrupt practices. He had served the time of his suspension.

In 2010, those who should have been mentors were instead corruptors. His captain, Salman Butt, was the very person who pulled him into a nefarious ploy. The culture he grew up in made it harder for him to resist the blandishments of his captain, and of the senior fast bowler, Mohammad Asif. My impression is that Amir was naïve. He was not, I believe, mainly interested in the money.

Shakespeare writes in *Macbeth*: 'As hounds and greyhounds, mongrels, spaniels . . . are clep't all by the name of dogs.' Crimes that fall under the same name likewise vary – in seriousness, in degrees of culpability. It is not only that 'the quality of mercy is not strained'; the quality of justice calls for differentiation. Murders committed in the heat of the moment, when under prolonged provocation, deserve lesser punishment than those committed in cold blood, or accompanied by cruelty. Amir sinned, but was more sinned against than sinning. He has paid his penalty, and we can now rightly appreciate his lively, whippy, at times lethal bowling.

As he himself said, he has learned his lesson, and a hard lesson it was.

27

THE SPIRIT OF CRICKET

The MCC has been responsible for the Laws of Cricket since 1787. In recent years, they have introduced a preamble to them referring to the Spirit of Cricket. There are those who think this unnecessary, and those who think it should be in the body of the Laws. This is my reaction.

'Mankading': Sachithra Senanayake runs out Jos Buttler, 2014.

Michael Atherton once suggested that the Spirit of Cricket is 'a lot of well-meaning guff'. Others criticize the Spirit of Cricket statements for being too vague; they lead to contradictory interpretations.

Ian Bishop, the West Indies fast bowler and now commentator, has said: 'Spirit of cricket is a noble and most welcome preamble to the laws as applied to this great game. But what is the use or fairness of that principle when it is invoked so inconsistently and conveniently?' He argues that many examples are cases of outdated social conditioning.

Atherton agrees with Bishop's response to one controversial instance: both assert that there is nothing wrong with 'Mankading' – the running out of the non-striking batsman for backing up too far.

Some years ago, I too struggled to accept this advocacy of the Spirit of Cricket and the placing of it as a preamble to the Laws of Cricket. My hesitation was to do with the risk of it sounding (or even being) patronizing, priggish or pompous.

In the days of empire and a more feudal MCC, the 'spirit of cricket' was, or could be, purveyed in a way that suggested hypocrisy and superiority. It could be used to stand for a set of standards that were proclaimed most loudly as part of the public school ethos, though not always lived out on the cricket field, let alone in other walks of life. The Victorian England of Empire was noted, for example, for swathes of sexual and financial irregularities among the upper and middle classes. One version of the English vice was hypocrisy; 'perfidious Albion' was how we were regarded in many parts of the world.

Another common failing seems to me to be an insistence on outward forms combined with a neglect of much more important moral or political shortcomings. To give one example: the MCC over-valued sporting contacts with official cricket in South Africa, ignoring for too long the shocking injustices of apartheid, especially in its impact on cricket and other sports. Moreover – and this is another failing, I think – when placed against the latter immorality, mere form, like whether one wears a jacket and tie to lunch, is in my view over-rated.

Today the atmosphere of the MCC has changed radically. It is now a kind of upper chamber of cricket, somewhat removed from the political and commercial issues that inevitably have to be faced and negotiated by the bodies at the sharp end, like the ICC, ECB or the Cricket Boards of different countries. As such, the MCC has a role in cricket akin to that of the House of Lords in the British Constitution, a chamber with little power, but with moral influence. Thus, the MCC is still the Custodian of the Laws of Cricket, and now has a respected World Cricket Committee. It can act, or at least speak, as part of the conscience of the game, without setting itself up on a pinnacle of self-righteousness.

Today, I am in favour of this Preamble. I like the fact that it is couched in simple and direct language. More importantly, we need to be clear that it is not meant to answer first-level questions about good and bad behaviour, but is rather a way of focusing on values that go beyond obeying the Laws. And third, we should beware of the risk of elevating cricket above other activities; the Spirit of Cricket applies to all sports, and indeed to the whole of life.

So: to answer the critics. They say the Spirit of Cricket is too vague. In my view it is meant to be vague, offering pointers to an attitude of mind that is to be expected and hoped for from people playing (and running) the game. Atherton himself wrote of the late New Zealand cricketer, Martin Crowe:

> Martin viewed his illness, initially, as an opportunity, given that it allowed him to confront the demons and the man that, he felt, cricket had made him into. So, latterly, his instincts for the game and people in it were invariably sound: he was against rampant ego, selfishness, boorishness, bullying (the takeover at the ICC made him livid) and the lop-sidedness of one-day cricket, which will, inevitably, swamp the longer form of the game.

This seems to me to be a good expansion of the Spirit of Cricket.

Certainly the Spirit of Cricket does not offer an answer to first-level ethical questions; for example, on what our attitude should be to

'Mankading'. Indeed, as with 'walking' (the batsman voluntarily and quickly leaving the field when he knows that he has edged a ball), there are arguments on either side. The words in the Spirit of Cricket don't decide the rights and wrongs of such issues.

But this does not mean that they are useless or meaningless.

I agree with Bishop that there are many situations where social conditioning is the main factor in what some group or other feels is correct. As a boy, I remember a hoo-ha when a player in my father's London club side, Brentham, was run out by a fielder for the Indian Gymkhana while prodding down the pitch; the ball had not become dead. One social group thought this was fine (as with Mankading), the other thought it was scandalously unsportsmanlike. This was a clear case of different social norms. Each thought they were in accordance with the Spirit of Cricket, as interpreted in different cultures.

There have been similar instances on the larger stage. In 1974, Tony Greig ran out Alvin Kallicharran in a Test in Trinidad, when the batsman was walking off the field before 'Time' had been called. Similarly, Ian Bell was run out when, on the last ball before tea, against India at Trent Bridge in 2011, he incorrectly believed the ball had gone for four, and had begun to walk off for tea when the stumps were broken. Both Kallicharran and Bell were called back to continue their innings, though both had been correctly given out according to the letter of the law. There is no absolute answer to these two ethical questions, and though one might hope for generosity by the fielding side, it is not something one should demand or rely on. In each case the reversal of the (legally correct) decision was possible only as a result of the fact that the immediately ensuing intervals allowed for negotiation, discussion and second thoughts.

The problem that Bishop and Atherton allude to is not so much the existence of the Spirit of Cricket, as the use to which it is put. There is a risk of its being used to justify Establishment views, or one's own views wherever one is, when what is being advocated, often passionately, is the outcome of merely local conditioning. But it is not inevitable that it will be used in such a way.

Not everything can be left to the Laws. As Doug Insole (then Chair of the Cricket Committee of the TCCB, the forerunner of the ECB) used to say annually to county captains: 'You can drive a coach and horses through the Laws of Cricket.' The Laws don't – and can't – cover everything. There will always be cases that arouse uncertainty, strange events, and shrewd but dubious or questionable actions that the Laws don't specifically address.

One such example occurred in 1979, when Somerset captain Brian Rose declared the Somerset innings after only a few balls in a one-day match at Worcester, thus ensuring progress to the next round of the competition on the basis of run-rate. That was legal, but against the spirit of sport, which involves playing the game, and allowing the opposition a chance of winning fairly. The strongest objection to Trevor Chappell's underarm delivery, rolled along the ground, as the last delivery in an ODI between Australia and New Zealand in 1981 (the latter needed, you may recall, six runs off the last ball) was that, *without using skill*, it allowed no room for the possibility of a stroke of genius and/or luck that could have produced a six. I would say that both acts were against the spirit of the game, without being, at the time, against any law.

Similarly, I would say that claiming a catch when you know the ball has bounced; appealing when you *know* it's not out; making it look as though the umpire has made a mistake (batsman looks at the ground, indicating that it was a bump ball) especially when the batsman knows the decision was correct – all these are (I would say) against the spirit of the game but not against its laws.

When I started playing first-class cricket, the official attitude, at least in county cricket, was that you should walk if you knew you were out. And most people, most of the time, did. However, walking invites hypocrisy. Many people would unfailingly walk if they had scored 54, say, or 71, or 105; or if they got a thick edge. But if they were on 0, or 99, or in the middle of a bad run and about to be dropped, or if it seemed to them an undeserving wicket to the bowler, or if they were enjoying batting so much they couldn't bear to leave, or if it was a marvellous piece of batting to get an edge to such a ball, or if the other side had been 'cheating' – in all these kinds of case, people would sometimes not walk. And this led to accusations of cheating even when the batsman believed he *hadn't* hit the ball. It also led to umpires feeling that they were accusing someone of cheating if they gave him out after he did not walk.

I'm not saying it's wrong not to walk. I think it's arguable. I admire people who do walk, unfailingly. My impression is that Adam Gilchrist walked, throughout his career. He was, I'm afraid, a better man than I am (or was).

What I do think is that, whether you walk or not, you should get off the field without a fuss and quickly. I have wholehearted admiration for Ian Chappell in this regard. Twice in a Test match, at Melbourne in 1974–5, Chappell was given out caught behind down the leg-side by Alan Knott, once off Chris Old, the second time off Tony Greig. Both decisions were wrong.

But on each occasion Chappell marched off to the dressing room without the crowd knowing that he was the victim of a mistake. As Ian wrote to me:

> I was taught always to look at the umpire when an appeal was made, and if I was given out to get on my bike and leave in a hurry without any fuss. I certainly did this both times in Melbourne, although not without a certain amount of swearing behind my glove as I walked off. However, on the second occasion, being doubly peeved at two bad decisions, and both when I was well set, my mood wasn't helped by Greigy telling me to 'Piss off, you're out.'

Ian then had words with Greig, right in front of the square leg umpire, but, he wrote, in extenuation, 'I will add I said all this while on the move.'

The vagueness of application of the Spirit of Cricket is what allows it to have so wide a range. It has to do with one's entire orientation, demeanour and attitude to the contests, to the opposition, and to the game itself.

Another issue that comes up from time to time is sledging (which I take to be systematic attempts to undermine a batsman by personal comments more or less within his hearing). There is of course no need for unpleasant language and bad mouthing, least of all for sledging.

Yet human nature is an unruly thing. Divide twenty-two pumped up, anxious young men into two antagonistic groups according to old tribal loyalties and you have a toxic mixture. You have, in fact, the makings of gang warfare. You have (for example) the Ashes.

Group posturing may become ritualized, both in order to increase bonding by working up one's own emotions, and to discombobulate the opposition's. The most striking example is the All Blacks' haka.

This reminds me of Greek tragedy and its possible origins. The word for its metre, its rhythmic building blocks – 'iambics' – is cognate with the Greek word for throw; so tragedy came into existence, we may infer, as a sublimation of insult-throwing, the latter itself a sublimation of throwing stones.

One central feature of gang culture is, as we've seen, mutual humil-iation. You score emotionally off the other lot, put them down, make them look small. If they humiliate you, honour requires you to return the compliment.

Such interactions occur at both group and individual level. The overall demeanour of the team sends its haka-like message to the other team; there are also individual recipes for destabilizing each opponent personally. He (or she) will have to deal not only with their private shame or smallness, but also with the discomfort of feeling they have let the team down.

Not that the Spirit of Cricket slogan proposes that these sporting battles, these Coliseum-like spectacles, should be tame. The phrasing includes: 'play hard but fair'.

Furthermore, it is fully within the spirit of the game to unsettle and disturb the opposition, which may be achieved by one's group solidarity, one's overt toughness, the hostility of one's bowling and batting, one's bearing, and indeed one's tactical ploys. The ebullient confidence of some great players, Viv Richards and Shane Warne, for instance, could intimidate opponents. Both had a magnificence and a strut that proclaimed that they were totally at home on the big stage. Ian Botham was not nicknamed 'Gorilla' for nothing. One of the sources of a fine sportsman's appeal and impact is to be found in his wholehearted, whole-bodied commitment. Ian Chappell's Australian team exuded belligerence.

As a captain, putting a fielder in a certain position may be based on several rationales. One is that he is likely to get a catch there to dismiss the batsman; another aim is to cut off run-scoring. But there is also bluff and counter-bluff, along with a combative message; for example, 'We don't need a mid-off for you!' Or – 'You don't like it at your throat, do you?' Or – 'You can't play this bowler, we all know that, so I'm taking off the bloke who's just taken three wickets and I'm putting him on.' The message may or may not require words. Actions and gestures often speak loudly enough.

Such messages may be conveyed with humour, or, less acceptably, with scorn. A young middle-order batsman, who on his way back to the pavilion murmured sycophantically but also perhaps patronizingly to the Yorkshire and England bowler, Fred Trueman, 'That was a fine delivery, Fred', received the brusque reply, 'Aye, and it were wasted on thee.'

The emotive message of such panache and self-assurance in the fielding side is plain; the batsman is not up to much. His confidence undermined, he either becomes timid, or he accepts the invitation to a fatal rashness in an attempt to assert himself. Playing for Middlesex as a young batsman, in the middle of a bad run, I remember being virtually shamed out by the chorus of disdainful moans and groans from Surrey's slip cordon. I found myself in self-denigrating agreement with them, I had no right to be there, sharing the spotlight with them. And soon I wasn't.

There is a narrow line between such more or less legitimate, dis-comfiting gestures and messages, on the one hand, and behaviour that goes beyond the spirit of the game on the other.

According to Steve Waugh, the aim is the 'mental disintegration' of the opposition, a notion he learned from Allan Border. As I say, verbal and non-verbal communications, on the field, including some of what the current players euphemistically refer to as 'banter', are part and parcel of wholehearted rivalry. But such 'banter' can tip over the top. And if mental disintegration actually occurs, partly caused by the gang-elements that lurk not far beneath the surface of high-powered teams, then the time has come to draw back, to reflect: does the problem lie in the vulnerability of the recipient, or has the banter degenerated into sledging. Has it all gone too far?

Guilt, justified or not, becomes a factor in mental disintegration. An adolescent may at moments, consciously or otherwise, wish his father dead. If the father actually does die, the guilt is terrible. If the opponent disintegrates and breaks down, the initiators of the disparaging remarks are liable to feel guilty, and need to remind themselves of the Spirit of Cricket.

Situations where such devastating consequences are liable to happen are times when firm fathers are needed, in the form of captains, coaches, umpires and match referees.

The great West Indian fast bowlers of my acquaintance never said anything at all to the batsman on the field. One might say: they had no need to – first, because of their superlative ability. They simply got on with the job, conveying their menace in the most direct and relevant way – by means of their speed and skill with the ball. Further, they were quite able to convey menace by their overall demeanour and their eye contact. When I played my first Test match, against West Indies, in 1976, it happened that both teams were staying at the same hotel in Nottingham. I ran into Andy Roberts at breakfast. He gave me a quizzical little look, not crudely unpleasant, but conveying, I felt, something along the lines of: 'Shall I be eating you for breakfast or for lunch?' Andy gave these looks on the field too; like Helen of Troy's face, which launched a thousand ships, Andy's conveyed a thousand words.

When England were about to tour India in 1976, not long after the infamous remark of England captain, Tony Greig's, that 'we will make them [the West Indies team] grovel', a group of players were talking, or listening, to Len Hutton, who came to the dinner the evening before we left. Tony asked Len for advice on going to India as captain. Len appeared characteristically guarded, enigmatic. We assumed we would hear some wisdom about tactics, or about the use of spinners on Indian pitches. After a long silence, Len uttered a single short sentence: 'Don't *say* too much.' (He did also give us one other piece of quizzical advice: 'Don't take pity on them Indian bowlers.')

In my view, the guideline 'Play according to the Spirit of Cricket, play hard but fair' is an encouragement to an as yet unspecified orientation or attitude to the game, its umpires, its traditions; to the opponents and indeed the spectators and administrators. It refers to a *je ne sais quoi*; it is an enigmatic signifier.

In this it is similar to many other moral or religious guidelines, such as 'Do unto others as you would have them do unto you' or 'Blessed are the poor.' Great teachers point out the spiritual shortcomings in hypocrisy and legalism; remember Jesus's comment that 'the Sabbath is made for man, not man for the Sabbath'. Or: 'Let him who is without sin cast the first stone.' Being 'pro-life' can pit one on either side of arguments about abortion or the death penalty. Similarly, Martin Crowe's injunction against *rampant ego, selfishness, boorishness, and bullying,* or the appeal to 'Respect umpires, captains, players and spectators', are valid moral statements, however contradictory the uses and judgements they may give rise to.

I see it as a category mistake to suggest that the Spirit of Cricket should be *part* of the Laws. It is *not* a Law; it does not dictate what should or should not be permitted. It is both more and less than that: it is an exhortation to keep certain values in mind in one's whole approach to the game, including to its Laws or rules. It is therefore appropriate that it should appear as a preamble. It is a comment on the Laws: it offers a context for them.

In the same article Atherton writes about Crowe's 'instincts for the game' – it seems to me that people's instinctual or spontaneous feelings and values are exactly what statements embodied in the Spirit of Cricket are designed to affect.

PART 6

GAME CHANGERS

28

SCOOPS, SWITCH-HITS AND
HELMETS AT SHORT MID-ON

When I was ten or eleven, the art teacher in his report at the end of a term put me down as 'Fair, but with occasional flashes of brilliance.' I was so pleased with this comment. I was used to rather more mundane ones. I was afraid I was too conformist.

I have always been drawn to innovations in cricket, to new possibilities beyond the orthodox. I think this was a source of strength – I wasn't too hide-bound – but also a potential danger – I might go against the grain for the sake of not complying; rather than focusing fully on that which has been tried and tested, I might seek out the quirky or the tricky.

At Cambridge I practised bowling underarm. Back in the 1790s, the first person to bowl round-arm – probably Tom Walker – had been, of course, iconoclastic. He was no-balled. But by 1835, this mode of bowling had been officially legalized and had become the norm. For the game to develop as it has, it took a bold invention, a preparedness to go against the grain and the rules.

It also took a certain nerve for me to go back to the antiquated form of bowling – underarm (subsequently banned) – in a 'proper' match in the early 1960s. One occasion was the final day of the game between Cambridge University and Sussex. We had almost got into a winning position. The Sussex tail, including slow left-armer, Ronnie Bell, were blocking us, fighting for a draw. The umpire was, I think, Arthur Fagg, the ex-Kent and England batsman. He was astounded when I told him I would bowl underarm. So was Bell. Unfortunately, so too was our wicket-keeper, Mike Griffith, who proceeded to miss a stumping.

On an MCC tour to Holland and Denmark in 1962, the South African Test player, Jonathan Fellows-Smith, known for some reason as 'Pom-Pom', bowled donkey drops. The idea was that the ball would drop full toss onto the top of the stumps. He had his own word for them, which sounded to me like 'spittegew'. (I've later been told that the word was in fact 'spedigue', derived from a short story by Arthur Conan Doyle, 'Spedigue's Dropper', about an un-athletic schoolmaster who defeated Australia with high donkey drops he perfected in village cricket.)

Charles Palmer, captain of Leicestershire in the 1950s, took 15 to 18 first-class wickets with these deliveries, including Frank Worrell's. Remembering Fellows-Smith, I tried it myself. I remember two incidents. One was when someone was caught, I think by John Emburey at mid-wicket, off such a ball, in Harare. The other was bowling a few donkey drops to the Zimbabwean, Brian Davison. Both Emburey and Davison thought this was not on: one was disgusted to have caught the catch, the other marched towards me with his bat held high; even without this threatening posture, he was an intimidating man, reputed to have fought valiantly in the Zimbabwe civil war. Davison emigrated to Tasmania, where he became a Liberal representative at the House of Assembly. I came to like him.

This delivery too has since been outlawed.

These were not so much innovations as throwbacks, as indeed was my ploy of putting all ten fielders, including the wicket-keeper, David Bairstow, on the boundary for the last ball of a limited-overs match against West Indies at Sydney in 1980, when they needed three to win. I remembered M. J. K. Smith doing just that against Middlesex a few years earlier.

More innovative was my use of head-protection during the Ashes series in 1977; I think this accelerated what became within a few months the widespread use of more substantial helmets in the game.

I also caused two tiny changes in playing conditions or Laws.

In early August, 1977, Middlesex had a remarkable win against Surrey at Lord's. We needed to win to keep in touch with Kent, with whom we eventually tied as joint winners of the County Championship. Heavy and prolonged rain interfered. At the end of day two, only five overs had been bowled, with Surrey 8 for 1. Had there been no play before the last day, the playing conditions would have allowed a one-innings match, in which more points would have been available than as bonus points. As a result, the match remained a two-innings-a-side match; the two teams had either to play for bonus points, or go in for declarations.

On that third morning, Mike Selvey, our opening bowler, looked at the pitch, which was green and damp, having been covered for so long, in such dank conditions; he sowed the seed, suggesting that we could bowl Surrey out twice in these conditions.

And when in little over an hour we had reduced them to 40-odd for 8, Clive Radley said, 'Let's put them in again. Can we forfeit our first innings?' The umpires had no idea if this was permitted. I ran off the field and went to the office of TCCB Secretary, Donald Carr, to ask the question. He told me that we couldn't; there was no provision for it in the Laws. So having dismissed Surrey for 49, we batted for one ball, declared at 0 for 0, and bowled them out again, this time for 89. When their best bowler for the conditions, Geoff Arnold, was unable to bowl because of a bruised foot, we won at a canter by nine wickets.

The longer-term outcome was that forfeiting an innings was made legitimate.

The second, more frivolous, episode involved the helmet. On a docile pitch at Lord's in 1980, Yorkshire were playing solemnly for a draw on the last afternoon. Philippe Edmonds and I thought we might induce the batsmen to play against the spin (and possibly get a leading edge) if we placed the helmet (usually parked behind the wicket-keeper when not actually in use by a fielder) at short mid-on. The point was that if a ball struck the helmet while in play, the batting side were awarded five penalty runs. We had a lot of fun moving the helmet a few inches this way and that, teasing the cautious and (by reputation) parsimonious Yorkshiremen.

The outcome? Henceforth, it was permitted to park helmets only behind the wicket-keeper.

Our resort to frivolity had a history. Back in 1971, in our first years as captains of Yorkshire and Middlesex respectively, Geoff Boycott and I had had a conversation at Headingley after a match in which, after I made an over-generous declaration, Boycott scored an undefeated hundred, and Yorkshire won with about fifteen overs, and seven wickets, to spare. Geoffrey came into the Middlesex dressing room with tears in his eyes, saying, 'What a good declaration, thank you for making a game of it, and if we can ever do the same for you we will.' They never did!

One-day cricket has been a source of rich innovation in both batting and bowling techniques. Bowlers have developed slow bouncers, wide yorkers, subtle changes of pace, and scrambled seams to deceive big-hitting batsmen with their new, powerful bats. Batsmen have developed what was known as the Dilshan 'scoop', or 'ramp' shot, and, more substantially, the 'switch-hit' sweep, also known as the 'reverse sweep', as well as developing a range of more orthodox sweeps.

Tillakaratne Dilshan was an aggressive Sri Lankan opening batsman. In 2009, he saw the possibility of 'helping' a fast straight ball over his own head, and over the keeper's head, into the unoccupied area directly behind them both. He played the shot to good length, usually straight, fast deliveries; placing his front leg forward as if to play defensively, lowering his right knee and his head, he would use his bat as a lever, the toe ahead of the handle, to deflect the ball upwards and backwards.

This took not only skill, but courage and chutzpah. If he missed, or if he got his angles wrong, the ball could smash him in the face (or more accurately, in the face-guard). I loved this courage and inventiveness. Not surprisingly, the shot is rarely seen. Perhaps it retired along with Dilshan himself, in 2016.

The other stroke, the switch-hit or reverse sweep, is now regarded as part of more or less orthodox armouries.

The crusty Jim Swanton referred once to the orthodox sweep, let alone the reverse sweep, as 'that infernal stroke', and there is indeed something less upright, less classical, less 'straight' about it than, say, the cover drives played with a full flow of the bat. In Edwardian terms, the sweep, with its humble name, had something of the backstairs about it. 'Playing with a straight bat' became synonymous with following the 'straight and narrow', derived from Jesus's 'strait gate' to salvation. (Though it can also mean being so narrow as to be merely compliant: or using narrow-mindedness to evade the point being made against one.)

But 'infernal'? The sweep shot is in fact in some circumstances – especially when the ball is not 'coming on' to the bat, but holding up on a dusty pitch – the best bet, safer than a straight-bat drive. The crucial thing is, as Alan Knott maintained, to keep still and not try to hit the ball too hard.

Interestingly, it was at Knott's Kent that the stroke had also occasionally been used against quicker bowlers, in particular by an otherwise dogged opening batsman, Brian Luckhurst. He developed it in the early 1970s as a mode of attack in forty-over games, against quicker bowlers. He once took apart Tom Cartwright, the meanest and hardest bowler of all to get away, with this stroke: Cartwright went for 72 runs in his 8 overs – an unprecedented event. The stroke required courage, especially in the days before helmets. It would have been all too easy to get a top edge into one's face.

The boldness of these two Kent players was a matter not only of technique and courage, but also of being prepared to face the scorn of selectors, committee men and writers like Swanton. Who wants infernal players in their representative sides? Who would allow them to influence the young!

Reverse sweeps smack even more of the sinister, the tricky; of the backstairs and the servants' quarters. Once again, the term includes a range of strokes. Some batsmen change their grip for the switch-hit, others don't. In one version, the right-hand batsman puts his front leg forward (as usual) but reverses his bat, playing a sort of backhand sweep towards third man. In another version, he switches his stance as the ball is bowled, puts his right foot forward, and plays a usually more brutal stroke square on the off-side. I have an image of Kevin Pietersen playing this stroke in a Test match against Muttiah Muralitharan, and hitting sixes over cover-point.

The reverse sweep has become almost respectable. It was not always so. Mike Gatting was scathingly criticized for getting out to a reverse sweep in the final of the World Cup way back in 1987. He had scored 41 runs off 44 balls; England were 135 for 2 chasing 254, and Allan Border had brought himself on, with his inviting slow-left-arm bowling, as a last resort. The ball was wide of Gatting's leg stump, so he had to 'fetch' it a long way to get it to go towards third man. In fact it went up off the edge and his shoulder for an easy catch. 'Impetuous' and 'ridiculous' were amongst the comments. The fact is, one can get out playing, or not playing, any stroke. I suppose that on this occasion, the ball was not well chosen (he could have let it go for a wide, or played an orthodox sweep); moreover, even had he connected with the ball properly, it's unlikely that he would have scored more than one or two.

Now, though, the shot is more or less accepted, and if played well, disrupts bowlers' field-settings, as well as their lines. Often its great benefit is forcing the opposition to place a fielder at deep third man for a spinner, which leaves a space elsewhere. Misbah-ul-Haq, until recently captain of Pakistan, used it to tremendous effect, a central part of his strong statement that slow bowlers should not be allowed to bowl. (He batted in the Ian Chappell mode: 'What are spin bowlers for?' he was asked. 'To get you from 60 to 100 as quickly as possible,' was the reply.)

Some have questioned whether the shot should be permitted. For one thing, bowlers have to specify which arm they will bowl with – why not an equivalent for batsmen? Others have questioned the parallel requirement for bowlers too, especially when a young man called Yasir Jan, from Pakistan, who was able to bowl at 85 mph with either his left arm or his right, appeared on this ambidextrous scene. If a batsman is permitted to change in effect to left-handed after taking up his stance as a right-handed player, should not the same licence be given to the likes of Yasir Jan? (On the other hand, it was felt that if it were possible for someone to conceal which arm he would bowl with until the point of delivery – itself questionable – there might be extra factors of danger for the batsman.)

And second, if the batsman gains an advantage by this flexibility, should not the bowler be given some compensatory benefit? Since there is ambiguity about which stump should be regarded as the leg-stump (according to initial stance the batsman is right-handed, according to final stance, left-handed), should the switch-hit batsman lose his or her immunity from lbws for balls pitching outside the leg-stump? Should we in effect regard the switch-hitter as having undone or scrambled the distinction between leg- and off-stump? In such circumstances, it was suggested, the very concepts of 'leg' and 'off' stump have been rendered otiose. (One problem with this idea is that the ambiguity arises only with the form of reverse sweep which involves jumping into a left-handed stance, and would thus require a quick differentiation by umpires between different forms of reverse sweep.)

A third objection to the reverse sweep was that it could result in a stalemate. If the batsman stood at the crease in an ambiguous position (taking neither a right-hander's stance nor a left-hander's) how could 'pitching outside the leg stump' be decided? And if the bowler refused to let the ball go whenever the batsman started to move towards another stance, and if this happened repeatedly, whose responsibility would it be to get the game moving?

In the end, however, I think it is a matter of whether the innovation enhances the game. I think it does. It calls for great skill, as well as speed of decision and execution. It enlarges the game as a spectacle. And one benefit the bowler gets arises from the element of risk for the batsman in making this complex adjustment to ordinary technique.

I welcome the innovation and the development. I would rather err on the side of quixotic experimentation than of routine respectability.

29

FATHER OF REVERSE SWING

Sarfraz Nawaz was a fine fast-medium bowler. Powerfully built and tall, he ran in straight, had a high somewhat military action (an impression perhaps enhanced by his erect poise and luxurious moustache). He was accurate, and with the new ball could bowl sharply, and swing the ball away. In 1974, I went in to bat for Middlesex against the Pakistan team at number three. My first ball, from Sarfraz, was quick, and nipped in from the off-side off the pitch. It hit my thigh. The next one was slightly slower, much fuller in length, round off-stump.

It invited a drive. Drive at it I did, the ball swung, conventionally, away, and I was caught at second slip. A sucker's dismissal.

In 1973, I was invited to go to Pakistan to play in two four-day matches for a World Eleven against a Pakistan team, to raise money for flood relief. The first was in Lahore. The so-called world team was composed mainly of West Indian international players, captained by Clive Lloyd. Also included were Lancashire wicket-keeper, Keith Goodwin, Essex and England leg-spinner, Robin Hobbs, and me. Clive Lloyd knew at least one word of Urdu, 'jeldi' meaning 'fast', and he and others worked the driver of the team bus up alarmingly with their enthusiastic exhortations of 'jeldi, jeldi'.

It was my second cricketing visit to Pakistan, having captained an MCC Under-25 team there five years before. In the match at Lahore on the earlier tour, I had gone in to bat late on the second day, scored four, and then got a ball that clipped my pad. Everyone in the ground appealed for caught behind, and the umpire's arm shot up. Later that evening I was given a message from the umpire via the liaison officer: he wanted me to know that he was 'Very sorry for the decision, but felt his arm going up and couldn't stop it.'

I had more success there on the later visit, scoring a century, on a flat, bare pitch, against Sarfraz and Asif Masood. I remember also Mushtaq Mohammad bowling his leg-breaks and googlies. At the drinks break in the morning, our twelfth man, I think it was off-spinner Salahuddin, said to me, 'Well played, sir, you are Rock of Gibraltar.' When he came out with the afternoon drinks, he said, 'Very well played, sir, you are Great Wall of China.' I took these somewhat stony and static images as a compliment, which I'm sure was what was meant. I was sorry not to be still there in the evening session, to hear which geological or humanly constructed massif I had come to resemble.

At some stage during the afternoon, Sarfraz came back for a second or third spell with the now old ball. Suddenly, it started to dart in from the off in the air. I remember looking up and seeing Sarfraz grinning at me. 'Where did that come from?' I wanted to know. He simply went on grinning.

In retrospect, I realized this was my first experience of reverse swing. And it is only recently, on reading Peter Oborne's book on Pakistan cricket, *Wounded Tiger: A History of Pakistan Cricket*, that I learned that Sarfraz was indeed its initiator.

With conventional swing, the ball swings more when new, sometimes just for a few balls only, at other times only after some overs have been bowled, by which time the bowlers have worked up a shine on one side, leaving the other side duller. The technique of orthodox swing involves action; the classic fast bowlers – Ray Lindwall, Fred Trueman, Ian Botham, Dennis Lillee, Andy Roberts – bowled side-on, their left shoulders facing the batsman in delivery, the hand finishing by their left shin, and swung the ball away from the right-handed batsman. They would put the shiny side of the ball on the right-hand side of their finger-grip, the seam pointing towards first slip. The idea was that the shiny side would offer less resistance to the air, so that as its speed diminished on its course down the pitch, it would start to swing in the air away from the batsman's body, towards the slips.

The in-swing bowler tended to have a more open-chested action, like Imran Khan, Wayne Daniel, Colin Croft, Bob Willis and Mike Procter, and was more likely to bring his hand down to the right-hand side of his body. These bowlers kept the shiny side on the left-hand side of the two fingers straddling the seam in their grip, and tilted the seam towards leg slip.

No one fully understands why one ball swings but another, looking identical, doesn't, but it has partly to do not only with shine and action, but also with the atmosphere and with the nature of the playing surface. On a grassy field and pitch, the ball loses shine and hardness more slowly than in bare, dusty conditions. No doubt details of the ball's constitution make a difference too – which is why bowlers are often keen to persuade umpires that a non-swinging ball is out of shape, and should therefore be changed.

Pakistan's pitches were, especially in Sarfraz's day, typically more or less grassless, and shiny. The outfields, several decades ago, were bare and sometimes rough. Conventional swing would last for a mere five or six overs. The ball would also lose its hardness after ten or twenty overs. In the old days of sub-continental cricket, fast bowlers might operate for that sort of period of time only, to be replaced by spinners. In subsequent spells, they might have to depend on the ball keeping low, though as the match progressed the surface would become rough and seam bowlers could achieve movement by 'cutting' the ball with their fingers, producing brisk leg-breaks or off-breaks.

But often the game would become attritional when the quicker bowlers returned. A batsman who had got in could see no reason to get out. (As Ken Barrington used to say of the old Pakistan and India pitches: 'Book in for bed and breakfast'.) All this changed with reverse swing (and indeed with the advent of the doosra).

As Oborne wrote, there was a further advantage in this new mode: 'In conventional swing, bowlers face a trade-off between swing and speed. In reverse swing the ball actually swings more at higher speeds, particularly when the bowler achieves a yorker length.' I think this may well be true, though throughout the history of cricket, the great swing bowlers have made the ball swing so late, at speed, that onlookers (not to mention batsmen) are often unsure whether the ball's movement was in the air or off the pitch.

Sarfraz himself had started to play cricket relatively late in his life, in 1965, aged sixteen, when he was working for his father's construction company putting up a wall at Lahore cricket ground. When the work was stopped because of the outbreak of war against India, instead of labouring on the wall, Sarfraz joined other youths playing the game. Soon this strong, six foot four inches boy learned he could bowl quickly. Within four years, he was in the Test team (but only for one match, being left out afterwards for the next three years).

It was in club and in domestic first-class cricket that Sarfraz learned how to make the old ball swing. He realized that if you roughed up one side and weighed it down with sweat, keeping the other side dry, the ball would swing in the opposite direction from orthodox swing with the new ball.

In the nets he tried out balls in different conditions. 'One day I shone one side of a very old ball and it swung. It was rough on both sides, but I shone one side and it swung *towards* the shine – it should not have done this.'

Like other inventors, in different walks of life, he not only studied and refined the new method, he also, cannily, kept his secret to himself. (If patents existed in sport, Sarfraz would have acquired one for reverse swing.) Even much later, when he played for Northamptonshire under Mushtaq Mohammad's captaincy, the latter was aware of reverse swing but had no idea how it was achieved.

The same seems to have been true of Michael Holding. Asked by me about whether he created reverse swing in the dry conditions at the Oval in 1976, when he took fourteen wickets in the match, he replied:

> Yes, that's how I bowled Greig out twice in the match! But all we knew then was that at a certain point the ball would tend to swing the opposite way to the newer ball, so we just switched it round in the hand.

Sarfraz even kept his secret from his opening partner, Imran Khan. During one match in Guyana on Pakistan's 1976–7 tour of the West Indies, he was making the ball reverse swing sharply, while for Imran, bowling alternate overs, deliveries were undeviating. Mystified, Imran complained, 'Your ball is moving but mine won't.' The roguish Sarfraz had, on his own admission, been 'roughing *both* sides of the ball on the last ball of [his] overs, so that it could not swing for [Imran]!' Next day he showed Imran in the nets. 'I only told Imran because he was not playing domestic cricket in Pakistan.'

As with the Australians at Cape Town in 2018, some bowlers illicitly used implements to rough up one side of the ball. Sarfraz himself mentioned Imran's confession that he had 'used a bottle top in an English county game', and reeled off a number of other leading players who had done the same. He was adamant that he himself obtained reverse swing by legal methods, getting team-mates to polish the ball properly. 'It is not necessary to gouge or scrape the ball,' he told Oborne.

I'm sure this last statement is true. The art of reverse swing, first used in international cricket by Sarfraz and Imran, further developed by Wasim Akram and Waqar Younis, is now used by fast bowlers the world over. Many skilful fast bowlers have become, in what had previously been considered graveyard conditions for their kind, more likely to take wickets with the old ball even than with the new.

To do this, they have to pitch the ball up and bowl straight, aiming to take wickets by hitting the stumps or getting batsmen out lbw. This means that there are bound to be more run-scoring opportunities – a tiny error in length produces a half-volley or a full toss rather than a yorker, small errors in direction result in a ball that is snaking past the leg stump, and can be clipped square on the leg-side, rather than one homing in to leg-stump. Boundaries are more frequent, but so are dismissals. This innovation has transformed cricket for the better.

Imran Khan himself tended to be a better bowler on the slower, batsmen-friendly pitch at Eastbourne than in traditional fast bowlers' conditions at Hove. He got less excited at Eastbourne, where he didn't bother trying to knock the batsman out rather than bowl him out.

I learned only recently that the main requirement for reverse swing is the condition of the actual strip. Graeme Fowler, Wasim Akram's team-mate at Lancashire, spoke of a demonstration at Old Trafford when Wasim showed how the ball swung sharply on a used dry pitch, but hardly at all on the strip next to it, which was damp, grassy and under-prepared. Presumably there are crucial differences in moisture content in the channels of air immediately above pitches.

There were few sights in cricket more thrilling that the sight of Wasim Akram and Waqar Younis in their pomp, racing in and using reverse swing at high pace. Waqar was powerful and athletic, with a big delivery stride and a high, menacing action. It was not surprising that he suffered from groin strains. Wasim was less flowing; short paces led into a very quick arm action. His back foot pointed backwards, his front one forwards, so for different reasons he too put strain on his groin.

Brian Lara told me that whereas with most bowlers he could tell from their approach and overall action which way they were aiming to swing the ball, he never could 'read' Wasim. This was one reasons for his rating him the best of all the fast bowlers he faced.

For such a big man, Sarfraz has a surprisingly quiet voice. He is an engaging and in some ways eccentric man. I think he likes to play the rascal, to provoke, to stir hornets' nests. He has always been outspoken. He announced that, when he spoke out against the spot-fixing scandal involving Salman Butt, Mohammad Asif and Mohammad Amir, he had received death threats.

As 'the father of reverse swing', he helped change the game for the better.

30

THE DOOSRA AND THE SPLINT

Sri Lankan star, Muttiah Muralitharan, revolutionized cricket with his bowling. He bowled sharply spinning off-breaks, with the occasional doosra (literally 'the other one') – a leg-break that looks like an off-break, the equivalent for off-spinners of the googly (the off-break that looks like a leg-break, invented by English leg-spinner Bernard Bosanquet in the early 1900s) for leg-spinners. These doosra deliveries (which he first bowled in Tests in 1997) have become part of the game's make-up, along with reverse swing and switch-hitting. Though he was not the first to bowl the doosra (that was Saqlain Mushtaq of Pakistan three or four years earlier), Murali, in his freakish way, has made new things possible with the cricket ball.

In his eighteen-year Test career, Murali took 40 per cent of the wickets captured by his team. It was neat that he not only set himself that percentage as a final target – in his retirement Test he needed 8 of India's 20 – 40 per cent – for the extraordinary record of 800 Test wickets; he also got them, albeit at the last possible moment.

Along with Australian Shane Warne (708 Test wickets) and India's Anil Kumble (619), he also helped revive spin bowling after decades of pace bowling dominance.

Murali is a remarkable human being. He has dealt with his immense success with equanimity. In the dressing room his humility and straightforwardness were a shining example to the rest of the team. He was, his one-time captain Kumar Sangakkara told me, 'grounded and simple, with no pretence. He has done more to unite the country in troubled times than any politician.'

He talks a mile a minute, and is happy to offer advice to spinners from all over the world. He also works tirelessly for charities. He is a Trustee of the Foundation of Goodness, which has rebuilt Seenigama, a village in the south-east of Sri Lanka that had been destroyed by the 2004 tsunami that devastated the coastline, centring its work on a wonderful facility with medical, dental, educational and training elements. They have also repaired cricket grounds and facilities in the vicinity. Murali and the Foundation have since embarked on a similar project in the shattered north of the country.

In assessing Murali one cannot avoid the issue of his bowling action. In 1995 and 1998, Australian umpires called him for throwing. And Bishan Bedi, the great Indian slow left-arm spinner, described him as a 'shot-putter' . . . For some of Murali's defenders, by contrast, even the raising of doubts has been regarded as a racist or nationalistic slur and prejudice.

My own response is more equivocal but also accepting, though I do understand the doubters. One thing I am convinced of: Murali's bowling has enhanced cricket. The range of his skills made him a fascinating bowler to watch and, I imagine, to bat against. Cricket is better for the presence of the doosra. Cricket's administrators have been right to veer towards wanting to make it honest in order to encourage this richness.

Once upon a time, round-arm bowling was forbidden, and cricket is a better game for its arrival (it was legalized in 1828). The question with all these innovators is: will others go along with them?

But Murali (and the doosra in general) is a more complicated case than those round-arm innovators, or than the schoolboy at Rugby school, who allegedly picked up a football and ran with it. For technology has shown that, contrary to what many experts would have believed, Murali himself is able to spin the ball either way with his arm in a splint. So, although he starts with a bent arm, he does not need to straighten it at the elbow in order to bowl either of his main deliveries.

The doosra is a leg-break bowled with the back of the hand facing the batsman. What is right in Bedi's claim is (at least) that most of us cannot deliver a leg-break in this way without throwing the ball (try it in the street or the living room). But as a result of his unusual anatomy and physiology, Murali *could* do this; and much of his prodigious spin came from the same physical features.

There are four elements at least to his physiological distinctiveness. First, if you or I hold out our arm in front of us, palm up, and try to bring our finger ends towards our forearm, the chances are that they will remain several inches above the arm. Murali's touch his forearm easily. His wrist has a congenital double-jointedness to it that enables him to flick the ball out with the back of his hand and wrist towards the batsman.

Second, his wrist is much more mobile in rotation than other people's. It was his wrist that did most of the straightening.

Third, technology shows that at least part of what looks to the naked eye like a straightening of the elbow is in fact the result of hyper-extension. If you or I stretch our arm out straight, palm up, the line from armpit to the middle finger-tip will most likely be fairly straight. In Murali's case, his arm bends down or back several degrees at the elbow. Hyper-extension has often been a feature of the anatomy and physiology of quick bowlers who have been accused of throwing but are not in fact straightening a bent arm. What people see is, at least in part, a whiplash flick of the hyper-extended arm.

Finally, Murali has some peculiarities in his strong and flexible shoulder muscles that enabled him to impart doosra-spin on the ball without straightening the arm; his arm, that is, remained bent throughout the action (or did not bend more than the prescribed amount).

All this put together meant that Murali was able to bowl doosras and sharp-spinning off-breaks without unduly straightening his arm at the elbow.

None of this proves, of course, that he never threw the ball, intentionally or otherwise; possibly, as some sceptics have asserted, when he was frustrated or when he put in extra effort.

Cricket has made use of technology in two ways in order to try to come to a view of what constitutes a fair action. One aim is to underpin common-sense. It turns out that experienced and knowledgeable watchers cannot in fact discriminate between a total lack of straightening of the elbow and roughly 10–15 degrees of straightening. Thus, though the law has not been changed, the ICC have brought in a modified regulation in the light of what technology shows us; what looks to the naked eye smooth, without jerking or straightening (with bowlers like Glenn McGrath, Sarfraz Nawaz or Bishan Bedi himself), often is not. But clearly these entirely orthodox actions should not be viewed as dubious. Within the 15 degrees allowed now, we have to accommodate to a reality that we can't see with the naked eye.

Second, common-sense may also mislead, in that it may, as I suggest has happened with Murali's action, confuse hyper-extension with other physiological peculiarities. Thus some actions that look dubious are not.

I remember batting for Middlesex in successive matches at Lord's in 1965 against Harold Rhodes of Derbyshire, who had recently been no-balled by umpire Syd Buller in a match against the South African touring team, and Brian Statham of Lancashire. It was impossible for me, as batsman or spectator, to differentiate between their actions, or to decide whether either, both or neither threw the ball. Current technology combined with current guidelines would have helped everyone, including the umpires (and Rhodes and Statham themselves), to decide.

Murali began his Test career at the age of twenty in 1992. To start with, he was primarily an off-spinner who turned the ball sharply, even on pitches where others couldn't do so, and with bounce. He operated rather like Lance Gibbs of the West Indies; both bowled with high actions, without drift from leg, and from wide on the crease, relying on bounce and spin beyond the normal. The stock ball of each was pitched wide of the off-stump. It was always hard for the batsman to predict how much the ball would turn.

Gradually, having seen Saqlain bowl it in Pakistan, Murali perfected the doosra.

Being able to do something remarkable is, of course, only the beginning. Such an art has to be practised and developed. Murali was one of the great workers at this skill. Sangakkara wonders whether his long net sessions, combined with marathon bowling spells, tired him prematurely. Hard work was, certainly, a main basis of his success.

One of his tricks was to bowl a top-spinner with the seam up to make the batsman think he could read this alternative to the off-break; then he would bowl a doosra with a scrambled seam, which fooled the batsman into thinking it was another off-break. As his wicket-keeper, Sangakkara could usually read him, but found it hard to spot the difference between the off-break that he spun most sharply and the doosra, since the wrist was in almost exactly the same position for each delivery.

Murali would often carry the Sri Lanka bowling attack. In the Test match at the Oval in 1998, when Sri Lanka stunningly won after putting England in to bat on winning the toss, and the latter scored 445 in their first innings, Murali bowled 113.5 overs in the match, taking 16 wickets for 220 runs – apart from anything else, a prodigious effort of stamina and concentration.

Towards the end of his career, his style had changed radically. The great Indian batsman Virender Sehwag told ESPN in 2010 that he was the most difficult bowler he played against. He added:

> Murali doesn't spin the ball so much any more. It's hard to believe this was the same man who could, at one time, pitch it well outside off and get the ball to hit the stumps. That changed when he began bowling a lot of doosras and straighter ones; they probably affected his turn. Yet the doubt remains in my mind. With Murali it does not matter if I am on 0, 10 or 100 – he is always a challenge.

Sehwag admitted that he could never read Murali's doosra, though he could pick that delivery from any other spinner. He also spoke of his subtle changes of pace.

Can one criticize Murali? I would tentatively suggest two factors that might have prevented him from being even more successful. First, he would sometimes go on the defensive too quickly. In a Test in Colombo in 2001, left-handed England batsman Graham Thorpe took a calculated risk against him, twice hitting him against the spin over mid-wicket. The bowler responded by immediately putting three fielders on the leg-side boundary, and keeping them there, thus enabling Thorpe to score ones and twos with freedom. Thorpe scored a marvellous 113 not out, followed by 32 not out; England won the match by four wickets. Second, Murali was, I thought, often too reluctant to bowl round the wicket.

In my view, Muttiah Muralitharan was a genius who shifted the horizons of what is possible in the game and transformed spin bowling. As Hamlet said of his father, we shall not look upon his like again.

31

'NAAAAAAGH, THAT'S NO GOOD!'

I always reckoned to read leg-spin, from the hand action, not from seeing the ball spin. In Pakistan, where the leg-spinners would often bowl with the low winter sun behind them, it was harder to pick out the exact hand angle and action. But on the whole I could do it, and fancied facing them. The best of those I played against was Abdul Qadir, he of the elaborate and elegant flourish and flair. Other leg-spinners I faced included Pakistanis Intikhab Alam and Mushtaq Mohammad, the unique Bhagwat Chandrasekhar from India, Kerry O'Keefe of Australia, and in county cricket Robin Hobbs and Bob Barber of England. I once batted against Sonny Ramadhin when he played for Lancashire.

Leg-spin delighted me. So when in 1993, a few weeks after the 'Ball of the Century' that bamboozled Mike Gatting, the young Shane Warne came to play in a charity match in Oxfordshire, and I was asked if I might keep wicket as there was no specialist present, I was very pleased to do so. This was a thrill to compare with anything in cricket. It was like being at Buckingham Palace for tea and being shown the Koh-i-Noor diamond close-up. Big leg-breaks, little leg-breaks, the odd googly, top-spinners, a flipper or two – the ball that skidded through low and pitched further up than the batsman anticipated: I only wish I'd had the sense and nerve to ask him about his whole range.

I could read most of his bowling. Oddly, two or three times the mistake I made was in seeing his big leg-spinner as a googly or top-spinner; for those deliveries I was looking down the leg-side, when the ball finished up two feet wide of off-stump. Could have been embarrassing if it had been a Test match!

There were loose rules for the match, involving how many overs a particular bowler could bowl, but I pressed Victor Blank, the host, to waive them for Warne, and he, Shane, seemed disarmingly pleased to display his skills. The batsmen for most of his spell were ex-England batsmen, Brian Close and Mike Denness, so they knew what to do, and they too thoroughly enjoyed in older age the chance to play against so special a bowler.

So what of *that* ball, the first bowled by Warne in a Test match in England? Leg-spinners who really spin the ball naturally make it curve, in the air, from off to leg. This ball did just that, landing on a full good length, a couple of inches outside Mike Gatting's leg stump. This drift or swing inwards tends to open the batsman out, so that he is liable to push against the spin towards the leg-side. Gatting was an experienced Test batsman, and a fine player of spinners. He would not have been unduly alarmed as the ball came towards him. He would have been confident that it could not get him out lbw, as it was clearly pitching outside leg stump. He was careful to get his substantial body behind the ball, bringing his back leg across towards off-stump as a second line of defence. He did not push at it unduly (which might have brought slip or short leg into play). However, the ball zipped across him, past the face of his bat, past the back thigh, and clipped the top of the off-stump. It was extraordinary to see so fine a batsman reduced to utter bamboozlement. He had no idea how it could have bowled him. He had played balls that looked like this without alarm, not quite, as it were, in his sleep, but not far off. And here he was, completely outwitted, like a man whose wallet has been pickpocketed in broad daylight.

The event was, to a large extent, like so much in sport, a piece of luck. The ball might just as well have brushed the pad and evaded the off-bail; or bounced an inch or two higher and gone over the top; or not spun quite so much so that it would have hit his leg and not been lbw. But it's also true that not many young spinners would have had the nerve, in their first Ashes delivery, to go flat out for a big spinner. Most would have been hoping to get through their first over, their first spell, without disaster. But not Warne.

He was picked in the first place because he had this natural attribute of being able to spin the ball, thanks to his slightly low action, his strong hands and shoulder, and the perfect amount of tension of fingers on the ball. And for his nerve and sheer delight in his skill.

Thus burst onto the Ashes scene this consistent shooting star of cricket, this genius at slow bowling, this ebullient, likeable and at times difficult character.

But was Warne a changer? He did not bowl doosras, as Murali and Saqlain did, nor did he introduce a totally new delivery into the game, as Sarfraz had done with reverse swing. More than anyone else, he brought spin to the forefront at a time when the focus was on speed, following the success and relentlessness of the attacks comprising four fast bowlers pioneered by Clive Lloyd for the West Indies. In fact four wonderful spinners arrived on the Test scene almost simultaneously: Anil Kumble, Saqlain Mushtaq, Muttiah Muralitharan and Shane Warne. This quartet resurrected spin bowling, in particular, leg-spin bowling, that had seemed to be a dying, antiquated craft.

The one man who'd recently preceded this crop of brilliant leg-spinners was Abdul Qadir, but he averaged 48 runs per wicket in Test matches outside Pakistan. Gideon Haigh, whose excellent book *On Warne* has been invaluable to me, suggests the title of the book by Middlesex and England off-spinner John Emburey, *Spinning in a Fast World*, offers an accurate picture of the world Warne and the others arrived into.

But was Warne an innovator or a throwback? And if an innovator, how?

Neville Cardus was said to have left Manchester before the last day of a county match, seduced by a typical Manchester weather forecast and an opera at Covent Garden. As it happened, Lancashire player, Archie MacLaren scored a century and a day or two later Cardus described it in the pages of the *Guardian*. A friend remonstrated with him. But you weren't there, how could you write about it? Cardus is reputed to have replied: 'If you really appreciate MacLaren, you don't need to see him score a hundred to capture it in words.'

This lofty Platonic attitude may express scorn for ordinary observation, favouring the a priori. But there is also some truth in it, as in another Cardus assertion, that he 'put words in his mouth that God intended him to utter'. And I find myself tempted to do something similar with Shane Warne. Not that I propose to put words in his mouth. Rather it's that one particular 'memory' of mine turns out to be incongruent with the mere facts, but I can't bring myself to give it up.

The memory/image is as follows. I'm in the old Press Box at Headingley, watching intently a Test match between England and Australia. Graham Gooch is going well, as are England, on something like 120 for three. The pitch favours batting. It is England's second innings. In the fantasy, Steve Waugh brings back Glenn McGrath, with a defensive field. McGrath closes up one end. Warne goes round the wicket, pitching the ball in the rough. Gooch pads him away. No risk but no runs either. The momentum dries up. After about four overs at each end, England have become becalmed. Instead of scoring at three or four runs an over, they have scored no more than that in eight overs. Eventually Gooch tries to drive Warne over the top, gets too close to the ball, and is comfortably caught at mid-on.

The trouble with this internal film is that its details bear little resemblance to detailed fact. McGrath didn't play in that series, nor did Gooch play in the next series. And Gooch was dismissed at Headingley by Reiffel and May.

Perhaps the passage of play occurred at Old Trafford, not Headingley. There, as I remembered 'it', Gooch was out to Warne, for 65. He had been playing fluently, along with Graeme Hick. He was caught by Brendon Julian, who was, Gooch himself recalls, at mid-on, with the score at 125 for 3. It was, he adds, a full toss.

Or perhaps it was a condensed memory, combining different facts, from different series, into a concentrated symbolic picture.

Warne and McGrath, what a combination! And this was one form of innovation from the leg-spinner: to be so variably useful, a superb defensive bowler as well as an attacking one. I had come across this line of bowling (round the wicket) from a leg-spinner from an earlier epoch, Intikhab Alam, who was also a clever bowler, and it helped me plan a line of attack for Derek Underwood. But no one did both as well as Warne.

You had to have a touch of genius about you to get on top of Warne when he was bowling round the wicket. Tendulkar did it, especially early in Warne's career, hitting him against the spin for six, then going 'inside out' over cover-point. So did Kevin Pietersen. But most players would get out in such an attempt. Even as strong and successful a batsman as Gooch was reduced to padding him away.

But this is not all. Warne was also a top bowler in conditions that suited the batsman or the seam bowlers. His figures in the first innings of Test matches were not far short of those in the second innings, when one might expect a much higher success rate on the dustier pitches – much closer than, say, Murali's.

As he got older, he bowled his big spinners less frequently, making use of greater variation, with a lot of balls that went straight on – just as dangerous to a batsman looking for prodigious turn. 'Part of the art of bowling spin is to make the batsman think something special is happening when it isn't,' he said.

Haigh suggests that his slider ('released from the front of his hand with the tops of the first two fingers across the seam, and the third imparting a nearly clandestine backspin', and developed in the early 2000s) was 'every bit as subversive as the doosra':

> as a bowler who had spun the ball as far as probably anyone in history, he turned his own reputation on its head, making himself into perhaps history's most skilful bowler of deliveries that went straight on or turned just a little.

Shane Warne was in his element on the Test stage. As the lead actor, he strutted his part. I like Haigh's paragraph starting with:

> his unvarying rubbing of the right hand in the disturbed dirt of the popping crease, [which resulted in the dust and grit trans-mitting itself to his clothing, so that] he appeared to acquire an earthiness, an affinity with the conditions . . . So although Warne bowled better in a greater variety of ecosystems than almost any other comparable cricketer, his caress of the crease always felt like an act of obeisance, of propitiation of the cricket gods.

'No matter how far they hit it, the ball always comes back,' Warne said once. Even sixes scored off him were opportunities. He was almost always optimistic, psychologically on top. He sauntered back to his mark. He threw the odd disparaging comment on the batsman's play, or, if verbally silent, expressed it in his look. And his run-up was actually a long walk-up, slow, almost hypnotic, with such strength and potency in the delivery stride and the action itself.

Haigh again: 'There was a leg-break, then there was a leg-break *from Shane Warne*'. I am reminded of a story told about a zealously behaviourist psychiatrist, William Sargant. Having seen a patient for consultation, he proposed electroconvulsive therapy (ECT). The patient objected that he'd had it twice and it hadn't helped. 'But you haven't had it from me, have you?' riposted the behaviourist.

For Shane Warne, every delivery was a part of a contest with a particular batsman, part of a personal confrontation. Shane Watson (Haigh again)

has explained how Warne subtly changed his whole attitude to bowling during the Indian Premier League. Warne interrupted his bowling one night, asking what he was trying to do. 'Oh,' said Watson, 'I'm trying to put it in the right place.'

'Naaaaaagh, that's no good. How are you trying to *get this guy out?*'

Warne was also polite and courteous off the field. Shaun Udal, who played under him at Hampshire, said of him: 'He has a sensitive side . . . which is never portrayed in the press. If I've got any troubles I can always speak to him. Warne used to say, "Manners are free".' And the Hampshire chairman, Rod Bransgrove, concurred: 'I once heard him telling his players to be sure to thank the dinner ladies.'

Like Ray Illingworth, he put pressure on the batsman with his accuracy. But part and parcel of his nagging accuracy were all the variations of a great leg-spinner. Like Ian Botham, he took wickets with half-volleys, but partly because of their great range: Warne's half-volleys dipped or swerved, deceiving in length or line. And they seemed also so rare! Batsmen must have felt an extra need to cash in.

Shane Warne changed cricket and its possibilities, largely by being better than anyone else.

PART 7

INDIAN BATSMANSHIP

32

SUPPING WITH THE DEVIL

To my mind, taking up the colonialists' game, and then beating us at it, is a sign of a robust capacity to overcome the condescension and worse of Empire (even in the 1950s, after Independence, a sign at the Willingdon Club in Mumbai still read: 'No dogs or Indians allowed' – a sign expressing an attitude so offensive that it's hard even to quote it). When Geoffrey Howard was about to leave as manager on the MCC tour of India in the 1950s, the one comment he had from the MCC President was 'I do hate educated Indians'.

For ex-colonial sides to beat England at cricket, making our game their own, in their own particular style, is a particularly robust strand of self-assertion, though it has over the years become sufficiently routine not to make such a mark.

You've only to look at Virat Kohli to know that he is a sub-continental batsman. He couldn't be European. It's a matter of the use of wrists, the last-second flick without risk.

Here, then, are four great Indian batsmen, all imbued with what one might call 'Indianness'. They span the time from the 1890s to the present. They represent, one might say, colonial India (Ranji), Independent India (Pataudi), commercially booming India (Tendulkar), and an India that aims at greatness in all spheres (Kohli).

Innovation is tinged – and often felt to be tainted – with transgression. Of Ranjitsinhji, who had burst on the English cricket scene in the 1890s, it was famously said (by a no doubt exasperated Yorkshire bowler, Ted Wainwright) that he 'never played a Christian stroke in his life'. C. B. Fry quoted a spectator: 'Yes, he can play; but he must have a lot of Satan in him.' The new, the unorthodox, the different – all this tends to strike the Puritan in us as a matter of the dark arts (and the word 'dark' has its own complexity). It's like psycho-analysts being dubbed 'trick-cyclists' – too clever by half, not to be trusted. Lord Harris, not one to doubt his own rectitude, or his own narrow values, attributed England's eight consecutive defeats in the early 1920s to 'Ranji and his conjuror's tricks *corrupting* a generation of batsmen'.

He who sups with the devil should indeed have a long spoon. The snake insinuates itself and glamorizes a tree of deceptive knowledge. Steer clear!

Yet Gilbert Jessop wrote that Ranji was 'indisputably the greatest genius who ever stepped onto a cricket ground'. And W. G. Grace said of him, 'I assure you that you will never see a batsman to beat the Jam Saheb if you live for a hundred years.' (The respect was mutual; of Grace, Ranji wrote: 'He founded the modern theory of batting by making forward- and back-play of equal importance, relying neither on the one nor the other, but on both.')

Cultural and racial differences, including in sport, are real differences; there are variations that are physiological, social, meteorological, psychological, matters of legacy. All such factors, and many more, enter into styles of play, levels of skill and behavioural norms.

When it comes to 'Indianness' in cricket, I have in mind two directions that one might go. The first is closely related to what has been hinted at with Ranjitsinhji, to do with deftness, unorthodoxy, fluidity and flexibility. He was noted for the leg-glance, presumably played sometimes against straight balls. When I think of words used to describe particularly sub-continental batsmen, 'wristiness' comes to mind. These players do not often bludgeon the ball. But by timing, playing late, and quick hands and wrists, the ball is guided, caressed or placed in unusual directions and often with surprising speed.

Players who fit this mould include Gundappa Viswanath, Mohammad Azharuddin, V. V. S. Laxman; Pakistani Zaheer Abbas, and Sri Lankan Mahela Jayawardene and Kohli. They are all *deft*; one might even say, subtle or persuasive with the ball. I would not include Sunil Gavaskar, Dilip Vengsarkar, Sachin Tendulkar, Rahul Dravid or Cheteshwar Pujara; nor Sourav Ganguly or Virender Sehwag, in this category. All were of course fine Indian batsmen, but the first five might, if anonymized, have been taken for solid English or Australian players. Ganguly and Sehwag were laws to themselves.

The other category consists of character-based descriptions of racial or cultural groups. Some (especially Indians themselves) have criticized Indian individuals and teams, or at least those of earlier generations, for lacking ruthlessness. Over many years, I was frequently told by Indian journalists that their cricketers never worked hard enough to make themselves fit, that they lacked appropriate 'Western' ambition. They needed a hard disciplinarian, preferably Australian, as coach. They played with flair and brilliance, but failed to drive home an advantage.

In an age of political correctness, are we permitted to speak of national characteristics? The danger is clear: we may start from a morality that assumes 'My values – cultural, aesthetic, moral, religious – are the only true ones. There is only one God. All other gods are false idols.' So other people's arts and skills are either to be disparaged and devalued, or to be mistrusted (they will corrupt our own purity). Satan had whispered in the receptive Oriental ear.

'Never played a Christian stroke' may be a dubious remark to our sensitized ears, but I think we know what Wainwright was getting at. It's not a risk-free business speaking of a concept such as 'Indianness' or of what it is to be 'characteristically Indian'. (Being married to one I have to be careful. Some of the old colonial arguments are repeated in our kitchen.)

The Duke of Edinburgh was not always over-cautious in this general area. Touring a factory in Preston about twenty years ago, noticing an electricity box bursting with tangled wires, he enquired if the factory's electrician was Indian. (My wife found it hilarious, actually, but not every Indian did.)

In 1973, I was in the Press Box in Calcutta. This was decades before emails and instant communication. Sending in one's copy to the UK was a matter of finding a telephone and a line that worked (passably) well, and shouting to your equally harassed copy-taker in London above a cacophony of others doing likewise. Connections would intermittently fail, the operator would interrupt every three minutes (scolding one, it felt, for extravagance in talking for so long). As you may imagine, writers with sore throats and pressing deadlines were liable to become intemperate and irate.

During one such breakdown of the system, K. N. Prabhu, the dry and learned *Times of India* correspondent, was sitting next to me. He murmured, 'What is five minutes against eternity?'

Are Indians fatalistic? Does this interfere with ruthlessness? Or was Prabhu being ironical, not only about us sweaty Englishmen, but also about his own countrymen?

Differences may, then, be invented or exaggerated from positions of superiority. Qualities that we don't like in ourselves are projected onto others, whom we can then belittle or patronize.

But there are also real differences. In 2012 I was in Trinidad when Usain Bolt won the second of his 100-metre Olympic gold medals. All eight finalists were black, and four were from the Caribbean. One was Trinidadian, so pride and excitement were appropriately high. We watched on a small television in the office of the Trinidad Indoor Cricket School. Deryck Murray was looking after me. He made me sit in the best chair (an act of typical hospitality and generosity) with the words: 'You chaps aren't very good at this; you'd better have a close look at how it's done!'

We *are* physiologically different. We are also psychologically different. I'm speaking in generalities, of course. No one means by a generalization that all people from such and such a stock or such and such a culture are like this or that, simply that there are tendencies, which will always be a mixture of inbuilt physiology, learned style, and traditions of work and play, in mixtures that can't readily be disentangled.

Years ago, on arrival in Western Australia after playing in India and Sri Lanka, where buildings, boundaries, and lay-out tend to be crooked, chipped, uneven, imprecise, I was struck by the straightness and sharp edges of Perth's wide roads, glass-and-concrete buildings and grid-streets. This sharpness of angle in Western Australia, two thousand miles from the nearest city, was matched by the crystal-clarity of light, stark, brilliant, clean-cut. In the sub-continent, light is often hazy, and no boundary stays still. The area laid out for animals overlaps with that for humans. Cows roam on traffic islands. It is tempting to carry this over into philosophy and personality. Among Indians, logic is alleged to give way to intuition, clarity about means and ends to a muddled melee of wish, motivation, and bending to developments. Is everything there higgledy-piggledy? Are proper differentiations allowed to be undone in the Eastern mind? Are contradictions embraced? What indeed is the point of worrying about winning or losing when your mind is immersed in eternity?

Or, of course, one might take the opposite position: that the Western mind is blinkered by its predilection for measurability and for a cold logic, for close focus rather than a synoptic view, for a limiting and inappropriate precision. I remember as a young lecturer interviewing a female applicant for a joint English and Philosophy degree at the University of Newcastle upon Tyne. The (male) professor and I were impressed by her. We then got a note from the rather stern female professor of Linguistics to say that the candidate was vague and woolly. The professor said to me, 'But a *creative* vagueness, don't you think?'

A robust account of the damage done by the English version of the straight and the crooked occurs in the closing pages of W. H. Hudson's novel about Uruguay, *The Purple Land*, where he has his protagonist observe:

> I cannot believe that if this country had been conquered and recolonized by England, and all that is crooked in it made straight according to our notions, my intercourse with the people would have had the wild, delightful flavour I have found in it . . . We do not live by bread alone, and British occupation does not give the heart all the things for which it craves.

If it is an Eastern, or perhaps Latin American, attitude to think more in terms of state of mind than of outcome, then again this is one aspect of success. Working on one's state of mind is what underlies Buddhist theories of martial arts – the aim (I think) being to learn to act with total concentration. If success results, it is almost as a side-effect. And if not, then we have done our best and will have learned something on the way.

Indian carpenters and builders often prefer to gauge things by eye, rather than by drawing exquisitely precise plans on graph paper in advance.

But then so do some traditional British craftsmen. A silversmith can tell a great deal by the feel of the metal – how even it is, how brittle, how evenly hammered. I remember Fred Titmus saying that the important thing was how the ball left his end when he was bowling, not the fate of it at the other. The latter was to some extent down to the man with the bat in his hand. In moments of decision as living beings we are all acting according to our sense of what strikes us as suited to the moment, and often any other, more calculated, more end-product way of thinking, may lead to stiltedness and sterility.

We (all) need both discipline and flair.

We need to practise, to be trained, to think clearly, not to let ourselves off the hook into dishonesty and self-delusion. We need to learn from mistakes, keep control of our recklessness, rein in some of our emotions. We need to be realistic. Yet it is not realism to deny a further fact of human experience: that we also need to give up our desire to control everything; that we have to let go of our attachment to the will, and allow spontaneity, freedom and flair their place. We have to trust the parts of our minds over which we have no immediate control. Provided we have a sound basis of discipline and an ability to monitor what we produce, we need something other than, wider than, deeper than, discipline and convention.

In 2002, when India toured England under the captaincy of Ganguly, India had lost the first match of the series by 170 runs; the second was drawn. Before the third, at Headingley, I was asked by the editor of the *Observer* to write on whether that Indian team was 'characteristically Indian'. I asked myself the questions I raised above. Did they lack discipline or ambition, either individually or as a team? Was there too much flair, not enough playing to a plan? Was there a shortage of determination?

In the event, India squared the series in that third Test. In my view, India showed enough to answer this question with a clear negative. They were confronted with a typically Headingley pitch and, early in the match, cloudy, chilly Headingley weather. The ball moved around; the bounce was variable. It was a pitch on which some sides might have played no front-line spinner. Yet India picked two, and moreover found their third seamer in the man brought in as a makeshift opener, Sanjay Bangar. They did not select as opener their player with Test experience, Shiv Sunder Das, who had just scored 250 in the previous county game. They risked Bangar, who had previously given evidence so far of rather ordinary medium pace and a useful middle-order resilience with the bat.

On winning a tricky toss, Ganguly boldly decided to bat. Here were cricketers willing to take hard decisions – to face the facts full-on. No shilly-shallying. They might have been bowled out for 150, anyone might, in the conditions. If England had had a lucky day, and India had played with any less skill and courage, they could well have been. Yet they read the pitch correctly in seeing that it would take spin as well as seam, and they backed their best available players.

The Indian batting was as disciplined as you like. Bangar exceeded all expectations, playing a crucial innings of truly Yorkshire grit. Dravid was quite wonderful not only in defence but also in his cruising up a gear into attack. And the little god Tendulkar limited himself, reined himself in. He struggled a lot, by his standards, scoring a large number of runs by pushing the ball for ones and twos square of the wicket. His innings, at least up to 150, was notable far less than usual for stunning shots. Capable of brilliance, he was not averse to honest toil. I think it was an innings that would have given him as much pleasure as many a more flamboyant century played on easy batting pitches. India closed on 628 for eight.

This dedicated attitude persisted in the field. India's quicker bowlers were determined and persistent, as well as hostile. Ajit Agarkar was decidedly slippery. He was so slight that a gust of wind might have blown him over, if it didn't miss him altogether. He had been suffering from a bad foot, I gathered, but in this Test showed pace and fire. Zaheer Khan (I noted) had the makings of a top left-arm fast-medium bowler, and was always challenging the batsmen. With the ball (as earlier with the bat), Bangar did more than could have been hoped, dismissing two top-order batsmen in England's second innings when they followed on. And then Anil Kumble and Harbhajan Singh – what terrific performers they were, and how good it was to see them together, in their totally different styles. Of the two, Kumble, the leg-spinner, was the more attritional, Harbhajan the more artistic, with his slower pace and more extreme spin.

All this application and determination came together in the Headingley match in such a way that any talk of 'Indianness' or 'Easternness' could be ditched. On this evidence – and I could also throw in their side's performance in the triangular one-day competition earlier that season – we could put this cliché in its place as a caricature.

Maybe Ashis Nandy was right: that 'Cricket is an Indian game accidentally discovered in England.'

33

'WHEN I FIRST SAW THE ENGLISH BOWLING'

I was invited to give the second Raj Singh Dungarpur Lecture in Mumbai, on 11 December 2011, following the Nawab of Pataudi, known widely as 'Tiger'. I was looking forward to renewing my contacts with him, the first of which occurred when we were about fifteen years old. Sadly, he died on 22 September that year, aged seventy. On 15 June of the following year, the MCC held a tribute dinner to him at Lord's. The following is an extension of my speech on that occasion.

Tiger – in the mind's eye – aquiline, still, slight, swift, hawkish. On the field he had presence, a regal touch; one's eye would be drawn to him, as eyes have been drawn to Imran Khan, Viv Richards, Ian Botham. A proper arrogance, or as Bishan Bedi put it, an 'imperious charm'.

He was of course in fact a prince, being brought up in the palace in Pataudi, a house of 150 rooms, with well over a hundred servants, of whom seven or eight were his own personal attendants from early childhood. His mother was the Begum of Bhopal, his father the previous Nawab, who scored a hundred for England at Sydney (his debut in Test cricket) in the Bodyline series, and later captained India on their tour of England in 1946–7.

His responsibilities began early, not to mention his interest in shooting. Aged six during the Troubles in 1947, he was given a rifle and told to shoot anyone who came within twenty yards of the window.

As a person, Pataudi was laconic and understated, wry not slapstick. He once convinced an Indian team member that the great white-marble Victoria Memorial in Calcutta (one of the Raj's great monuments) was another of his personal palaces – a story whose English analogy might perhaps be one of the other Sussex amateurs announcing to a young pro on his first visit to London that St Paul's Cathedral was his private church – which might almost have been true for the Right Reverend Bishop David Sheppard.

After his maiden Test hundred in 1962 against Ted Dexter's MCC team Tiger was asked when after the injury in which he lost most of the sight in his right eye, he first believed he could play Test cricket. His reply was: 'when I first saw the English bowling' – which reminds me of Mahatma Gandhi's response to the question (put to him in 1933): 'What do you think of Western civilization, Mr Gandhi?' He replied: 'I think it would be a good idea.'

As a batsman Tiger was by temperament a dasher, who, contrary to Indian batting approaches of the 1950s and '60s, hit over the top. At the age of fifteen, playing for Winchester against the Sussex XI of which Robin Marlar was captain, he kept lobbing Marlar's off-spin back against the sight-screen; Marlar said he enjoyed it the first four times. After the injury, Tiger was inevitably more circumspect, even at times tentative.

He also had one Test wicket to his name, at Kanpur, in 1964, when he took the second new ball. 'Cowdrey lbw Pataudi 38.' The appeal was answered by the umpire with the words: 'That's out, your Highness.' Tiger claimed it was a sound decision.

As captain of India and, for a year, of Sussex, he insisted on total commitment in the field; whites were to be got grubby, regardless of the – as he put it – abysmal service provided by English laundries. Bishan Bedi again: 'On my debut, he didn't have much to say about my bowling beyond acknowledging with a nod of the head that I was doing all right. But he had plenty to say about my fielding.'

Pataudi brought the Indian team together as a unit, rather than, as had tended to be the case, as a group of disparate individuals or regional clusters, speaking different languages and sometimes forming cliques, whether from Delhi, Calcutta, Bombay, Hyderabad or Bangalore.

In a way, Tiger was the Denis Compton of Indian cricket – the first cricketing superstar in India, whose appeal involved a similar heady mix of brilliance, charm and charisma. To top off the Indian version of the fairy story, in 1969 he married the glittering film star Sharmila Tagore – someone who in India's celluloid pantheon seems to have been a combination of Peggy Ashcroft and Marilyn Monroe, with a bit of Joan Sutherland and Margot Fonteyn thrown in for good measure.

Aside from Tiger's aristocratic air, he also had the common touch. Cricket writer John Woodcock told me a story of meeting a country labourer he (John) knew, while fishing on the banks of the Avon. This fellow turned out to have been one of the beaters at a partridge shoot at Druid's Lodge that Tiger had been part of, and clearly had taken to him as one of his own. And Peter Vallance, who played with him for Wisborough Green, a village in Sussex where his guardian lived, spoke to me of Tiger's approachability, and of his pleasure in village green cricket – Tiger played for the village on a Sunday in the middle of a match against Yorkshire at Hove. There was, he also said, 'nothing of the Nawab about him'; I imagine that not to be entirely true, but what was true was that there was a lot of the ordinary man in the Nawab.

Tiger had a rebellious streak too. He once invited Woodcock and Henry Blofeld to the back of a (dry) Indian Airways flight from Bombay to Calcutta to share a bottle of vintage brandy he'd quietly removed from the cellars of the Bhopal palace.

More notoriously, he got into trouble for shooting a black buck, a protected animal in India. The historian Ramachandra Guha, who wrote the excellent book on Indian cricket, A Corner of a Foreign Field, told me how, when they were both on a TV panel together shortly after the black buck affair, Tiger, surrounded by intellectuals of one kind and another, murmured that no doubt he had been invited as the panel needed a convict to provide balance.

By repute, or possibly by scurrilous rumour, his son Saif, now a film star like his mother, had also a streak of his father in him. Shortly after Saif left Winchester, a young boy in the same house announced that they were glad Pataudi had gone, because now they could get onto the billiard table. Did he spend a lot of time playing, came the natural question. No, said the boy, but he was often asleep on it.

I played against Tiger in 1956, when he was fifteen and I was fourteen, for Middleton-on-Sea Sunday Eleven, a team that went all over Sussex, playing on often pretty and always rustic grounds, such as the one at Wisborough Green. I was in awe of this already renowned schoolboy. If my memory is right, our combined total for the day was two runs, and I outscored Pataudi.

By 1959, he was at Oxford. The following year I went to Cambridge, where we read about his achievements with admiration, even apprehension. He scored two centuries in a match against Yorkshire, with their full bowling attack, including Fred Trueman. Hardened, even cynical, county cricketers spoke about his batting as unique. He had more than a touch of genius. And then, of course, the apparently innocuous car accident happened, on the sea front at Hove; feeling no pain in his head, he had no idea that a sliver of glass from the windscreen had entered his right eye.

He was left with little sight in that eye – only the ability to discern some shadow and light. One problem was, he saw two of everything. The story he tells is that in his first important match after the injury, against the MCC at Hyderabad, he got to 35 despite seeing two balls apparently six or seven inches apart, of which he found it more productive to play the one to the left. At this point in his innings, he got rid of the contact lens and made the most of his one good eye, doubling his score.

This innings, like his life, ended prematurely, at seventy. But it resulted, extraordinarily, in his being picked for India only a few months after the accident. And he scored a hundred at Delhi in the fourth Test. He says it took him five years to get used to batting with this huge impediment, by which time he had been captain of India for four years. But there is another story about this. In 2001 Saba Karim, a wicket-keeper batsman who played thirty-five times for India, was hit in the right eye during an Asia Cup match in Dhaka while keeping to Anil Kumble. The ball reared up off the top of the stumps. Tiger visited him in hospital, 'making his presence felt without shouting from the rooftops', as Karim put it. Tiger helped the younger man to accept fate and move on; to make the kind of adjustments that allow life to be worth living. Saba asked him how long it took him to recover. 'Saba,' he said, 'I never recovered.' But Tiger made a life, including of course a major cricketing life, for himself, despite the accident.

Tiger's baptism as captain of India came when he was only twenty-one, in 1962. It happened as a result of Nari Contractor's notorious near-death, when his skull was broken by Charlie Griffith in the

Barbados vs Indian match; an injury followed twenty minutes later by Vijay Manjrekar being hit in the face by the same bowler. In that match, Pataudi himself was twice bowled by Griffith for a duck.

A few months later, in 1963, he and I were captaining Oxford and Cambridge at Lord's, an altogether more peaceful, less menacing occasion. He scored 50 or so; we had a sporting game, in which those other sons of famous cricketers, Richard Hutton and Mike Griffith, also made half-centuries. Tiger declared 45 runs behind, and we set Oxford 194 to win in two hours and twenty minutes. We had them six down for 101, at which point they called off the chase, and the match was drawn.

Tiger won the respect of cricketers and followers all over the world. Ian Chappell came from Sydney to Mumbai to speak in his honour. Ian described his two innings in the Melbourne Test in 1967. Tiger had pulled a hamstring and missed the first Test, which India lost. He played at Melbourne despite not being fully fit. India lost the toss and were put in under heavy cloud cover. Pretty soon they were 25 for 5, all five to McKenzie, who was quick and strong, a fine fast bowler. Pataudi then scored 75, followed by 85 in the second innings. As Ian put it, not only was he batting on a green pitch in bowler-friendly conditions; not only was he coming in at 25 for 5 after being put in to bat, with one of the leading fast bowlers of his time against him; not only did he have just one fit eye. He also had only one fit leg. Chappell remembered two shots during that first innings: a hook that went in front of square for a one-bounce four on the biggest square boundary in world cricket; and a back-foot straight drive off McKenzie over mid-on for another one-bounce four.

Ian told a couple of stories about Tiger. One was when he asked Tiger what he did after retirement. The reply came, 'I don't really do anything.' 'No,' said Ian, 'what do you do for a job, now you're not playing cricket? What do you do from nine to five?' 'I don't do anything in particular, I'm a prince.' Ian said, 'We don't know much about princes in Australia, so what do you actually do?' 'Ian,' said Tiger, 'I'm a bloody prince' (expletive not deleted, as used to be said in reports of the Nixon files, but diluted).

Chappell also remembers asking Tiger how it was that he would come in to bat after intervals with a different bat; Pataudi said he picked up the nearest one to the dressing-room door. Once again, shades of Compton; a sense of a capacity to do things other top players could never emulate, the sense of his being a law unto himself. Compton, too, borrowed bats. Both of them were incredibly untidy.

The last paragraph of his book *Tiger's Tale* includes the following: 'in the country of the blind the one-eyed man is king. In the keen-eyed world of cricket a fellow with just one good eye and a bit has to settle for something less than the perfection he once sought.' And of cricket itself he wrote: 'It is difficult to explain the appeal of cricket, but to me it has charm, style and depth.'

Like the writer!

34

THE INDIAN BRADMAN

Don Bradman said of Sachin Tendulkar that when he first saw him batting on television he called to his wife to come and have a look. 'I felt the fellow plays much the same as I used to play,' he said. 'I can't explain it in detail but there is a similarity. It's his compactness, his stroke production. It all seems to gel. That was how I felt.' Bradman rated him and Brian Lara as the greatest of their generation, Lara slightly more aggressive, Tendulkar marginally ahead all round.

I agree. If I wanted someone to play for my side in all conditions, I'd have chosen Tendulkar. He is the most complete batsman I have seen. If I was looking for sheer brilliance: Lara.

Australians Ricky Ponting, who was in the same bracket as the other two, and Ian Chappell both opted for Lara, on the grounds that he could turn a game more quickly and devastatingly than Tendulkar, and that he more often won tight games off his own bat.

Lara could be impossible to bowl at. If you bowled straight at him he would get across his stumps and with wonderful wrist-work play you through the leg-side. I once saw part of a Lara master-class in which he hit the same ball – well pitched up outside his off-stump – anywhere between backward cover and wide mid-on. But in 2013 South African bowler Makhaya Ntini, who bowled rather in the style of Mike Procter, with a pronounced in-swing action from relatively wide of the crease, remarked that he had bowled Lara behind his legs no less than four times. And he felt that if Lara moved across his stumps less, he had a good chance of getting him in the slips. I remember Stephen Harmison, somewhat similar in his deliveries to Ntini, though less unorthodox, pummelling Lara with short-pitched stuff that followed his body and gloves from the leg-side, and then having him caught in the slip cordon by pitching the ball up around off-stump.

I doubt if Tendulkar gave any bowler such rays of hope. His technique was more orthodox. He was a short man, and like Bradman was compact at the crease. You wouldn't know from his style of play alone that he was Indian. He could have been from anywhere. He was firmly grounded, his feet apart in his stance. He had a perfect defensive technique, along with a wonderful ability to turn defence into attack with the minimum of flourish. (Here too a contrast with Lara, who had more of a flourish in his stroke-play.) Tendulkar transferred his weight onto either foot without ever losing balance (which explains some of his combination of power and solidity). He had economy of movement. At the same time, Tendulkar could play a straight ball wide of mid-on with minimal risk, along with equal freedom on the off-side. Like many shortish batsmen, he was quick to pick up the length, and a magnificent puller and hooker. In Tendulkar one saw a living example of elegance as simplicity.

Apart (apparently) from Bradman, the player who most (to my eyes) resembled Tendulkar was Sunil Gavaskar. When Tendulkar gained the record for Test centuries, with thirty-five, it was Gavaskar's record that he overtook. Gavaskar was also short, firmly grounded and quick to judge length. He was occasionally quixotic, and occasionally could get bogged down. But what a player! And when in good enough form, if he got a ball that could be hit early on, he would play an attacking shot. He rarely missed out on a half-volley or a short ball. And Gavaskar had a fantastic tally of runs against the West Indies, much of it achieved in the days of their prime; he has still scored more runs and centuries (thirteen) against them than any other batsman.

All this is well known.

I want to discuss two other aspects of Tendulkar's personality and play. First his guts, second his modesty.

Courage takes many forms. He had it in plenty, of course, in facing and taking on the fastest bowlers of his time. But I have in mind another expression of courage, here combined with humility. He himself said there were many times when he 'did not feel comfortable at the crease. And not only on occasions when the bowling was exceptional and the conditions against him.' In other words, top form, or a feeling of relaxed concentration, from time to time evaded him. He had to struggle. He even became pedestrian. This was most striking when he suffered from long-term injury.

In England in 2007 he had both tennis elbow and a shoulder injury. But he was willing to fight it out. He never took refuge in glory shots, or in a form of self-excuse, that he was 'above' the need to work for every run. He tolerated being an ordinary good player rather than the genius that he had been, and would again be. After eighteen years of wonderful stroke-play at the highest level, he settled for the (almost) humdrum. He batted, and battled, with humility to put his side into match-saving, and ultimately match-winning, positions. He was willing to let short balls hit him on the body, rather than run any risk of being caught – as he had been in the first match of the series – off glove and chest, or glove and hip, on the leg-side.

Second, his modesty. I had the privilege of interviewing Tendulkar at Chandigarh in December 2008. In the aftermath of the terrible terrorist attack in Mumbai, the previous Test, due to have been in Mumbai, had been swiched to Chennai. In a remarkable match, India scored 387 for 4 in the last innings to beat England on a turning pitch, against an attack containing two fine spin bowlers, Graeme Swann and Monty Panesar. Tendulkar scored a not-out century, reaching this landmark with the stroke that also won the match. Shortly after, he was greeted in the middle of the ground by a groundswoman in a red sari, whose job had been to sweep the ends of the dusty pitch at intervals during the match. She approached Tendulkar diffidently, wanting to greet him and offer *Namaste*, salaams.

I had been struck by the generosity and modesty of his response. He gave her his full attention. I started the interview by commenting on this. I told him it must have made her day, if not her year. His reply was humble: 'We don't play for ourselves; we play for India. Thanks to God, I have been able to play for India for twenty years. It is wonderful for the nation to have a victory in such a fine match, after the events in Mumbai.'

He went on to speak of his gratitude to others; to his father, who took him to play in one cricket match after another as a child. 'Not only for what my father said, but for his whole way of being . . . If I can give my children half what my father gave me I will be happy. My father is my hero . . . I'm grateful to my wife, Anjali, who shares everything I think and feel, the bad times and the celebrations of the good times . . . To my brother, who organizes so much for me. To my coach. And particularly to Sunil [Gavaskar] – for the way he organized himself and his innings – and to Viv Richards, who could dominate attacks. If I have something of each of these I would be a good player.'

As we spoke, I wondered if he was too good to be true. Was this false modesty, over-egging the pudding of humility? I tried to push him on this. Was he, for instance, at all relieved to get away from the hero-worship that dogged his every footstep in India? Were there times when he hated the adoration and demands? Did he relish the fish and chips of Yorkshire (for whom he played in the early 1990s) and even the ale?

'Not ale, no, I wasn't one for bars.' He went to a bar only once, he said, at the end of one season. If he had been brought up differently, perhaps . . . But he always wanted to play in England. He was thrilled when the offer came, from Yorkshire, he wanted it and it worked for one season. Yes, he did eat fish and chips, and burgers, he could get away with it then, when he was a young man of nineteen, but not now, he has to look after himself more carefully.

In our hour-long conversation, Sachin never fell into any trap, never hinted that it might be a burden to carry the expectations of a nation, that there might be relief in being less recognizable, that he might have enjoyed being able to drive his fast cars at times other than 2 a.m. (due not only to the density of traffic in Mumbai during the day, but also to the human traffic of people queuing up to get a touch or a glimpse of him). He was assured, modest, controlled and unfailingly polite. And as a break-out from being the perfect young man, driving one of a collection of cars on the streets of Mumbai, even at 2 a.m., seems a rather tame, conservative form of rebellion.

There seems, then, to be no chink in his goodness. Neither was there in his batting. You can never have everything in one player. You can't have in a single player David Gower's elegance and cover-driving on the up and at the same time Geoff Boycott's soundness. You can't have Lara's brilliance and Rahul Dravid's reliability. With Tendulkar, and of course Bradman himself, you got as close to that ideal as was humanly possible.

35

THE BRIDGE

The year 2017 was the seventieth anniversary of Indian independence. During the summer, a celebration of cricketing links between India and England over these decades was held at Lord's, hosted by the Indian High Commissioner in London. A hundred and fifty or so guests, perhaps, mainly of Indian origin, were invited, along with a few cricketers from different generations, plus those minor divinities in their smart dark blue blazers, trim haircuts and beards, fit-looking and on the whole dashing – the Indian cricket team. The senior god was their captain – the handsome, severe and charming, Virat Kohli.

The format of the event started with drinks and chat in the Long Room. When the players arrived, the social world clustered around them, avid for selfies. After a while, order was called, the Commissioner welcomed the guests and made a few appropriate remarks about how important cricket was in the links between our two countries. Both teams were in the semi-finals of the Champions Trophy, and devout hopes were expressed of their meeting in the final (not to be: Pakistan beat England in the semi-final; and then defeated India in the final at the Oval ten days later).

An interviewer went from one cricketing celebrity to another with a microphone, for short conversations about their experiences against each other. The audience quickly became restive. The buzz of their conversations grew louder, distracting from the interviews.

Suddenly Kohli stepped forward, asking for the microphone. He was blunt. You should keep quiet and listen to what people have to say, he pronounced. It's impolite to talk among yourselves.

People were shocked into silence, but only temporarily. The last interviewee was Kohli himself. Again he was forthright about the rudeness of the guests, before acquitting himself admirably, with modesty and frankness in the more ordinary aspect of his task.

I was impressed by this. It's one thing to respond to questions when given the floor and the microphone; one's right to speak has been underlined, one's duty clear. It is quite another to interrupt the flow (both of interview and of distracting conversation) without invitation. His confidence, his ease with the mantle of leadership, his authority, all were strikingly evident. Here was a man with an independent and courageous mind. He has charisma, part of which is expressed by his articulacy.

Many of these qualities are apparent on the field in his captaining of India. Watch Kohli and you sense from his reactions a great deal about the way the game is going. He wears his emotions on his sleeve. He is fierce and forceful, keen-eyed, absolutely focused, dynamic.

Along with passionate desire and high standards go the huge pleasure of joint success and the desolation of disappointment, each emotion at times plainly visible. He will speak his mind bluntly, as at the High Commissioner's party, if he feels the opposition have behaved badly. He is aggressive, sometimes even brash. He is totally involved. As a fielder too, he is keen, lean, active and aggressive. It's hard to take one's eyes off him.

Tactically he strikes me as shrewd and inventive, looking for opportunities to attack. He lives by, and expects from his team, a strong work ethic. He demands attention to detail. He himself is an excellent example of fitness, notably when he is chasing a target, when he will turn every potential single into a two. There have been times when less athletic partners have been run off their feet. I suspect he has little patience with laziness.

At press conferences he is also articulate, open and challenging. He will use sarcasm to deal with what he thinks are foolish questions, while at the same time being frank about the team's shortcomings. He is up for an argument about his changing of sides from match to match, even often when the team has won; he refuses to go by results only. 'We have a large squad because there are that many players who can do the job.' He is always on the look-out for improvements. The players have to be hard on themselves.

He had long been singled out as a potential captain, since before leading India Under-19s to victory in the World Cup in 2008. He is the only player in the history of cricket to have scored hundreds in each of his first three Tests in charge – a tribute to his feeling that this is where he belongs.

He has known hard times. His lawyer father died when Virat was sixteen. The family had to move. He has moved a long way in the next fourteen years.

His run-hunger is apparent for all to see. As a batsman, he is hawk-eyed, quick-witted, quick-footed. He is all energy. His conversion rate in turning fifties to centuries (57.1 per cent) was recently second only to Don Bradman's (69 per cent). The third-highest was a long way below him – Steve Smith at 51 per cent. Joe Root's conversion rate was 26.5. Kohli states that to win international matches you need individuals who turn in big hundreds, and pairs who build partnerships of 150 not just 70. He has stamina, drive and persistence, and does himself what he expects of others.

Kohli is clearly the best batsman in the world. He averages over fifty in all three formats. He has a fantastic record chasing targets in one-day cricket. As ex-New Zealand cricketer, Martin Crowe, put it in 2014: 'Kohli exudes the intensity of Dravid, the audacity of Sehwag and the extraordinary range of Tendulkar. That doesn't make him better, simply *sui generis*, his own unique kind.'

But actually he may now be the best of all Indian batsmen, past as well as present. As Suresh Menon wrote in 2016 of his fantastic ability to make use of the classical alongside the innovative: he has made a 'bridge across two cultures' – the culture of Test cricket and that of limited-overs cricket. He adds:

> For every cringe-evoking shot played by a desperate batsman for whom the end justifies the means, Kohli has a phalanx of answers, both visually pleasing, and thoroughly effective. His understanding of space and time is unrivalled.

Truly an Einstein among batsmen.

It is as if, Menon suggests, Kohli is saying 'Hey, we haven't fully explored the possibilities in traditional stroke-play yet'. As in music, art and film . . . the essential difference is not between the highbrow and the lowbrow. It is simpler than that. Something is either sound or unsound.

He has the full range of classical technique, with great capacity to judge length. His bat-speed is itself exceptional – he is not a caresser of the ball. Kohli has also at least one extra skill, a stroke to be seen in his Test innings as well as in shorter forms of the game. This is the top-spun drive. (The other batsman to play it was Kevin Pietersen.) Many fine attacking batsmen drive the ball on the up; that is, they drive balls that are well short of half-volleys, allowing their hands to flow through the line of the ball, hitting it alongside the bent front leg. The risk of the shot is, of course, that if the ball moves an inch or two in the last couple of yards, the batsman may edge it. Kohli's stroke is a variant. Instead of letting the ball come to him, he reaches forward in front of his left leg, making contact with the ball well ahead of himself and sooner after it has pitched; with his wrists he plays what is almost a hockey shot, cuffing or top-spinning the ball. He plays it on either side of the wicket. He reduces the chance of edging the ball. He is less likely to hit the ball in the air. It requires speed of vision and dexterity of wrists and hands.

Kohli has one Achilles' heel to overcome. His record in England in 2014 was poor. In ten Test innings he averaged 13.4 with a top score of 39. The pitches and weather suited England's fine opening pair, Jimmy Anderson and Stuart Broad. Anderson in particular repeatedly dismissed him with out-swing, caught at the wicket or in the slips. He played too far away from his front leg, pushing at the ball. No doubt even the exuberant Kohli lost confidence as the failures mounted.

So the tour of England in 2018 will have been a personal as well as a team challenge for Kohli and India. Everything may of course be different. But if the weather is again damp and cloudy, if Anderson can make the ball swing late in either direction, will Kohli have found an answer? No one knows in advance. But what we do know is that, like Kumar Sangakkara in 2014, Kohli contracted with Surrey to play at least three four-day games for them in June shortly before India's tour begins. The BCCI agreed with his suggestion that he miss India's Test against Afghanistan in order to acclimatize himself by playing these matches in English conditions. In the event, he had to cancel because of a neck injury.

(Postscript: this book went to print after the first Test of the series, which was at Edgbaston. It was a fascinating, seesawing match, which England won narrowly by 31 runs. The contest within a contest was its highlight – Anderson vs. Kohli. The great swing bowler bowled fifteen overs consecutively at the start of India's first innings, many of them to Kohli, who had adapted his technique against the swinging ball, getting as far forward as he could, leaving whatever he could leave and playing as late as possible, without following the ball with his hands and bat. At one point, Kohli scored off only two of the 37 balls Anderson bowled at him. He had played and missed, had been put down off a half chance, and several edges had not quite carried. Off the last ball of this fifteenth over, with his score on 21, he gave an orthodox chance to Dawid Malan at second slip. Possibly distracted by his colleague at third slip (Keaton Jennings), who dived towards the ball, Malan dropped it. Kohli proceeded to drag India back into contention. In his personal battle for confidence, he had endured a torrid time, and made the most of his luck. He scored 149 and 51, his morale and form completely revived. Not only was he set up for the series; he offered a mode of approach that other batsmen in the team could try out for themselves. He showed it could be done.)

As Kohli himself says, we must pay attention to detail. We must be hard on ourselves. He has the skill, the drive and the maturity to make himself the best player in all conditions.

No human being has all attributes; no attribute is without its damaging converse. A second question-mark against Kohli has been raised by cricket historian and writer, Ramachandra Guha, who was one of the Committee of Administrators appointed by the Supreme Court to implement the Lodha panel recommendations for the restructuring of Indian cricket.

In June 2017 Guha resigned from this Committee, citing BCCI's failure to address continuing examples of conflict of interest, and their over-deference to the great names of Indian cricket.

In January 2018, he wrote in *The Telegraph* (Kolkata) newspaper about his apprehensions about Kohli. In his view, Kohli is one of those liable to be the recipient of a damaging deference.

Guha describes how, watching Kohli 'play two exquisite square drives against Australia in 2016', he concluded, not without sadness, 'there goes my boyhood hero [Gundappa] Viswanath from my all-time India XI'. (His current first five in the batting order are: Sunil Gavaskar, Virender Sehwag, Rahul Dravid, Sachin Tendulkar, Kohli.)

Having remarked that captaincy 'only reinforces Kohli's innate confidence', he writes: 'No one in the entire history of the game in India has quite had [Kohli's] combination of cricketing greatness, personal charisma and this extraordinary drive and ambition to win, for himself and the team.' He adds that he has 'manifest intelligence (not merely cricketing) and absolute self-assurance'.

But – and here is the 'but' – when Kohli has so much influence,

> this is precisely the time to remind ourselves of how we must not allow individual greatness to shade into institutional hubris . . . To the corruption and cronyism that has so long bedevilled Indian cricket has recently been added a third ailment: the superstar syndrome. Kohli is a great player, a great leader, but in the absence of institutional checks and balances, his team will never achieve the greatness he and his fans desire.

In other words, to balance his own strength, Kohli needs strong men around him. He needs, Guha suggests, people to challenge his views, to stand up to his convictions. He needs a coach of the calibre of Anil Kumble.

All this makes sense to me. As US President, John Kennedy had an inner group whose task was to question and argue against all his plans and proposals. He needed his own checks and balances. To prevent proper pride crossing the narrow line into arrogance, so perhaps does Kohli.

PART 8

COMMENTATORS

36

FROM THE COMMENTARY BOX

In 1973 that doyen of cricket writers and commentators, E. W. Swanton, invited me to write a 'Diary of the Season' for *The Cricketer* magazine. When I demurred slightly, uncertain, he wrote that 'to a mind as facile as yours, this should not be a great burden'. I thought this subliminal ambivalence was salutary. 'Facility' meaning fluency, ease, degenerates into the facile, the superficial. But it's also salutary for the writer – how easily, facilely, one can convey the wrong impression, or indeed possibly the right one (but not the one we want to make public).

There is bound to be some tension between commentator and player. The latter wants praise; he wants any criticism to be sympathetic, to take account of his difficulties; he wants allowances to be made in his case. The commentator or writer wants a good story, or even, possibly, to be truthful. At times, the one significant expectable drama is whether, when or how someone will topple from his perch; we look for signs of promise, of blooming talent, but also for signs of terminal decline.

It's not quite all one way. Swanton had a stentorian voice, orotund, pontifical. One hot day Peter Richardson, who played for Kent, Worcestershire and England as an opening batsman in the 1950s and '60s, was playing at Canterbury. The commentary box was over the sight-screen. He walked up to the umpire and pointed towards the box. He told him he was being distracted by a loud voice coming from the sight-screen area; would the umpire please investigate and see if this could be quietened. Richardson well knew that it was Swanton commentating. As the umpire approached the box, Swanton of course was speculating on the reason for the conversation and the pointing. He had to shut the window.

As an ex-player turned part-time journalist, I admire the ability of the full-time writers not to put their foot, or perhaps their whole leg, too far in it too often. I think it difficult for ex-players not to harp on about the old days, with subtle or not so subtle self-reference. I enjoy and admire the television coverage of cricket on Sky; the commentators do a good job of educating us all, showing features of technique or approach that are illuminating both to other experts and to beginners.

As for writing, it is a truism that a varied and rich literature emerges from cricket. The standard of writing is often high. The game is dense in its texts and sub-texts, and the time it takes conducive to reverie, reflection and constructive analysis. There are fascinating issues of technique, as well as social and psychological depth and range.

37

'DESPERATELY GOOD'

It is not an empty cliché to say of John Arlott that he was the voice of cricket. In his early days at the BBC, the house style was pukka, formal and, whenever possible, scripted. John brought the eye and tongue of a poet; the accent and timbre of a Hampshire grave-digger's son; and the courage to describe a whole scene, to give the game its setting. As a member of the Radio 3 *Test Match Special* team, where the individuality and informality that his own example among others had encouraged would sometimes descend to triviality, John gave the commentary a needed ballast of objectivity and seriousness.

He knew cricket more in the way of a lover than of a critic, and as such tended to romanticize the performers.

John befriended me when I was playing county cricket in the early 1970s, inviting me to dinner with another old friend of mine and his, Tom Cartwright, during Middlesex's game against Somerset at Taunton. Tom was a totally honest cricketer, hard-working and with exacting standards. He was also one of the most difficult bowlers to score off in the history of county cricket. Socially, he could be an acerbic commentator on the foibles of our class-ridden game. I seem to remember that being the match when I rushed down the pitch at Tom in desperation, and skyed the ball to mid-on. At the dinner with John later that evening, Tom grinned at me, 'Poor man's Denis Compton!' He may however have recalled this from an earlier match – though I can't find such a dismissal in the relevant scorecards.

This was the first of my many social meetings with John, often as the recipient of his generous hospitality, more often than not at his home, where an icon like Ian Botham might join Hampshire stalwarts Brian Timms or Leo Harrison. If he liked you, John was utterly loyal.

His own disappointed aspirations as a player (he appeared for Hampshire Club and Ground in 1937 as an opening batsman) never soured into envy or rancour. He saw professional cricketers, with few exceptions, as honest and likeable craftsmen in a worthy tradition, and valued the invitation from the Cricketers' Association to be its first president, a post he held from 1968 to his death, as a great honour.

John was born in Basingstoke in 1914. His father looked after two cemeteries from 1918, so from the age of four, young John was linked to death. He was an only child in a happy family. Hating his sadistic headmaster, he left school at sixteen after failing the School Certificate 'spectacularly'. He worked in local government; then as a clerk in a mental hospital, calculating the amounts of each item of food needed daily by the wards.

In 1934 he joined the Southampton police force. He enjoyed his eleven years on the beat. He must have been an unusual policeman, composing poetry on quiet duties and freelancing as a writer of programmes for the BBC. This led in 1945 to his first job with the BBC, as a staff producer.

In 1946 the opportunity came to broadcast cricket. He toyed with the idea of modifying his country accent – one person said he had a crude voice but an interesting mind – but, thankfully for him and for the rest of us, was dissuaded. With his humanity, his gravitas and his fine voice, Arlott became a major figure in cricket.

After his retirement in 1980, John moved to Alderney, in the Channel Islands. This step may in part have been motivated by the need for clean air, to help with his deteriorating chest problems. But the idea of living on an island was also a dream for him, satisfying some longing for solitude, for the rhythm of the sea and no doubt for much else. He was a very special character, not part of the main.

John's commentary, and to perhaps a lesser extent, his writing, had a weight and depth that was unique. The pigeons described by him were solider than those described by some of his colleagues. He had a feel for images, a poet's eye and voice. 'Botham runs in like a shire horse cresting a breeze.' A shot by Clive Lloyd was 'the stroke of a man knocking a thistle top off with a walking stick'.

Rod Marsh told me of Arlott's perfectly understated pointing up of the inevitability of a particular mode of dismissal, while commenting one early evening on the Test match at Old Trafford in 1972. 'And as the train departs from Stretford Road station, so Boycott departs, c. Marsh b. Lillee.' Boycott's departure, and the manner and timetable of it, like that of the 6.17 from platfom 2, were routine and ineluctable.

John had too a streak of show-biz. John Samuel, his sports editor at the *Guardian*, wrote:

At a long table in their Fleet Street pub, he would say, 'D'you want me to say a few words?' He knew he had presence, those heavy eyes in a moment all of a twinkle, his mind composed and memory sharp at a hint of an audience.

But it was not only the content that made him so special; it was the whole manner of delivery in speech or writing, the hinterland of values and perceptiveness from which his words emerged.

It was said of Arlott that he spontaneously offered immigrants and visitors from the Commonwealth a sense of the England many hoped, even expected, to find – liberal, literary, open-minded, and with a degree of sentiment and nostalgia for cricket and its roots in the English countryside.

Art critic David Sylvester once took my wife and me after hours to an exhibition of Bonnard's paintings that he himself had hung. We got to the last room, the culmination of the show, with its four large paintings depicting Bonnard's wife in the bath. We were alone. We were silent for several minutes. David said to me: 'I'm so glad you didn't say anything.'

John, too, knew the value of silence; the need for time to take things in. In this he differed from most of his colleagues, indeed from most of us, so often eager are we to impress others, and to relieve anxiety by filling every gap with chatter.

(Though it should also be said that towards the end of his career, after lunches liberally washed down with Burgundy or Beaujolais, a few of his pregnant silences during John Player League broadcasts – these matches, 40 overs per side, were far from Arlott's favourite form of the game – were, it turned out, signs of a less intentional kind of blessed release: John had nodded off on air.)

In 1984 I was invited to interview John for Channel 4. He was not well; we had to do the shooting in the morning, with glasses of red wine at hand, before he became (at that point in his life) too sad, too heavy, too (not to put too fine a point on it) inebriated. The producer gave me some advice. 'Don't rush to fill silences. Wait to hear what he goes on to say.' The resultant programmes are full of gaps in the conversation, as the four hours on screen were distilled from only five hours of filming. These programmes must hold some sort of record for coughing, gasping, swilling, the clearing of throats, the sound of gurgled wine and repetitions. But these (verbal) silences also had a virtue; they opened out – at times – into second thoughts that went beyond the 'official' story.

In 1949, when he stopped off in Sicily on his way home from the MCC tour of South Africa, John was introduced to the local wines. Thus began another passion and career, on the fruit of the vine, and on food, particularly cheeses, that enhanced the wine. He always regretted that cricket is scarcely played in wine-producing Latin countries.

John Arlott managed to combine qualities that do not often come together. He was both passionate and moderate in his opinions. He was a lover of tradition – policeman, cricketer, historian, collector – and a rebel against many authorities: he was outspoken in his antagonism to the regime in South Africa, and had little time for sports administrators, dismissing Lord's as 'feudal'. Among all else, he found the time and energy to stand as the Liberal candidate in two parliamentary elections in the 1950s.

He regarded his part in bringing Basil D'Oliveira to England in 1960, to play in the Central Lancashire League, as one of the best things he did. As a diplomat and negotiator, he sometimes found that the need for restraint was tested by his sentiment and conviction, but he nevertheless steered the Cricketers' Association towards a constructive role in both the major divisive issues of the past fifty years – South Africa and Packer.

The hinterland I referred to became increasingly ingrained with loss. John suffered two tragic losses. On New Year's Eve 1965, his eldest son, Jimmy, aged twenty-one, was killed in a motorbike accident. Then, in

March 1976, came the death at forty-four of his much-loved second wife, Valerie. After his son's death, John's tie was always black. Deep down he felt there could be no underlying meaning in life. His vision was changed. The second loss increased his tendency to lugubriousness. The pleasures of life, of friendship, family, cricket, wine, food, poetry, were real enough, but even the best moments were tinged with an awareness of their inevitable endings. As he rolled the first tasting of a bottle of excellent wine lasciviously inside his pendulously extended lower lip, he would say, in a mixture of growl and murmur, 'Good, good, desperately good', his protruding eyes filling with tears, his look one of intense misery. There was indeed desperation in the transience of all good things. I'm reminded of Samuel Beckett's phrase, 'birth was the death of him'.

When I hear the first movement of Schubert's Piano Sonata in B flat, with its lyrical sweetness interspersed with growling rumbles from the lower depths, I think of John.

Yet John Arlott was fully engaged in life in all its detail, and was, like the rest of us, worried about the ordinary smaller and larger things of life; about cricket, or racism, or whether there would be a table at a favourite restaurant he'd like to take one to. He was by no means all serious-minded weightiness.

He became, though, increasingly overweight, less healthy and less handsome. Too much tobacco, wine and food left him with chronic chest problems, and eventually the emphysema that killed him. Then the growl became at times an expression of primitive vulnerability.

John spent the years of his late middle age worrying about not having enough wine laid down to see him through, and the years of his old age worrying that he wouldn't be granted the time to drink it all.

Over the last two or three years, he needed constant care. This he received with steadfast love and patience from his third wife, Pat. Others, too, were tolerant and affectionate, moved by glimpses of the old Arlott, by the person he had been and by the depredations of time. Now he often feared being alone and demanded company. He was, as his son Tim put it, 'dying most nights', suffering from 'terminal hypochondria: where two pills would be good, four would be better'.

He once said to his son, Robert, 'You'd make a lousy nurse', to which Robert retorted: 'There's only one person who would have made a worse one: you.'

He was also afraid of dying, but the end came peacefully, in his sleep in the early morning of Saturday 14 December 1991. Pat and his much-loved sons were with him in the house, and had spent the previous evening at his bedside.

Until this last painful phase, John was generous and lovable. He was a marvellous raconteur, ranging brilliantly over past and present, all the while from time to time shaking his head and hand as if to say: 'But what does it all matter?' He acknowledged that cricket, wine and aquatints are in the last resort marginal, so, recognizing this, he would in mid-flow subtly (with, as I say, this characteristic little demurring, self-dismissive, pushing-away gesture with his hand and fingers) undermine the importance of his story before embarking on another.

As to generosity, I think of it as a wide-ranging attitude of thought and deed. His hospitality was rich. He liked strong foods, pâtés, smoked eel, meat, matured cheeses; he was not bothered about delicacies much – sweets, salads, chocolates. I suppose you would call it a man's taste – with perhaps an apple pie permitted as a robust dessert. He was generous in thought too, though he could be savage about those he found to be beyond the pale of decency and kindness.

He was generous also with his time. In the company of friends, John never made one aware of other commitments and anxieties; he wanted to talk throughout a meal and long beyond. I once sat down to Sunday lunch with John, his family and some friends at two o'clock, and we didn't get up from the table until ten at night – except for a shocking moment in the middle, when someone reported that Robert, aged ten, had fallen in the river. I never saw John move so fast. Fortunately, Robert was only wet.

The tragic view of life can't be maintained full-time, but it is there, in the background, for us all, even though most of us keep it far in the background so as not to have to deal with it in any way that allows us to recognize it as such. We forget the spectre at the feast. Not so, John. Cricket, John didn't let us forget, doesn't matter a jot compared with one life lost in Northern Ireland. The tie was the same; knitted, untidy, always black. The growl, with its elemental grit of realism, of awareness of transience, of the robust and the vulnerable, was never far away.

38

'ANOTHER TIME, ANOTHER TIME'

In October 2007, nominated by Doug Insole to succeed him, I became President of the MCC for a year. One of the pleasant duties of the role is to invite speakers to monthly dinners for members during the winter. My first two speakers were Matthew Engel and Vic Marks. I should have liked to take credit for this being a statement of political intent (to start with Marx and Engels), or if not intent, ironical provocation, but if so the credit is to my unconscious only. Another speaker was Sir Harrison Birtwistle, the composer. He compared cricket to opera, and told us how the team that ought to have been selected and announced for the MCC's tour of Australia in 1946–7 would have featured, between 'Bedser, A.V., medium-fast bowler', and 'Wright, D.V.P., leg-spinner', the name 'Birtwistle, H., bowler of googlies'.

Subsequently, I invited Harold Pinter to speak. Unfortunately, ill health made this impossible. But I had the beginnings of my welcome prepared. Here it (more or less) is, tinged with regret.

Harold Pinter is the person I most hoped to welcome as speaker at one of these dinners. I have no idea what he would have chosen to say to us, except that he loved cricket. Waiting to hear what *he* would have said fascinated me more than knowing or not knowing what anyone else would say on the subject. Why?

Partly because it's not often that you get the chance to hear talking about one's own love a man who is one of the great writers of the twentieth century, of any century. Harold had the highest honour the country can give to an artist – he was a CH, Companion of Honour. He also won the Nobel Prize.

But it goes beyond that. We are confronted in life by the reality that we are specks of dust in the vast aeons of space and time; that when we die we go (I believe) into nothingness; that our importance in the long run is nil; that we live always on the brink of 'death's dateless night'. But we believe that at the same time, or in the same breath, there are things (if one is lucky) that make life fascinating and well worth living. Literature, love, family closeness, art – all these and others may do so. Even sport quickens the apprehension, lifts the spirit, engages and challenges the whole being physically, psychologically, emotionally.

And cricket – a rare team game each of whose dramatic moments is a contest between individual protagonists, the only game that goes on seven hours a day for the best part of a week, and at the end of which neither side may be much nearer winning or losing than they were five days before – cricket has (for me) the capacity to enthral, bore, enchant and also evoke argument to a greater extent than any other.

So we have to consider not only John Arlott's dictum, that the whole of cricket is not worth the death of a single young man in

Northern Ireland, but also Bill Shankly's comment that 'Some people believe football is a matter of life and death. I am very disappointed with that attitude. I can assure you it is much, much more important than that.'

Pinter felt the same. He was once asked by an interviewer: 'Isn't cricket a game with a lot of rules . . . For a rule-breaker, somebody who's bucking against the system all his life – that's what makes me confused about cricket. And you.' Having said that he had never been asked this question before, Pinter responded:

> I like rules which are for the benefit of mankind. And I think there are some good rules and there are some lousy rules. And I think the cricketing rules are totally respectable.

So here is a man who faced more courageously and rigorously than almost anyone else our cruelty and aggression, but also the failures and loneliness of life, and our tendency to hypocrisy and defensiveness, who also finds that this strange game, which may have originated in France, but certainly came into its own first in England, helps make life worth living.

Pinter scatters cricketing references throughout his plays. Near the end of Mick's wonderful riff against the feckless Davies in *The Caretaker*, when Mick tells Davies that

> You remind me of my uncle's brother. He was always on the move, that man. Never without his passport. Had an eye for the girls. Very much your build. Bit of an athlete. Long-jump specialist. He had a habit of demonstrating different run-ups in the drawing-room round about Christmas time . . .

We suddenly hear another sublime inconsequentiality: 'Used to go in number four for Beckenham reserves. That was before he got his Gold Medal.'

In *No Man's Land* the characters' names are Hirst, Spooner, Foster and Briggs. George Hirst was a Yorkshire all-rounder, Reggie Spooner the Lancashire batsman, Frank Foster played for Warwickshire, and Johnny Briggs was a fine spin bowler, also for Lancashire. For Pinter, contests between batsman and bowler echo verbal sparring and menace. Cricket provided Pinter with metaphors for life. I am reminded of a feature of my own analysis, in which interpretations were sometimes referred to as fast bowling, and I brought dreams of bats going rubbery, or of not being able to get my pads and box on in time to bat – dreams that were revealed as being parts of my repertoire of ways of representing various insecurities, including feeling unprepared for pressing challenges of everyday life.

Harold wrote a famous poem about his hero Len Hutton. It reads, in its entirety: 'I saw Len Hutton in his prime. Another time, another time.' He sent the poem to fellow-writer Simon Gray. Not hearing back from him for a few days, he couldn't bear to wait any longer. He phoned. 'Did you get my poem?' 'Yes.' 'Well?' Pause. 'I haven't quite finished reading it yet.'

I'm aware of only one published piece by Pinter that deals directly with cricket: his tribute to Arthur Wellard, the old Somerset and England player, who, in older age, played for the team Pinter played for, captained and then ran as chairman, 'The Gaieties'. Harold loved Wellard, his shrewdness, his pugnacity, his directness. An ex-team-mate of Wellard's at Somerset, Eric Hill, said: 'He got Arthur down to a T.' He also beautifully describes his own humility and deference to Wellard. 'Sorry, Arthur.' 'Yes Arthur.'

He writes:

Occasionally I would perform respectably, under Arthur's scrutiny. Once, when we were in terrible trouble, forty for five or
something, against Hook and Southborough, I managed to get
my head down and stayed at the wicket for an hour and a quarter,

for some twenty-five runs; thus, with my partner, warding off disaster, On my return to the pavilion Arthur looked at me steadily and said: 'I was proud of you.' I don't suppose any words said to me have given me greater pleasure.

One of *my* greatest pleasures was performing that *Caretaker* speech at a celebration of Pinter's life held in the Long Room at Lord's in September 2009, nine months after his death. I cast Mike Gatting as the bewildered caretaker, flummoxed for words. Being for these few minutes an actor alongside very distinguished actors, including Sam West, Jeremy Irons, Robert Powell, Roger Lloyd Pack and Penelope Wilton, I knew how the actors who play in cricketers' benefit matches sometimes feel – frightened, flattered and pleased!

39

ENDGAME

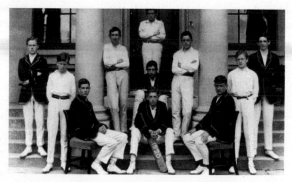

Samuel Beckett (second from left).

I can't resist including one piece that links John Arlott, Harold Pinter, Samuel Beckett and Wilfred Bion.

The first version was written in 2013 when I was asked to write something that touched on sport for the eightieth birthday Festschrift *for James Knowlson, then Emeritus Professor of French at the University of Reading, where he had founded the* Beckett Archive *(now the 'Beckett International Foundation') and the* Journal of Beckett Studies. *He was also the dramatist's biographer.*

Some years before, Knowlson had come to the Institute of Psycho-analysis to speak about Beckett's therapy with Bion. More recently, he had been a guest at the box I hosted at Lord's when I was President of the MCC. Pinter was also there – his last visit to cricket before his death a few months later. Beckett loved cricket and had played a few first-class games. Pinter famously compared cricket to sex, to the advantage of the former. Bion had, as far as I know, no interest in cricket, but played rugby and swam. I imagined that Knowlson admired Arlott, as I did. I knew Pinter loved Beckett. Hence the article, consisting of a few thoughts about, and links between, the four men.

Wilfred Bion was Samuel Beckett's psychotherapist between 1934 (when Bion was thirty-seven, Beckett twenty-eight) and 1936. They met three times weekly.

I have often wondered who had the greater influence on whom. Like Beckett, Bion was vividly aware of disconnection, anomie and our tendency to lose contact with others and ourselves. In his autobiography, he wrote about an occasion when he found himself immobilized and unable to respond to his very young daughter in distress; she needed him to go to her, but he could not.

Both had a dry humour. Beckett: 'The sun shone, having no alternative, on the nothing new.' And: 'All of old. Nothing else ever. Ever tried. Ever failed. No matter. Try again. Fail again. Fail better.'

Bion (to a patient): 'I don't know why you are so angry with me. I wasn't trying to help you.' And, about another patient: 'It's fascinating how boring the patient is.' When someone said to him, 'I think I understand what you mean', Bion replied, 'I was afraid you might.'

These remarks of Bion seem to me to come from a quintessentially psychoanalytic frame of mind, revealing someone fully aware of human difficulties and pretensions, shrewd, and above all, curious. They are remarkably similar in spirit to Beckett's many gnomic, paradoxical and thought-provoking comments.

At the age of eight, Bion had been sent away from his parents and ayah in India to boarding school in England. He was lonely and isolated. He was a swimmer and rugby player – sport helping to fill gaps in his life, and no doubt in his psyche. Awarded a DSO and a

Legion d'honneur as a tank commander in the First World War, he later wrote of the near-psychotic states of terror and automatism that gripped him at times in this horrific world. He thus illuminated the concept of courage, unsettling it (and the reader's presuppositions) but also thereby deepening and reinforcing it. He wrote: 'the only difference between getting a VC and a court-martial is the direction you run'.

Bion wrote, about his work with groups:

> I think my interpretations are disturbing the group. Furthermore, that the group interprets my interpretations as a revelation of the nature of my personality. No doubt attempts are being made to consider that they are in some way descriptive of the mental life of the group, but such attempts are overshadowed by a suspicion that my interpretations when interpreted throw more light on myself than on anything else, and that what is then revealed is in marked contrast with any expectations that members of the group had before they came.

Bion and Beckett both grew into wisdom, a wisdom rooted in a radical refusal to deny the bleak aspects of reality, to espouse facile hope, or to take refuge in reassuring words or in an aura of respectability. In the facing lies the growth. Fail again. Fail better (I like its ambiguity; is failing better failing less badly? Or more badly, becoming a better type of failure?). 'Truth', Bion said, 'is food for the mind.' And: 'Wisdom or oblivion – take your choice. From that warfare there is no release.'

Harold Pinter did not claim wisdom: 'I never think of myself as wise. I think of myself as possessing a critical intelligence, which I intend to allow to operate.' As a young writer, he met Beckett when the latter was his cultural hero. Pinter described a trip to Paris where they drank through the night, ending up at 4 a.m. at Les Halles. He had a hangover. Beckett set off on foot across Paris for the nearest all-night chemist, and returned an hour or two later with a packet of Alka-Seltzer.

Pinter wrote: 'I don't think there's been any writer like Samuel Beckett. He's unique. He was a most charming man and I used to send him my plays.' (I love this: a great writer willing to allow a sense of his youthful affection and admiration to come through in this child-like switch from acclamation of his mentor as a writer to touchingly naïve, almost banal, hero-worship – 'I used to send him my plays'.)

Both dramatists were essentially kind and generous. Both were loved and admired by actors. Pinter was the more overtly political, capable of trenchant and public rage.

Like Bion, Pinter felt truth was both to be aimed at and elusive (which didn't stop him being forthright – 'I could be a bit of a pain in the arse. Since I've come out of my cancer I intend to be even more of a pain in the arse'). He also stated: 'There are no hard distinctions between what is real and what is unreal, nor between what is true and what is false. A thing is not necessarily either true or false; it can be both true and false.'

He wrote: 'Beckett had an unerring light on things, which I much appreciated.'

Beckett is I believe the only Nobel Prize winner to have played first-class cricket. Pinter said he tended to 'think that cricket is the greatest thing that God ever created on earth – certainly greater than sex, although sex isn't too bad either'. Bion, so far as I know, had no taste for cricket. But of all cricket people, perhaps John Arlott would have appealed most to them all.

Arlott himself worked in all sorts of jobs, including being an attendant in a mental hospital and a policeman. In 1946 he was assigned to cover a cricket match. He became a major figure in cricket, with his fine deep voice – something in common with Pinter there – his humanity, and his gravitas. And humour. When bowler Tufty

Mann (of South Africa) caused problems for batsman George Mann (captain of the MCC), Arlott commented: 'A clear case of Mann's inhumanity to Mann.' And he once described Cunis, the New Zealand all-rounder, as 'neither one thing nor the other'.

Like the other three men, Arlott had a deep-seated sense of loss, as I've described.

Like Pinter, though not quite of the same political hue, Arlott was capable of anger and passion in his politics. In a debate at the Cambridge Union in 1969, soon after the D'Oliveira affair, he said:

> It is political commitment and political belief that can make a man think that his opponent's views are so obnoxious that he will abstain from playing any game against him, as a protest against what the other man believes and also, lest it should be assumed that by taking part in any activity with the supporters of that view, he gives it his tacit approval. Any man's political commitment, if it is deep enough, is his very personal philosophy and it governs his whole way of life, it governs his belief, and it governs the people with whom he is prepared to mix.

I heard on the radio a comment of Arlott's that reminded me of Beckett's dry, even sardonic, remark about the sun having limited choice in the matter of shining or not. Introduced to the commentary box with the words: 'And now, as the sun sets in the West, John Arlott will commentate on the remaining half-hour's play', Arlott began: 'And if the sun sets anywhere else than in the West, you will be the first to hear of it.'

40

'THEY'VE NOT GOT
THE SINGLES GOING'

I have long enjoyed conversations with Ian Chappell, and appreciate his views on cricket. His position opposite Ray Illingworth in the early 1970s brought together the two shrewdest, toughest of cricketing brains. I also enjoy listening to Ian Chappell commentate. Here I write about his commentary during the Ashes series, 2017–18.

Ian Chappell was a shrewd, uncompromising captain, and a gutsy, resolute batsman. Now he is one of the best commentators on TV.

I love listening to him. First, he knows the game inside out. Second, he is frank, fair-minded and wry.

And third, like all of us, he has his pet attitudes, but they aren't all one way. Compare and contrast Geoffrey Boycott and Kevin Pietersen. With each you get the impression that their pre-judgements (if not prejudices) are one-sided: to parody – for Boycott, if a batsman gets out caught at slip playing an off-drive, he should have let the ball go, while for Pietersen, if you get out blocking, you should have been trying to hit the ball out of the ground.

Chappell is more rounded. The second day of the Perth Test began with England 305 for 4, Dawid Malan (on 110) and Jonny Bairstow (75) having transformed the game in England's favour. The day started with four consecutive maidens. Chappell's comment was: 'They've not got the singles going.' A few overs later, he criticized the running between the wickets: 'It's not been good at all. England have failed to take into account the "Freemantle doctor" – there is always one for the throw when the fielder is throwing against the wind at Perth.'

For Chappell, squeezing out runs is a matter of almost moral significance, not to mention pragmatism. The underlying motto is: 'waste not want not. Make the best of a bad job.' I imagine a trans-generational history behind this attitude; long experience of scraping a living from ungiving soil. I can't imagine this basic assumption in someone who has been brought up on abundance.

Another of Ian Chappell's core values is resourcefulness. Don't let anyone get on top of you; rotating the strike is a small but key expression of a refusal to be kept down. If you're a small man faced with a huge aggressive fast bowler, don't die in your hole; be shrewd – if he's physically stronger than you for a while, or on top, use all your wits as well as your guts and stubbornness to resist and defeat him.

Another element: don't worry too much about looking good; it's results that count. I once asked Ian why he thought Mark Ramprakash had done less well in Test cricket than his undoubted skill and technique promised. His response was that Ramprakash was more interested in playing a classical-looking shot than in manoeuvring the ball for a one or a two. He blocked the ball impeccably when he might have steered it into a space. Instead of looking for a single, he held his shape for a split second at the completion of a shot.

Chappell does not put defence first. He advocates taking the contest to the bowler. He says: make the bowler think, don't let him settle into a feeling of power and superiority. Talking about England in the field, he comments that Jimmy Anderson and Stuart Broad are too defensive-minded in terms of field-placing. He notes how much they talk to each other whenever one or other was about to bowl. If he were Joe Root, England's captain, he wouldn't like it. He'd want to get between them and encourage a more positive attitude.

I also admire his attitude to playing the bouncer. If you get out hooking, he says, the answer is not to stop playing the shot but to go into the nets and learn to play it better. You don't give up the cover drive if you get out cover-driving, you work at it, and at judging when to play it.

You have to choose your moment for hooking, too. A year or two ago, I mentioned Andy Roberts to him. He agreed that Roberts, whom the other West Indian fast bowlers of the late 1970s, '80s and '90s regarded as the father of the renaissance of their art in the Caribbean, was a great and shrewd bowler. Ian remembers finding short balls from Roberts harder to play than anyone else's. 'It was never wasted, always chest or shoulder height, always straight.' As a batsman he jumped around, fended the ball off, got hit, scored a few ones and twos, stuck it out. And waited for a short ball round off-stump that he could free his arms at and play the pull shot. Just once, in a World Series match, Roberts gave him such a ball, and Chappell gratefully pulled it for four in front of square. But only once! Years later, he met Andy in Antigua and asked him if he remembered this moment. Yes, the fast bowler replied, he did. 'But I never gave you another to hit like that!'

To return to Perth, 2017: the third day's play began with Australia in a powerful position. Steve Smith was 92 not out, and had looked in total command the evening before. Chappell was critical of Root. When fielding, he said, you have to think in terms of any batsman starting again on zero. Grim realism might have told Root that his bowlers, on this pitch, had little chance of finding the edge, and if they did, it probably would not carry.

But there is a tension between realism (truthfulness) and conviction (sometimes based on illusion). Is success in sport more to do with facing the facts – in this case, in these conditions, that England's bowlers were up against it, pea-shooters against tanks – or is it more important to build one's collective confidence? To do many things in life well, including playing sport, we need energy and conviction. Delusion is one route to conviction. But is it the only one? After all, a really unrealistic approach will, more often than not, lead to massive defeat.

I think there is truth in both positions. Team members infuse each other with optimism and determination. Emotion invigorates; energy (like apathy) is catching. Proper hope *is* based on reality. As no one knows for sure in advance what will happen next (even when bowling to a determined and in-form Smith in conditions favourable to batting) hope is both justifiable and necessary. So bowlers, batsmen, fielders, captains have to come out fighting, believing in their chance of successes. Proper pride keeps at bay a sort of helpless shame, even despair produced by the cold light of day which can be self-fulfilling. Nothing of this involves delusion.

I doubt if there was much more Root could have done on that interminable third day, when Smith and Mitchell Marsh added 300, and England took one miserable wicket in 90 overs. Especially without Ben Stokes, we were outgunned in the match by the three tall Australian strike bowlers. An overall difference of 10 km per hour for each fast bowler is a huge disparity – the difference means that there is that much less time for the batsman to get into position; the bounce of the ball is steeper, and variable bounce is exaggerated. Edges carry further, even on slow pitches. In this match, Josh Hazlewood rivalled Glenn McGrath for accuracy, pace and movement. What's more, fear and apprehension become more of a factor. Think of Curtly Ambrose, who once took 7 for 1 on a typical cracked Perth pitch.

But I agree with Chappell: we must hold on to gritty hope, combined with a shrewd range of possibilities, even, as someone put it, when you get down to plan Z.

41

WHAT DO THEY KNOW
OF CRICKET...

C. L. R. James, who died aged eighty-eight in 1989, was a Trinidadian historian and social theorist. In his exceptional 1963 book on cricket – *Beyond a Boundary* – he puts this challenge to us: 'What do they know of cricket who only cricket know?' The phrase echoes Rudyard Kipling's question: 'What do they know of England who only England know?' James originally intended this as the title for the book; now it is in effect a sub-title.

James commented on cricket from the perspective of a literary man, a cultural historian, and a passionate lover of the game. He offers a picture of the game, and of phases within it, much broader than that of most commentators.

Beyond a Boundary is among other things a celebration of the appointment in 1960 of Frank Worrell as the first black man as captain of the
West Indies for a whole series (George Headley – 'the black Bradman'
– had captained them, but only for a single Test in 1948). But it is
wider and more embracing than this.

One way of characterizing the book is: it offers an account of the
significance of cricket for a whole society. James describes W. G. Grace
as the most famous Englishman of the Victorian age, unifying the
country in a way that no one and nothing else could. Through him,
'cricket, the most complete expression of popular life in pre-industrial
England, was incorporated into the life of the nation . . . Directly and
indirectly, he took what he found and re-created it. It came his way at
the perfect historical moment.'

Grace, as Ranjitsinhji (the first non-white to play for England)
wrote in 1897, 'united in his mighty self all the good points of all the
good players, and made utility the criterion of style. He was not only
the finest player born or unborn, but the maker of modern batting. He
turned the old one-stringed instrument into the many-chorded lyre.
He discovered batting; he turned its many narrow straight channels
into one great winding river . . . The theory of modern batting is in
all essentials the result of W.G.'s thinking and working on the game.'

James notes Grace's immense popularity, and links him (and this
phenomenon) not only with the cricketers of his, James's, childhood,
youth and manhood in the West Indies, but also with the athletes at
the ancient Olympic Games in Greece. Through these sportsmen,
people experienced artistic and expressive delight and passion, were
put in touch with the fundamental elements of human life – attack
and defence, courage, steadfastness, grandeur, ruse – but also with
pride, that 'one of us' could do such things.

In parallel to this, James shows how important the game was in
the variedly coloured strata of Trinidad, how vital for the pride of the
black man. He knew from his early experiences of playing (for Maple)

against Shannon what pride meant. It shows how success for individuals represented a victory over the colonial and class-ridden upper ranks; how such successes enabled the man and woman in the street to walk taller, to conceive that they have a right to regard themselves as the equals of their social superiors. James himself wrote: 'The cricket field was a stage on which selected individuals played representative roles charged with social significance.'

He showed how, alongside colonialist superiority, British values included the idea of fair play, and (to greater or lesser degrees) embodied it on the cricket field. He linked such values of fair play to the qualities of English literature he studied at school.

Beyond a Boundary itself is an example of its own epigraph. James knows a lot more of cricket than only cricket, and it is his wider historical and social understanding that gives depth and force to his writing, including to his arguments about Worrell.

James's question prompts further questions: 'what is "knowledge of cricket"?' This is a Socratic question, inspired by Socratic irony. For an implication is that the person most devoted and experienced in cricket, as player or coach or commentator, doesn't, without other knowledge, know what cricket is. This was Socrates's mode of approach. He persuaded generals to admit their ignorance of what courage is, priests their ignorance about piety, rulers and judges about justice. At the end of the discussions, everyone, reduced to perplexity by the Socratic examination, agreed with his conclusions – no one knows what courage, piety or justice are.

Partly this was an outcome of Socrates's logical sleight of hand (the fact that no definition of these complex concepts covers all cases doesn't entail that no one knows what these things are). But Socrates goes beyond this, forcing his interlocutors (and us) to realize how hard it is to be courageous, pious, just or virtuous. In his book A *Case for Irony*, philosopher and psychoanalyst Jonathan Lear links the Socratic moves to those of Danish philosopher, Søren Kirkegaard, who said that in all Christianity there is no (real) Christian. Socrates challenges all ordinary claims to excellence or virtue. He raises questions that are more radical than the ordinary ones about our practical identities and roles.

If we take James's question seriously, we, like Socrates's generals and priests, have to interrogate our assumptions about knowledge of cricket, and about what it is to be a cricketer.

For one thing, there is a range of possible forms of knowledge here. There is, first, practical knowledge (how to play, how to be a batsman, bowler, fielder). Second, there is a coach's or commentator's knowledge (including the making of critical judgements and the spotting of real talent). And third, James may have in mind a more reflective knowledge (being able to say what cricket's importance is, socially and psychologically, being able to relate cricket to other matters, as in *Beyond a Boundary*). Are the first two kinds of knowledge not really knowledge? Are they somehow too limited to count as knowledge?

What does being practically knowledgeable, or critically knowledge-able, call for? Surely those who really know cricket are those most closely, professionally and devotedly committed to it, embedded in it?

The player's knowledge of cricket

Let's consider those in my first category, the performers, who may be said to know cricket neither in the philosophical or comparative way evinced by James himself, nor in the overall way of the coach or commentator.

I would say that James has a point even here. For the player, too, needs to understand more than his own particular niche within the game. One thing I liked about the Yorkshire tradition in cricket was that players were brought up to think about the game as a whole. By contrast, I heard recently of an international bowler fielding at fine leg in a one-day international. At a break in play he had no idea of the situation of the game, how many overs were left, what sort of run-rate the opposition were faced with. All he could think of was whether his wrist was at exactly the right angle in delivery. We might ask: what do bowlers know of cricket who know (or are interested in) only the mechanics of bowling?

Professionalism in sport can atrophy into a narrow focus on one's own task, so that each player is imbued with guidelines about his own performance, based perhaps on computerized attention to how to bowl to each batsman in the other side, at the expense of an appreciation of and emotional involvement in the tactics of the game and/or in the problems and skills of his team-mates. He becomes a cog in a machine, rather than a thinking team-member. In American football, entire teams change when a defensive role is replaced by an offensive one. The division of labour is extreme. The role of the defensive lineman, say, can become so specialized and limited that the person fulfilling it need know nothing at all about the play of or the strategy of the team. His job may become routine. Such developments can rob one of one's full humanity. No longer having to consider the process as a whole makes it impossible for him to understand how his world makes sense. Like Charlie Chaplin in *Modern Times*, the defensive lineman becomes a conveyor belt attendant and his task is reduced to a small range of repeatable, automated skills.

As captain, I tried to turn the players into a team of potential captains, of thinkers about the game. Their responsibilities did not cease when they were not involved in their individual first-order skills of bowling or batting. I wanted them to be thinking about the whole situation, and about each other's strengths, weaknesses, vulnerabilities. They might then be able to offer ideas or advice to others or to the captain or to the team as a whole. No one (in any team or organization) knows where the next good idea will come from.

I believe, too, that the effort to see things from other points of view helps in the development of the individual's own skill – as a batsman he can see the anxieties and doubts that even great bowlers are not exempt from, as a bowler he can appreciate the nervousness even behind the great batsman's confident way of carrying himself.

In this sense, too, James has something important to say. A batsman, however skilful and correct, is not fully a batsman unless he can build an innings and pace a run-chase, unless he can assess early on, and convey to the team, what a good score on a particular pitch might be, unless he has a good sense of when to chance his arm in the interests of the team, and when by contrast to conserve his wicket even if his approach then risks being interpreted in some quarters as selfishness. The excellent bowler can make the best of difficult circumstances – a pitch that doesn't suit him, being put on at the wrong end (from his own selfish point of view), or not being given the new ball when he thinks he deserves it. Batsmen and bowlers can be creative in their development of a broader range of options, for themselves and for others.

And all cricketers, like all sportsmen, have to deal with 'those twin impostors' success and failure. Some react better than others to both.

A really good player is not liable to fall apart at the first sign of failure or difficulty; nor will he become reckless or complacent in moments of triumph.

So: at this first level (what does a performer have to know in order to know his cricketing onions?) the ideal player is capable of understanding more than how to hit a cover drive or bowl a fast out-swinger. He who (in a narrow sense) knows only cricket (only cricketing technique) is not going to be as good a player as he might be. Though articulation of the understanding is not necessary, he needs to be more broadly knowledgeable and curious; to be capable of a greater range of assessments; to have strengths of character that go beyond flamboyant or exceptional personal or technical ability.

The knowledge of the coach or commentator

What then about those in my second category: coaches or commentators?

A person may, as the great Sussex and England cricketer, Ranjitsinhji, put it, 'grow grey in the service of the game and learn nothing'; but I'm not talking about such people, who may be narrow or bigoted or unimaginative. I'm talking about those who are rooted in the game, in its techniques, its lore, its values, its character and the characters of those playing it.

An expert of this kind may know cricket through and through, without understanding its actual and potential social role. But such a man would understand a lot about character, about relaxation and concentration, about building an innings or working on an opponent's weakness. This expert knows the game tactically and psychologically as well as technically; he is shrewd in his assessment of who to pick, who (for example) can be relied on in a crisis. He recognizes the need for a balanced side. In his day-to-day coaching he would constantly be switching between, on the one hand, talking to the players at a technical level and, on the other, subtly or directly making suggestions or opening up discussion about matters of character and personality. 'Tiger' Smith, the old coach, asked me once, noticing how tense I was, why I frowned when playing shots with his walking stick. Did I think I would hit the ball harder? He was questioning my unacknowledged assumption that doing well is based on trying harder, which itself seemed to imply to me a sort of rigidly tense effort of concentration. In fact one can't hit a ball well when one's body is tense. Smith might have spoken to me in terms of technique or physiology: instead he addressed my emotional orientation. He understood all this.

Graham Gooch, England's batting coach from 2012 to 2014, said that he doesn't so much coach batting as help with run-scoring; by which I think he meant that what he emphasizes is not so much technique as the whole approach to batting. He tries to cultivate in the player an orientation favouring big scores, or recovering from bad patches. He is, one might say, coaching more elements in the players than their batting per se.

Some of the most perceptive in this category are ex-players who have devoted a lifetime to the game. They may have moved into professional cricket in their teens. Once retired, in their late thirties or early forties, they went into coaching or commentary or umpiring. They are steeped in the practice and in watching the game and its players. I am thinking of people like Ian and Greg Chappell, Ray Illingworth, Keith Fletcher, Michael Holding, Michael Atherton, Geoffrey Boycott, Andy Flower, Graham Gooch, Rod Marsh, Sunil Gavaskar.

The knowledge of these men includes much that is wider than technical knowledge of cricket. It includes knowledge about risk and safety, about teams and individuals. It requires understanding of people, and assessment of personal as well as technical qualities.

Presumably, too, such coaches/commentators understand the role of proper pride, like that which motivated the West Indians in their almost-two decades of world dominance, and which in some degree lay behind their utter determination to be the best. Coaches and commentators may not be able to express such knowledge in James's fluent prose, but it would be there, in their attitudes. The true coach or leader recognizes and draws on intangible and hard-to-describe sources of ambition and dedication in members of the team. Like a good parent or teacher, he knows intuitively about the balance between telling, showing and consulting. He understands that learning involves learning for oneself, that we all need to respect others' opinions (and be open to learning from them), while at the same time holding on to our own.

Someone may object: but *is* this a case of knowing 'more than cricket'? Or does cricket itself include and teach more than cricket? But such a move concedes James's point. 'Cricket' includes more than cricket. This does not, of course, mean that someone could, like a career Civil Servant, be shipped in as coach or leader in, say, another sport than that which he knows first-hand. These broader qualities can't be abstracted from the context in which they count.

To sum up so far: knowledge in a practical activity like cricket involves levels of understanding and knowledge that go beyond the acquisition of, beyond the capacity to sum up or convey, technical skills. Such comprehension includes a sense of self and a sense of others. It includes a capacity to grasp or sum up the game as a whole. It includes a wealth of human insight. And however good our ideas, can we get them across? We have particular skills, but can others tolerate us being part of their team? We put others off, so they don't want to hear what we have to say. Gubby Allen once said of England vice-captain Bob Wyatt: 'he had excellent ideas, but no one would give sixpence for them'.

The social historian's knowledge of cricket

C. L. R. James himself was a social historian. His book is about the social history of cricket, and to some extent, of sport. He writes of the significance of sport socially, personally, aesthetically, culturally, politically. Clearly, he has to know about all sorts of things other than sport per se. The scale of his map for sport ranges far and wide, wider than that of the successful player, wider too than the successful coach or commentator. Here the breadth of knowledge is obvious, and could hardly be contested.

Further thoughts on focus and scale

We need both narrow and wide focus. In the Middlesex team, the person I always got good advice from about what to do next, or right now, was Clive Radley. He was perceptive, down to earth, pragmatic. Moreover, if I didn't follow his suggestion, and things went wrong, he would still be open to my request for help an hour or a day later. He was the perfect person to check out immediate plans with. Mike Smith was different. He was less direct, more vague when it came to what to do now; but he had often helpful suggestions on more strategic matters, on wider issues of which younger players had class, what the balance of the side should be, the longer-term prospects of the side. He was more reflective; almost, one might say, more philosophical. A third player, Roland Butcher, was even more capable of making wide-ranging observations. I remember two such comments. One was when I called a team meeting after we had lost four games on the trot (after winning the first eleven completed matches in the season). Many people had opinions, including me, and several of them were relevant. Roland said something like this: 'I think we have started to count the trophies on our mantelpieces at the end of the season. We are speaking as if we only have to turn up to win. Our attitude has become complacent, very different from what it was early in the season. We have to stop thinking about the distant future and concentrate on each ball, each over, each hour, each session.' And on another occasion, when I was unhappy about one or two players sulking when dropped, or when not given the prominence they thought was their due, Roland came in with: 'But do you appreciate what it feels like to be left out of this side?

One minute you're part of the set-up, the next minute you're changing down the corridor, and no one really talks to you in the same way.' No wonder, he might have added, one or two are prone to sulking. Butcher's comments were more like those of a psychoanalyst, inviting thought about one's deeper, subliminal assumptions.

Here are three invaluable contributions, none more or less useful than any of the others, though each more relevant in different contexts. For a full understanding of a team at work one would need each kind of intelligence, each kind of contribution. Socrates (or Plato) with their elevation of verbal intellect, might place the three in the hierarchy: Butcher on top, then Smith, then Radley. A pragmatic professional might reverse the order. I see them as having equivalent weight. Sometimes one needs more of one than the other, but all are valuable.

It is rather as if one were to say which kind of scale is of most value in a map. The answer is: it depends what you need at the moment. The closer the map is to a replica of the environment, the less it becomes a map, but also the more one can see detail. The larger the scale, the less one sees one's route in relation to other places, other journeys; but the more detail one can pick up. With a small-scale map, we may be slower to discover that we are going in entirely the wrong direction. Sometimes one needs one kind of scale, sometimes another.

The microscope and the telescope, the minute particulars and the panoptic vision – we need both. Each complements the other.

Perhaps there is an analogy here to the values of professionalism and amateurism. The typical professional knows the game close to. He has to; his living depends on it. He has to put in time at the technicalities; he practises and trains assiduously. He has to know the processes involved, recognize the differential factors. The old pro can read a pitch, since he's seen similar and different pitches over many years. He knows cricket from having played in and watched games in a variety of conditions, including ground and atmosphere. He has ideas of how to combat a range of opponents. The amateur may be less closely acquainted with the detail, but at best he plays with a spontaneity that comes from love of the activity. He can, we hope, take risks and be more independent; his livelihood doesn't depend on it. He can relax. He has other things in life, so cricket can be seen as not the be-all and end-all of everything; failure is not, customarily, so devastating.

I don't mean to suggest that professionals don't love the game, or that those who aren't paid to play don't work at it. Both sets of qualities are invaluable, and need to be held in balance. My argument applies more to attitudes and temperaments, rather than to differences related to whether or not one is paid to play; there are plenty of people who did not and did not need to get paid to play cricket whose approach was of the former kind; and vice versa. Think of Trevor Bailey's batting (the amateur who played like a professional) and Colin Milburn's (the professional who batted like an amateur). Think of the two professionals Graham Gooch (who emphasized work, training, practice, dedication, and was marvellously successful against the pace and skill of the West Indies) and David Gower (elegant, lazy; hating training, without much time for practice, with an ironical attitude that could at times veer over into the lackadaisical, but whose batting was a delight of timing and touch). As bowlers and all-rounders, Ian Botham epitomized the 'amateur' approach, while Ray Illingworth was more the hardened 'pro'.

Finally, an analogy. I'm writing about cricket. Many readers will not, I assume, be experts on cricket. Yet we assume (or I at any rate hope) that what I'm saying will have echoes and resonances, with other situations. I believe that such analogies apply across many different fields and skills.

The specific analogy I want to end with is this. I read recently of Mozart's support for democracy, not in politics itself, but in the music of his operas. How so? Mozart gave his minor parts complex characters, with complex music. They are not just pawns, either in the plot (content) or in the music they are given to sing (their form). He shifted music away from a hierarchical tradition. Rather than there being a totally dominant top line, with others in unison beneath it, supplementing, harmonizing, fitting in, in short, *serving* the dominant tune, Mozart gave each instrument and voice a unique line of its own.

PART 9

WICKET-KEEPERS

42

BEHIND THE TIMBERS

I was once a wicket-keeper. It kept you in the game all the time. It got me into the Cambridge University side in my first year, batting at number eight. Rodney Hogg recently raised this role with me on air, asking with apparent innocence, 'Why did you give up wicket-keeping, Mike?' 'I wasn't very good at it,' I replied. 'But you carried on batting?' he said.

Point taken! But my early experience in the role gives me more confidence in commenting on the state of the world's wicket-keepers. In my view, this is one cricketing skill that has deteriorated over the past half-century.

In the 2016 Lord's Test match between England and Sri Lanka, I saw both keepers, Dinesh Chandimal and Jonny Bairstow, fail to take straightforward chances. (I have dropped similar ones in the past, but not in Test matches.) Chandimal had missed Alex Hales the ball before, a difficult one-handed chance down the leg-side. Tail-ender Steven Finn edged the very next ball, also bowled by the unfortunate Nuwan Pradeep, giving a routine chance, at hip height slightly to the wicket-keeper's right. Chandimal, perhaps remembering the ball before, had shifted his weight to his left foot, as if the ball was bound to come down the slope at Lord's and would, if it took either edge, take the inside one. Completely wrong-footed, he did not move to the ball at all, and it flew to the boundary behind him for four runs.

The really good wicket-keepers, like the top batsmen, remain poised and ready to go either way, for as long as possible. They move late, but surely and quickly. They don't miss chances like this, let alone not get a glove on them.

Another feature of keeping at Lord's (and indeed of fielding at slip there) is that the ball sometimes dips or swerves after it has been edged. I don't know if this is more frequent there than elsewhere, or why, assuming it is, this should be so. But it certainly happens. It may have been a similar wobble or dip that foxed Jonny Bairstow in that same match, when an edge from opener Dimuth Karunaratne hit him on the thigh rather than the gloves.

Bairstow and Chandimal are not alone; they are part of a trend. They gave the impression of having been fashioned into the role, not 'to the manner born'. Many cricketing skills have improved over the decades; fielding, athleticism, hitting the ball over the bowler's head, improvisatory stroke-play, swing bowling (in particular reverse swing), and (surprisingly) leg-spin. Unlike wicket-keeping. Long ago, we were of course pleased if our keepers could score runs, but we put a higher premium on their unique skills as keepers than is done in the era of T20s. Nowadays, the first consideration for selection in this position seems to be: how good a batsman is he? How fit and athletic, how quick and resourceful in getting up to the stumps? How busy in preventing singles?

There are pay-offs, of course. One is epitomized by the freeing up of Bairstow's batting. Having two strings to his bow, he can play a wider range of notes. I remember Alan Knott saying that he could never have developed his own idiosyncratic batting style had he not been primarily in the side for his keeping.

And some of those who started in this way became better and better at the skill. I think of people such as Bairstow himself, but also keepers of earlier eras, such as Jim Parks, Matt Prior, Alan Gilchrist and Jeffrey Dujon. With all, proficiency in the specialist skill grew on the back of their skill and, in some cases, their brilliance as batsmen.

Nevertheless, wicket-keeping as an art, a special craft on a par with that of a fast bowler or a spinner, is less and less in evidence. Too often even international keepers look like fielders with gloves on.

Most counties in the old days would have had a master of the trade, capable of standing up to medium-fast bowlers, or against spinners on uncovered pitches. He would take chances that an amateur in the role would never catch, and would also lift the side in the field. Everything revolved around him. These professional keepers were deft, shrewd, often unobtrusive. I am thinking of cricketers such as Keith Andrew of Northants, Jimmy Binks of Yorkshire, Bob Taylor of Derbyshire, Eifion Jones of Glamorgan, Derek Taylor of Somerset, or Roy Sweetman and Arnold Long of Surrey. Knott himself rated Wasim Bari, of Pakistan, as the best keeper of his time. Another excellent exponent was Syed Kirmani of India, who kept to the four great Indian spinners. He hardly spent any time standing back.

Most of them had style too, making the job look easy, though I remember a comment by the pragmatic Wally Grout of Australia, when asked whether to catch the ball with fingers down or up: 'Catch it whatever way you like,' he said. 'But catch it!'

So here are pieces on four wicket-keepers I've admired.

43

ELEGANCE

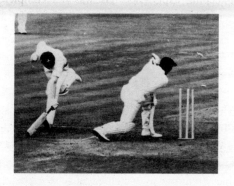

John Murray had a remarkable career spanning neatly the third quarter of the last century, since 1950 when, at the age of fifteen, he came on the MCC staff, having learned his cricket at the Rugby Boys' Club in Kensington. There were no facilities at his school, but the Boys' Club, for whom his father had also played, had a good ground and gave him the opportunity to play competitive cricket, football and boxing. J. T. was talented in all these sports – he was offered terms by Brentford in 1952, and was a champion junior boxer in his area.

He decided early on to concentrate on cricket. The start of his wicket-keeping career was fortuitous; the regular keeper broke his finger during a game and John stepped in. From 1953 to 1955 he played for a strong RAF team. He took over from Leslie Compton at Middlesex at the end of 1955, won his cap the next year, and was for twenty years an automatic choice for Middlesex. He played for England between 1961 and 1967, and went on MCC tours to all the major countries. I was surprised to discover that he played only twenty-one Tests. In my memory he was as much the England wicket-keeper of most of the 1960s as Knott was of the 1970s. He broke Herbert Strudwick's world record of 1,493 dismissals from behind the stumps; Murray's tally was 1,527, including 1,270 catches, also a record.

By the time he became a regular county player, he had had very little wicket-keeping experience. He was not completely confident of his own ability until 1961 and his first series for England. He never worried – nor did he need to – about standing back; he was superlatively agile and reliable. He regarded standing up as the real test of one's ability. A feature of his career was his alliance, for both Middlesex and England, with off-spinner Fred Titmus, who was three years older than him. Fred was not easy to keep wicket to. For one thing, he bowled very straight; for another, he only really spun some deliveries. And Lord's used to be, in my limited experience of keeping there, a harder pitch to stand up on than most, because the bounce was unreliable. Fred and John helped each other enormously, but I should say that the debt Fred owed John was the greater, since the latter so often could 'feel' what sort of pace Fred should bowl at on a particular pitch, on which line, and so on.

My clearest image of his keeping is of the way he caught the ball. There could be no better model – fingers down, hands relaxed, a long easy 'give' to one side or other of his body.

During his later years – I can't speak of the earlier part of his career – his keeping could, I think, be criticized in two ways. Sometimes he stood a little deep, though on pitches with variable bounce the right distance is hard to gauge. Second, when standing up, he tended to take the ball on the leg-side with his feet a long way from the stumps, so that batsmen had more time to get back, and the elegance of his 'take' – the long 'give' – lost mini-seconds in getting his hands forward for a potential stumping. However, it may well be that overall his results were better his way, in that although a few near-chances did not become chances, fewer were missed.

John was always an entertainer, a man for the occasion. He often saved his best county performances for Middlesex's greatest rivals, Surrey and Yorkshire (three of his nine Championship centuries were against Yorkshire). He was less likely to sparkle on a damp Thursday at Ashby-de-la-Zouch. His whole game, especially his keeping, gave an impression of ease, such that when I first really noticed him, probably in 1961 when I had my county debut as his substitute during a Test match, I felt he was inimitable. I could derive none of the reassurance that seeing, say, Ken Barrington bat had given me earlier that same season, the sense of a shared frailty. Barrington seemed always to have to try and often to struggle; Murray seemed not to need to.

This impression was, of course, immature and partial. J. T., like everyone else, had to work at his skills. He says himself that quite often he had to 'turn on' a performance when the body was unwilling and the mind bored; that his style was something he could put to use as a professional when initially his heart was not in it. I do not mean that he merely went through the motions. We whistle to raise our spirits. There is a respectable, anti-Stanislavski theory of acting which says that the actor should let feeling follow bodily movement and gesture, rather than the other way round.

At his best, J. T. was also wonderfully fluent as a batsman, especially against fast bowling (he was a fine hooker), and against spin (he used his feet and hit beautifully over the top). His heart was not always fully in his batting. He agrees that he never worked at it as he would have done if it had not been his second string. And it is unlikely that anyone could be both a front-line batsman and a wicket-keeper over a long period in county cricket without losing something of his zest for and concentration on the latter job. For a man with such talent, he was too often bowled, both 'through the gate', and by just missing a straight ball. He was less likely to succeed against bowlers he regarded as blatantly second-rate.

He was exceptionally elegant in all that he did on the field. He stressed the importance of rhythm and balance. John's own mannerisms, the tips of the gloves touched together, the peak of the cap touched, helped to give him the feeling of relaxed rhythm that came across so characteristically. Of his contemporaries as keepers he most admired Wally Grout, who was 'never on the ground except when actually taking a catch'.

Retiring gracefully, in any walk of life, requires strength of personality. One regrets past shortcomings, now one knows but cannot do, bitterness – often a defence against recognition of loss – may poison the withdrawal. For a cricketer, retiring may bring additional worries; unlike the footballer he is often considered too old for a new career, but unlike the pensioned-off bank manager, too young for paddling with trousers rolled.

J. T. retired, as he played, with grace, warmth and a sense of timing. There could hardly have been a nicer crowning of a splendid career than for his last match to be the Gillette Cup Final (except perhaps winning it), followed a few months later by recognition in the New Year's Honours List as an MBE. He was not bitter about retiring; he was, rather, proud to have achieved so much, and touched by the response of friends and supporters.

He worked hard over the last few years towards a second career. He joined D. H. Robins's company, and continued when retired to work for the same concern. He managed and captained Robins's sides in England, and was an important figure on his overseas tours. These occasions brought out some of the best in him – his ability to organize and handle people, his charm and good company, not to mention many masterful performances on the field. He was influential in deciding which of the younger players deserved opportunities to prove themselves in a wider sphere. He also served as a Test selector for two years (when I was captain). He resigned, partly, I think, because he could not agree with the selection of a player as wicket-keeper more, he thought, for his batting qualities than for his keeping.

When I asked him about his disappointments in cricket, the one thing he mentioned was that Middlesex had never won anything during his career, though in his last year we did at least appear in two Finals, which gave him exceptional satisfaction, and towards which he contributed greatly, both by his own performance and by his help and advice to me and others.

The best Middlesex sides he played for were, he reckoned, those of the late 1950s and early '60s, though he admitted that one tends to bring together in memory people who did not, in fact, overlap, or were not at their best together. During his time, Middlesex always lacked one or two top-class bowlers to support Titmus and, at various times, John Warr, Alan Moss and John Price.

I imagine too, though I've never heard him talk on the subject, that he must have been disappointed not to have been appointed captain of the county. He was vice-captain for five years, under both Titmus and Peter Parfitt, so he did of course captain the side when they were away. When he had the chance, he liked to attack. I remember once that he placed eight men around M. J .K. Smith on a placid pitch, and the ruse worked, Smith padding up to Price and being lbw for nought. At the same time he was fairly conventional in his ideas about tactics and field-settings.

He had strong views about the spirit in which the game should be played, which included looking to get on top whether batting or fielding, and unquestioning acceptance of the umpire's decision. It is a nice question whether J. T. might have been an outstanding county captain as well as everything else. I believe he was unlucky not to have had the chance to try.

John believed that standards of cricket declined overall during his playing career, and connected this with the lessening of discipline in cricket and life in general. For him, 'discipline' entailed hardship and knowing one's place. When he first came to Lord's, his place was clear, and low in the hierarchy. He never resented the fact that he had to sweep the stands, that he had only one session a week reserved for net practice, or that he was not allowed in the pavilion unless he was playing in the game. This made ambition clearer and stronger; he could see exactly what he wanted to get away from and what he wanted to achieve. By the mid-1970s, he believed it was too easy for young cricketers; too many of them thought they knew more than they did.

At the same time, J. T. was always aware of the limited rights a cricketer had in the face of arbitrary, whimsical or uninformed decisions by administrators, and of the limited say players had in the running of the game. He was one of those responsible for the launching of the Professional Cricketers' Association, and was for many years its Treasurer.

John Murray always enjoyed his life in cricket and outside. At a pre-season lunch in 1976, he said to the younger Middlesex players: 'Play properly, and enjoy yourselves.' He did both for twenty-five years.

44

'WHAT DO YOU THINK THIS IS, RANDALL?'

In 1977, Richard, the five-year-old son of an old friend, unselfconsciously modelled his batting stance and style on Rod Marsh. I put his picture in my first book, *The Return of the Ashes*. (His brother Tom appears on the same page, bowling like Thommo.)

I can see why. If you were to summon up a picture of the essence of belligerence, of pugnacity, on a cricket field, Marsh would be a prime candidate, whether with bat or gloves.

Whereas some players would grin, exchange a joke or a word, Rod would not. Not exactly growling, but resolutely, absolutely, intransigently, present, Marsh would not give an inch.

One story I love was of Derek Randall coming in to bat in the Old Trafford Test in that same series. He was, as always, scratching around the crease, fidgety, chattering. (Rodney Hogg later said of Randall: 'He's always trying to get my goat. He's always saying something stupid.'

I think it's fair to say that Randall's peculiar sense of humour didn't always endear him to Australians.) On this occasion, Marsh was up at the stumps. Randall said: 'Eh oop Marshy, how're you going?' Marsh barked back, 'What do you think this is, Randall? A fucking garden party?'

Wonderful line: 'garden party' – it makes me think of Buckingham Palace, of smoothness and gentility, of niceties. It is suggestive of 'perfidious Albion'. Almost as if Randall of Retford were one of the English toffs who so got (and presumably still get) up the noses not only of Australian larrikins but of ordinary residents of Nottinghamshire!

I like both sides of this story. And both characters. On one side the impish, irritating, fussy, provocative Randall, never short of a word, his restlessness of body and of mind a sign not only of abrasiveness but also of anxiety. And on the other, this pocket battleship of combativeness, who wouldn't waste his breath on an opponent, not on the field. Who expected and gave no quarter.

Marsh was a magnificent wicket-keeper and a more than useful aggressive batsman. He formed a vital part of Australia's emergence under Ian Chappell in the early 1970s as a power in world cricket, an emergence that had a good deal to do with the brief efflorescence of the Jeff Thomson/Denis Lillee partnership. 'Caught Marsh bowled Lillee' was as regular a dismissal as 'Caught Knott bowled Underwood'. Nicknamed 'Iron Gloves' after a poor debut (against England in 1970), the term could later only be used as one conveying admiration for his toughness.

Marsh was also the epitome of the old Australian virtue of mate-ship. It was in Melbourne in 1856 that workers (in the form of stonemasons) for the first time won the right for an eight-hour working day to be regarded as a full shift. Eight hours' work, eight for sleep and eight for yourselves. Stick by your mates, who equally stick by you. This attitude is, or perhaps was, not exactly class-less, since there was an atavistic sense of the oppressive presence of a class system that ran an empire, but it's as close as can be.

And though Australians have been known to sledge, to voice disruptive remarks half in and half out of the batsman's ear, I never heard any such from Rod. He simply got on with the job. I doubt that he ever appealed unless he thought there was a good chance it was out. Famously, he called back Randall at a tense stage of the Centenary Test at Melbourne earlier that same year, 1977, when he knew the ball had bounced as he rolled over to try to catch it. He would not allow such a decision to stand uncorrected.

(Though again, in typical Aussie style, Rodney said later that, as a matter of fact, not only had the ball not carried, but Randall hadn't hit it; but *that*, he added, was the umpire's business. Australians have a clear code of right and wrong. Never claim a catch if you know it's bounced, but never walk, and never question an umpire's decision on an edge, either.)

And after the game, or the series, there was a different Rod – genial, modest, respectful of the skills of others, even of Englishmen. When I wore the little plastic head-protector under my cap, I imagined he would scorn it – rather like the spectator at Nottingham who, when my cap, together with the guard, fell off while I was running between the wickets, shouted, 'Why don't you stick it on with a six-inch nail, Brearley?' But at the end of the series Marsh simply said, 'You're right, but it has to be bigger and stronger', and within six months virtually everyone was wearing helmets similar to what is now commonplace. And after the series in 1979–80, won 3–0 by Australia, he told me, kindly, that I'd played better, straighter that series than before. For an ageing English blocker, that felt like generous praise.

There really is a place in Australia called Bacchus Marsh, which is where Rod's nickname 'Bacchus' came from. But it can't have been entirely irrelevant that Bacchus was, two millennia ago, the Roman god of wine. His namesake enjoys the red stuff, even going so far in the direction of the British aristocracy to relish more than a single glass of MCC port.

But wait a minute. Being a mate has its other side. What about those within the team who aren't quite your mates?

I think there was also in Rod, though I've never talked to him about this in any depth, some feeling of hurt, anger and perhaps especially frustration, at the choice of Kim Hughes to captain Australia. When Greg Chappell made himself unavailable for the tour of England in 1981, Hughes was appointed captain. He was something of an Establishment favourite; the biography of him by Christian Ryan was titled *Golden Boy*. Handsome, dashing and personable, he was also untarnished (as the Australian Board would have seen it) by Packer (having been young and not established by 1977, when the whole extraordinary phenomenon broke out onto, and within, the cricket world).

Like his older colleagues, Marsh and Lillee, Hughes was from Western Australia. He was a fine player, though a touch erratic, his loose approach diametrically opposed to the steely technique and personality of, say, Ian Chappell. He was raw, keen, eager to impress, excitable, perhaps naïve. Hughes was chosen ahead of Marsh himself, who had had an excellent record captaining Western Australia. I imagine appointing Marsh would have been a step too far for the cricketing establishment.

Lillee later said frankly that Marsh should have been captain. Marsh's trenchant exterior only partly concealed a thoughtful, empathic and dynamic person. He may well have been the best captain Australia never had. John Inverarity, a fine captain of Western Australia himself, wrote: 'There are a number of good but very few outstanding captains. Rod was, certainly, one. People respected him and responded to him. He had an outstanding reading of the game and the tactics. If you worked out ten criteria for captaining a cricket team, he had a tick in every box.' Whereas of Hughes he said, bluntly: 'Mercurial. And such mercurial players are better off not bearing the burden of captaincy.'

A situation made for tension. The appointment was not easy either for Marsh or for Hughes. I recognized the scenario, as I had felt some of the same feelings, from the viewpoint of the younger intruder, when I became captain of Middlesex in 1971 (as I daresay John Murray did, from the opposite side). These situations are extremely difficult, on both sides. And at that time I may, like Hughes ten years later, have been, or appeared to be, unwilling or unable to listen and learn. When things started to go wrong for Australia in 1981, I imagine any tension became worse.

Establishing his authority over Marsh and Lillee cannot have been easy for Hughes. He and I had one conversation, just before the Oval Test in 1981, when we had already won the Ashes with the three remarkable victories that owed a huge amount to Ian Botham and to luck: Australia could easily have won the series 3–1 instead of losing it by that margin. Their best bowler during the series had been Terry Alderman, yet another Western Australian. Lillee, who had been unwell for much of the summer, was still a fine bowler, but not quite the great bowler he had been. Our conversation was about the problem of whether to give choice of ends to Lillee or to Alderman. A year or two before there would have been no question. But now?

It may be that mate-ship linked Marsh and Lillee in a way that left out the more naïve, sometimes narcissistic, less obviously tough (though physically courageous) Hughes.

Rod Marsh has always been completely straight. Perhaps this has sometimes meant that he can't hide his feelings of frustration and disappointment. But nor does he hide his feelings of joy and pride. I happened to meet him in a box during the 2004 Test match between England and the West Indies at Lord's, when Andrew Strauss scored 137 and Rob Key 221. Rod, who as the first Director of the England Coaching Academy at Loughborough had coached both players, was as happy as if he'd scored the runs himself.

In 2011 I became Chair of the MCC's World Cricket Committee, a think-tank on international cricket composed mainly of ex-Test players of various vintages. One of our very best appointments was Rod. He cares deeply for cricket, especially Test cricket. He speaks directly but considerately. He listens to what others say. He is delightful company. He is a true friend.

And I can't wait to attack a bottle of port with him when he's next in England.

45

THE FLEA

Alan Knott was a great cricketer. He was also, in my view, the best wicket-keeper of his time. He had a good physique for the job – short, low-to-the-ground, agile and quick (though he foresaw a new breed of tall keepers by analogy with tall goalkeepers, and maintained that he had to stretch so much because he was not particularly supple, especially in the hips). He had marvellous hands. Physically, he kept himself fit, and practised assiduously.

His technique was not classical; he took catches with one hand when he might have got two to the ball, and he sometimes dived when he could have reached the ball without falling. He had sound reasons for both – simply that for him these methods were more natural and more effective. His judgement about what to go for was unerring. As a first slip I always seemed to know when Alan would go for a catch in front of me, and I was never balked by him or distracted by any tentativeness on his part.

Standing up to the stumps, he took the low ball without bending his knees and with his legs together. This gave him the right amount of give, against his legs. Moreover, if he missed the ball with his hands, his pads would prevent byes, and if the edge beat the gloves, there was no knee or elbow sticking out to obscure first slip's view, or to deflect the ball.

His constant exercising was a reflection of his perfectionism, as was the care he took to have essential equipment in perfect order. He kept and rehabilitated an old bat especially for Tests; he spent the afternoon before the Melbourne Centenary Test in town getting a loose stitch from the webbing of a glove repaired, just in case he should uncharacteristically have to rely on the webbing to make a catch. He was also prepared to be unconventional in his gear, if it helped get the job done. He once saw the New Zealand wicket-keeper, Ken Wadsworth, struck on the inside of the knee by an awkward throw-in; his pad had swivelled round as he moved towards the ball and had left the knee unprotected. As a result, Knott took to taping his pads to his trousers rather than using the middle strap and buckle; he thereby also reduced chafing. He did not mind that the result looked untidy.

I have never known a cricketer who was less concerned with style for its own sake. Though brilliant, he eschewed the flamboyant. He stood back to medium-pacers more than his predecessors, not at all for safety-first reasons or to avoid errors, but as the result of a cool calculation as to the overall effectiveness to the side.

He would have been, in my book, a more or less automatic selection for any team on the strength of his keeping alone. With Derek Underwood, bowling his particular brand of almost medium-paced left-arm spin, he was unbelievably good, especially on rain-affected pitches.

When his batting was put into the scales, any possible doubt fell away. For he was also a genius, a minor genius, with the bat. Here too he was no purist for the sake of orthodoxy. Against fast bowling he realized that he had a better chance of playing a lifting delivery if he changed his grip so as to have his top hand behind the handle. This method enables a batsman to hold his hands high, in front of his face if necessary, and still keep the bat straight. He evolved a kind of French cricket technique for use when he first went in against the quickest bowlers; but soon took any opportunity to attack them, clipping the ball square on either side of the wicket, cutting deftly, often intentionally over the slips' heads. He reckons that if he were starting his career now he would learn to hook fast bowling, and cites the hours of practice Viv Richards went through in the nets against his Antiguan team-mate Andy Roberts during the torrid time he went through in the first four Tests (when he averaged 21). (In the last two, he scored 30, 101 50 and 98.)

Against fast bowlers, Knott's grip, stance and technique were totally different from those he adopted against medium-pacers and spinners. He might start an innings in an orthodox vein, but quickly ventured into the unusual. He played a sort of off-glide to good effect, especially against off-spinners.

His sweeping was unique. On a drying pitch at Canterbury, he once played fifteen consecutive balls from Phil Edmonds and John Emburey with this shot and never missed or mis-hit one. His secret was to get low, keep his head still, watch the ball and not try to hit it too hard. (Many of us could of course follow these instructions and still make a hash of it.) He was able to hit the same ball to fine leg or even in front of square with different versions of the sweep. Setting a field when he was in this mood was like playing chess against a Grand Master.

I remember an innings in the fourth Test against India, at Bangalore, in 1977. The pitch had deteriorated to the point where good spinners were almost unplayable (and India had three great spinners). Yet Knott, whom we nicknamed the Flea, kept dancing down the pitch to Bishan Bedi and Erapalli Prasanna, and chipping them, often against the spin, over mid-wicket or extra-cover. He finished up marooned on 81 not out, after an innings that was unparalleled in cheek and verve.

Behind all the idiosyncrasies as a batsman (as with his keeping) were the basic skills. His head was always steady, and he was capable not only of quixotic aggression, but also of long defensive innings. Completely unselfish, he was courageous too, physically, and also in terms of mental strength, having the guts, the confidence, even the stubbornness to stick to his method if he felt that he was right, whatever anyone else might think about him.

Personal health was one area in which these attitudes were expressed. If not hypochondriacal, Alan was at least keenly interested in the state of his own body. One evening in Delhi he fell ill in the middle of the night. Without delay, he knocked on the physiotherapist's door, bearing a sample of what had recently been in his intestines. He wanted no sketchily based diagnosis. He was equally fussy about what went into his stomach from the other end. No meat or cheese at the same meal, for instance. He drank little and avoided parties. He needed eight hours of sleep, yet had to have a couple of hours clear in the early morning for ablutions and exercises before breakfast (so it was not always easy to find room-mates for him on tour). After hurting his neck in two car accidents in the mid-1970s, he had his car seat remodelled. And he was so chary of draughts that he would come away in the team bus from a day's play in India wearing three sweaters, an anorak with the hood up, and dark glasses. The lack of a surgical mask must have been an oversight. He was never unfit for a Test, though once, in 1976, he played too soon, he felt, after breaking a finger.

Tactically he was sound, though not without his biases. He had an exaggerated respect for pace, and would usually advise his captain to keep the pacemen on. He sometimes over-rated players he knew best, though he was capable of hard judgements as when he said of a colleague that he had 'learned nothing during his years in the game'.

Politically he was involved in both the major cricketing 'rebellions' of his time – signing for Packer in 1977, and going on the South African Breweries tour of 1982. Typically, his views were well thought out, courteously expressed and tenaciously held.

The man is all of a piece, and at the heart of his life lie close family ties and religious convictions. Leaving his wife and son behind for four months at a time while he was on tour became an insupportable wrench for him. One of the attractions of World Series Cricket was the welcome given to families; he was able to take a flat in Sydney with his family and use it as his home base for the World Series season, whereas the English cricketing Establishment were in general less sympathetic to wives on tour, and in particular failed to understand his reasons and attitude. Some felt it outrageous that Knott should lay down conditions for being available to tour for England (that he should not be separated from his wife and young son for longer than a month).

He was not in an ordinary sense 'one of the boys', but he was a complete professional and team man. Even his stretching exercises on the field were viewed in some quarters with hostility, as if it were for show. Nothing could have been further from the truth. Traditionalists (a term that includes blimps), some of whom were suspicious of his idiosyncrasies, found it much easier to forgive his Kent and England team-mate, Derek Underwood, for joining Packer than to forgive and accept Knott.

To this day (2018) Knott remains I think the only one of the twenty England players who have played 85 or more Tests not to have been given a national honour. Though four others who played in the 1981 series have not received one, Knott, one of the most distinguished players in the side, stands out in this regard. I consider this prejudiced and unfair.

As for religion, he became a Christian in 1974. This, he said, changed his whole attitude to life. He came to see his own behaviour during the ill-tempered and probably badly umpired series in India in 1972–3 as reprehensible. From then on, he was an unfailing example of sportsmanship on the field.

He was generous to others. Paul Downton, who moved from Kent to Middlesex as he was unlikely to have a first-team place for some time, acknowledged the many tips and kindnesses received from Alan while on the Kent staff and afterwards. In 1977, when we won the Ashes at Headingley, Knotty seized a ball as a souvenir for the young Ian Botham, playing in his second Test, who was off the field injured at the end of the game.

Alan Knott's religious convictions also helped him to a more philosophical attitude to his own performance. He became less concerned about the *outcome* of his play, focusing more on simply trying as hard as he could, in ways he felt he was most likely to succeed. His view was that it is the inner attitude that counts most; the results will then look after themselves. He was utterly modest, and equally free of false modesty.

Alan Knott retired from the game (in 1985, aged thirty-nine) while still playing at a high standard. He was even then regarded by most of his fellow-professionals as the best 'keeper in England. Ray Illingworth said of him that he was 'streets ahead of any other wicket-keeper'. His decision to go was in part determined by an ankle injury that he was told could get worse if he carried on.

Knott was part of a great tradition of Kent wicket-keepers. His own fortieth birthday more or less coincided with Les Ames's eightieth, and Godfrey Evans's sixty-fifth, both great predecessors for Kent and England.

In my view, though many skills in the professional game have improved since Alan Knott's day, one that has not is wicket-keeping. Selectors have been inclined to pick fine batsmen who are stoppers; first slips with gloves on, rather than the skilled craftsmen of an earlier period. In retirement Alan coached for some time, but was not, I suspect, given the recognition he deserved or the opportunity to produce further England wicket-keepers comparable to himself. No job offer as specialist coach in the England set-up materialized. Perhaps this entered into Knott's decision, in 2002, to move to Cyprus. He and his wife, Jan, enjoy the beaches, playing tennis, dancing, and the sunshine. His son James played professional cricket for Surrey and Somerset, and is now head of sports administration and cricket at Stowe School.

Alan Knott was more than a cricketing genius. He was also wise, kindly and thoughtful, and his own eccentric person.

46

NOT YET THE KING OF ALBANIA

Kumar Sangakkara played his first Test for Sri Lanka in 2000, as wicket-keeper and batsman. Between then and June 2006, he played in sixty Tests, forty-seven of them as wicket-keeper. Over this period he averaged 46.90 – 68.15 in the thirteen as specialist batsman. From July 2006 to his retirement from Test cricket in 2015 he played in seventy-four Tests, averaging 65.65. (And these figures were slightly lower than they would have been had he not been asked by the Sri Lanka Prime Minister to play in two extra Test matches 'for the honour of the country' after he had announced his retirement.)

I have subscribed to the general view that the three finest batsman of the past twenty or twenty-five years were Sachin Tendulkar (India), Brian Lara (West Indies) and Ricky Ponting (Australia). But I wonder if in this judgement I failed to give due credit to Sangakkara, as also to the South African all-rounder, Jacques Kallis. There have of course been great wicket-keeper batsmen in the past; England's Les Ames of Kent and Alec Stewart of Surrey; and Australia's wonderful Adam Gilchrist. Sangakkara's overall Test average is 57.40 – the highest of the five. To mention just one further statistic: he reached 12,000 Test runs faster than any other player, taking twenty-three fewer innings than Tendulkar. And he kept wicket successfully and competently to the great spinner, Muttiah Muralitharan.

Kumar Sangakkara's batting was a perfect combination of skill and technique combined with gritty determination and application. He played as classically as anyone I saw, and combined this with total ambition, for side and for self. Others might be more flamboyant – Mahela Jayawardene, his own team-mate, comes to mind, a consummately, exquisitely wristy player, as does Virat Kohli. Joe Root is friskier than Sangakkara, not far off in technique, but not so sound.

Sangakkara was usually the rock around which his team's batting success, and sometimes its survival, was built. He was the most sturdy, the most correct, of them all. If he were a motor bike he'd be a Harley-Davidson – well-built, stable, packing a punch. The ball always made a solid clunking sound on his bat. He played with a steady head, strong body and hands, and exceptional ability both to judge length and line, and to adjust his balance accordingly. He made the bowlers bowl at him, but not with an exaggerated movement (*à la* Steve Smith), just an easy judgement and capacity to line up the balls he had to play. He moved seamlessly from defence to attack. I could not imagine a better model for a young cricketer.

In the Lord's Test against Sri Lanka in 2014, England scored 579 for 9 declared, Joe Root scoring a double century. In reply, Kumar Sangakkara, scored 147. It was a terrific match, which ended with Sri Lanka hanging on for a draw with nine wickets down.

This was Sangakkara's thirty-sixth Test century in his two hundred and tenth Test innings, an average of more than one every six innings. On the Friday night, he was 32 not out. In the morning, I reckoned his chance of scoring a hundred (it was to be his first in a Lord's Test) were about one in two, though he had to bat in cloud and some drizzle on the Saturday morning. His first ball, from Jimmy Anderson, squirted between body and stumps for two, but, apart from that, he himself could remember only one other false stroke in his 258-ball innings, when shortly before reaching his century he played Liam Plunkett airily between gulley and point. He is not a person to be fazed by near-misses or mistakes – after the lucky break early on Saturday morning, he soon 'creamed' Anderson through the covers for an effortless boundary.

I also saw him score two other centuries in England. Two weeks before the Lord's Test he had played a perfect one-day innings, scoring a run-a-ball hundred after taking twenty-four balls to score his first four runs.

I also watched him make a match-saving 119 at Southampton in 2011. The conditions there were more challenging for the batsman. The ball moved for the seamers, and sometimes bounced uncomfortably. Sangakkara was courageous and unflinching against Anderson, Chris Broad and Chris Tremlett (who had taken six wickets in the first innings), but never missed an opportunity to get forward and drive firmly whenever they pitched the ball up. These attacking shots were never more elaborate than a firm push, but his ability to put his body-weight and the full face of his bat behind the ball resulted in surprising power.

It was typical of him that planning and preparation had played a part in this success. He had arranged to arrive in England three weeks before the rest of the touring party, so that he could play two County Championship matches for Durham. There he had made small but definite changes in method. Instead of taking leg stump guard, he took middle-and-leg; he did away with the tap of the bat on the ground, and hardly moved at all. His aim was, by giving himself a stiller base, to enable himself to watch the swing longer, and to play the ball fractionally later.

I first met Kumar in Galle, Sri Lanka, during the third Test in 2007. Someone arranged a Q and A session one evening with him and me. Immediately, I was impressed by his physique, bearing and straightforward charm. His handshake was firm and strong, his body muscular, well toned. He frankly stated that his ambition was to be the best player in the world. I could see the ambition lived out in the determination to score that hundred at Lord's seven years later.

Kumar Sangakkara's interests and capabilities go well beyond cricket and the technicalities of wicket-keeping or batting, though I'm sure he brought many of his wider qualities to bear on these apparently narrow areas of life. One could sense that integrity shining through in his batting. He is also articulate and wide-ranging in thought. As a young man, he began a training in law, a process temporarily on hold during his cricketing career and his time as father of young twins.

He has been, and still is, a valued contributor to discussions on the World Cricket Committee, even though his cricketing commitments meant that he was until recently often unable to attend.

His Cowdrey Lecture (2011) stood out in an excellent field. He described with a novelist's touch the ordeal of being in the team bus blocked and shot at for twenty minutes on the way to the ground during the Test in Lahore:

> Everyone dived for cover and took shelter in the aisle or behind the seats. We were all lying on top of each other. Then the bullets started to hit. It was like rain on a tin roof. The bus was at a standstill, an easy target . . . Tharanga Paranavitana, on his debut tour, is next to me. He stands up, bullets flying all round him, shouting 'I have been hit' as he holds his blood-soaked chest. He collapsed onto his seat, apparently unconscious. I see him

and think: 'Oh my God, you were out first ball, run out the next innings, and now you've been shot. What a terrible first tour.' It is strange how clear your thinking is. I did not see my life flash by. There was no insane panic. There was absolute clarity and awareness of what was happening at that moment. I hear the bus roar into life and start to move. Dilshan is screaming at the driver, 'Drive . . . Drive.'

Fortunately, no one on the bus was killed. The bullet that hit Tharanga was lodged 'lightly in his sternum, the body of the bus tempering its velocity enough for it to be stopped by the bone'.

Sangakkara referred, movingly, to his family's taking in scores of refugees during the civil war, when he was a small boy.

In the talk he also told truth to power, robustly taking on the administrators of Sri Lankan sport for their self-interest, and for their lack of integrity and of commitment. He spoke frankly against the damaging interference by his government in his country's cricket.

In the early 1920s, C. B. Fry, described by John Arlott as 'the most variously gifted Englishman of any age', was apparently offered the vacant post of King of Albania. He turned it down. When Sangakkara retired from Test cricket in 2015, he was invited to be High Commissioner for Sri Lanka in London. Not quite a kingdom, but quite something for a sportsman not yet forty! He too turned the offer down. But it will be interesting to see what course he will take up for the second half of his life, both serving his country and developing himself and his own career.

PART 10

AESTHETICS

47

THE ART OF THE MASSES

Sport is the art of the masses. It might also be their – our – opium. Or our invitation to gang warfare – supporters who travel to fight, or who indulge in banal, dreary, unpleasant chanting.

But art comes into it.

I once saw a photograph in a Sunday newspaper. A footballer had just headed the ball, which was on its way into the goal. The football was in the foreground, but not in close focus. What was in focus was a section of the crowd. I was impressed by the intent expression on every face. Of perhaps a hundred people, not one was looking elsewhere. Each face expressed pure concentration; there was no smiling, no yawning, no distraction, no anger. Simply absorption in this dramatic moment. These supporters may identify with the scorer, or with the goalkeeper who has failed to reach the ball in time. But they also occupy a more neutral, less partisan, position. It's the same when a fielder is about to take (or drop) a catch on the boundary.

What else – apart from the arts – brings people together in absorption and fascination, in relation to moments or passages of play, in activities that have no direct bearing on everyday worries or the more obviously serious matters of life?

I am not denying that element in sport. Football – like art, music or literature – is a more serious matter, as we heard from Bill Shankly, than mere matters of life and death.

And these shared moments, short or long, which are exhilarating, enlivening and passionate, have much to do with aesthetics, which includes beauty. Kevin Pietersen, captaining England for the second time, stood at mid-on or mid-off while Sachin Tendulkar scored his match-winning, undefeated century at Chennai in 2008. Pietersen told me after that game that it had been an honour for him to be in the pound seats, as it were, to watch the Little Master play. *Watching* someone *play* . . . yes, appreciating skill, elegance, timing, poise, balance and so on. It's not unlike watching dance, or theatre.

Of course, Pietersen had, or should have had, other matters on his mind, other priorities; not least how to stop this show, how to set Tendulkar challenges or temptations to do what he least wanted to – in other words, to get him out. But alongside that, there was the sheer aesthetic pleasure of seeing his batting up close. I had similar feelings when Greg Chappell was batting against us. And I once stood at extra-cover at Cambridge to the great Garry Sobers. Apart from my alarm at the likelihood that he would middle one of his wonderful off-drives – played with the highest back-lift, the purest pendulum of bat-swing, and the most complete follow-through, sometimes slapping himself in the middle of the back with his bat at the end of the great arc of the stroke – straight at me, I have a vivid image from that afternoon fifty years ago of the style, the power, the classicism and freedom of his arms and hands, and recall it better than I remember most of the pictures I've seen in art galleries.

My Middlesex colleague, Mike Smith, who played in five one-day internationals, but was never picked for a Test match, remarked that, all things being equal in terms of efficiency, international selectors should select those who play with style. One proper aim, he implied, was to give value to *grace* in selecting for the biggest showcase of the game.

Pleasure of this kind occurs at every level of skill. Moreover, the pleasure of watching mimics the pleasure of playing. As spectators, we imagine our way into the mind-set of the sportsman, we occupy his or her body-mind. Freud said, in accounting for aesthetic pleasure, that we are moved by *Oedipus the King* because we all in our unconscious are little Oedipuses. The role resonates. Similarly, we become mini-Federers as we watch Roger play a cross-court forehand, or mini-Warnes when Shane bowls a perfect leg-break, or mini-Chappells when we see Greg playing a back-foot stroke off his hips with sumptuous elegance. It's not that we are under an illusion. We know we're not Federer. But we enter the mind-set. We know they are beyond us, but just for a moment we have a sense of its possibility (or at least its imaginability).

I once heard a small boy say excitedly to his friend while watching a firework display: 'Look how I dance, look how I jump.' These pleasures are as much aesthetic as sensory.

And we all, at every level, have our moments. Warne bowled the ball of the century; on the village green the blacksmith (or computer scientist) bowls a ball that pitches on middle and hits the top of off. Not often, of course, but who does? For the weekend cricketer, as for us all, the dream of perfection, occasionally intimated if not achieved, is one of the lures that keep him at it, keep him turning up at Lower Slaughter, or Ambleside, or at the local recreation ground or wherever, in the hope of dreams coming true.

Even now, in my mid-seventies, I had an explicit and detailed dream of playing a perfect on-drive, my balance exactly right, weight going into the stroke, the ball speeding through the gap between stumps and mid-on. In 1979, I stood at mid-on while Sunil Gavaskar, on his way to 221 for India against England at the Oval, toyed with me. He could play the same ball in just the way I recently dreamed it, or he could at the last millisecond turn his wrists and play it to my right. The precision of timing, placement and sheer deftness was a thing of beauty.

Timing and placement: I was privileged to be asked by art critic David Sylvester to discuss the aesthetics of sport and in particular cricket, of which he was very fond, and these were the two qualities we focused on to start with, along with a degree of repeatability.

In writing about Tom Cartwright, I compared his values with those of Caleb Garth, George Eliot's character in *Middlemarch*. She writes of Garth's valuing the 'myriad-headed, myriad-handed labour by which the social body is fed, clothed and housed . . . All these sights in his youth had acted on him as poetry without the aid of poets. His early ambition had been to have as effective a share as possible in this sublime labour.'

In response to that comment Sylvester said: 'You're talking about the aesthetic satisfaction which the poet gets, I take it, from finding exactly the right word . . . *the* word you need for that line at that moment.'

'Poetry without the aid of a poet.' Art without the aid of the artist. Batting and bowling, these humdrum activities with bits of willow and lumps of cork and leather, may, at best, be poetic, artistic expressions. Something is done just right. All is in balance. Poetry in action.

Some of the best cricket writers have emphasized these links with art. In *Beyond a Boundary*, C. L. R. James writes about himself as a young boy, watching cricket standing on a chair in the bedroom of his grandmother's house behind the bowler's arm at Tunapuna recreation ground, Trinidad.

Here was 'shaped one of my strongest early impressions of personality in society', he writes. There follows a description of a neighbour, Matthew Bondman, a ne'er-do-well, an

> awful character . . . generally dirty . . . would not work . . . an almost perpetual snarl. He would often without shame walk up the main street barefooted 'with his planks on the ground', as my grandmother would report . . . But Matthew had one saving grace – Matthew could bat. More than that, Matthew, so crude and vulgar in every aspect of his life, with a bat in his hand was all grace and style.

And his grandmother's 'oft-repeated verdict' on Matthew – 'good for nothing except to play cricket' – puzzled James. How could a person's ability at cricket make up for his 'abominable way of life'?

James goes on to quote an eighteenth-century account of the great cricketer William Beldham: 'It was a study for Phidias to see Beldham rise to strike . . . Men's hearts throbbed within them, their cheeks turned pale and red. Michelangelo should have painted him.'

Thus, James's childhood passion for cricket touches quickly on aesthetics, especially as revealed in classical Greece and in the Renaissance (he refers to the impact of Bondman's batting – 'a long low "Ah" came from many a spectator and my own little soul thrilled with recognition and delight'. Phidias and Michelangelo should have sculptured Beldham's cut shot, which the eighteenth-century cricket writer lyricizes.) Thus, understanding cricket at James's level includes not only seeing its place in society, but also knowing on one's pulses its aesthetic appeal.

It is a nice question how far beauty lies in the outcome of an action. Is salvation achieved by works or by faith, by successful actions in the world, or by right attitudes? When David Gower, the languid genius of left-handed batsmanship, caressed the ball through the covers with effortless ease, and impeccable timing and placement, was his stroke any different from the one where the ball deviated a few centimetres, found the edge, and was caught at slip? Had elegant beauty degenerated into a careless waft? Would we have been right to bemoan and castigate his 'carelessness', his not going on? Yet both strokes were identical, both balls pitched in the same place, at the same speed, perhaps from the same bowler. Had these unpredictable centimetres turned virtue into vice, beauty into ugliness (the 'waft')? If we ignored the fate of the ball, we have exactly the same movements of the batsman. Phidias could have constructed his sculpture on the basis of either.

Yet outcome does, must, come into it. Partly because we see the event as a whole. But also because part of the aesthetic beauty in a person's actions lies in truthful attention. It involves seeing things in the world for what they are. Gavaskar had a mental image of exactly where the fielders, and the stumps, were, and on form he could place the ball into the gaps, even wrong-footing a fielder to make the gap wider. All too often we refuse to see what is in front of our eyes as a result of wishful or lazy thinking. We go for glory shots. We opt out of the need to embed the precise field in our mind's eye.

We are suckers for temptation, as I was when caught second ball of Sarfraz Narwaz.

And aesthetics is not just a matter of skin-deep beauty. There are the signs of effort and of inner conflict. We admire not only the elegance but also the sheer bloody-mindedness of the beleaguered Mike Atherton, say. Like Rembrandt in his self-portraits, he was intransigent, willing to face whatever came at him. As Maurice Leyland, the Yorkshire batsman from the 1930s, said: 'Fast bowling keeps you honest.'

Scyld Berry compares with sculptures by Donatello, Bernini, Castagno and others, an early action photograph of Wally Hammond playing a cover drive at Sydney in 1928. The picture was taken on a 'Long Tom – a new type of camera between four and six feet long' – by English-born photographer Herbert Fishwick, who had settled in Australia as a youth. Berry stresses the structure of the photograph, the triangles, the way the lines of the feet and gloves of wicket-keeper Bert Oldfield move into the also-horizontal lines of the batsman's back leg. He also stresses the power, lightness and poise of the latter's feet. He compares Hammond's power – the strong shoulder and back muscles to be seen through the shirt, the stride forward – with various sculptures of the young David with his sling, victor over Goliath. He sees all as representations of masculine power and grace.

I admire the attempt, but I think Berry goes too far in trying to capture in rules the essence of form. For instance, he values, as did conventional accounts of batsmanship from the late nineteenth century onwards, front-foot shots over back-foot ones (as when 'getting on the front foot' means being positive and taking the initiative, and its opposite, 'being stuck on the back foot', means indecision and tentativeness), and off-side strokes over leg-side ones. The pull shot, for instance, is 'the most primitive shot, the nearest to natural. It may even be termed "savage"' – perhaps he means closer to baseball. Whereas my dream was of that difficult stroke, the on-drive, and one of the images that stays with me is of Greg Chappell's off-the-hip ability to guide the ball through square leg off the back foot, which unlike most players, he could do with upright elegance and grace. Then there is Ranji's leg-glance, and the beauty, power and courage of Botham's hook shots off his eyebrows. And there are various forms of lithe and whirlwind beauty in bowling, not only the classical, sideways on, high front arm, of Berry's exemplar, Ted McDonald, the Australian fast bowler of the 1920s.

Like Sylvester, Berry emphasizes outcomes. He says the picture would lose its perfection if the ball had in fact bowled Hammond, and dislodged the bails.

I suggest that aesthetics also includes the appeal of the ugly, the depiction of the shrewd, the determined, even of the absent – Simon Barnes writes of Gower: 'People said Gower would be better if he put his mind to it. It seemed to me that Gower's basic strength was that he didn't put his mind to it. Rather he gave himself up to his gift.'

It's hard to sum up the roots of beauty, let alone of aesthetic appeal. But that it exists, that we find in sport approaches to perfection, that sport offers countless examples of grace, style, courage and fortitude, of this I have no doubt.

Not so different: driving Derek Underwood
for four (MCC v. Cambridge University, 1964).

48

THE BEAUTIFUL GAME

Recorded in David Sylvester's London house on 21 April 2001, only six weeks before he died, this interview is a typically passionate and energetic affirmation of his enjoyment of life, art and cricket. A fuller version appeared in London Recordings, *a posthumously published collection of Sylvester's interviews.*

DS: This interview is meant to focus on a topic – the differences and likenesses between the aesthetics of sports and the aesthetics of arts. You're peculiarly qualified to talk about these, first because you've been a professional sportsman and a successful captain of your country, second because you're a professional psychoanalyst and third because you spend a great deal of your time as a consumer of the arts, all of them.

As a point of departure, the other day I heard a phrase used by a television announcer giving notice of various sports programmes. Out of the blue he said: 'Timing, that's what sport is about – timing.' This made me ask myself whether this remark was a truism.

MB: Timing. If you play a stroke as a batsman or bowl a ball as a bowler, timing is of the essence. There is an exquisite feeling attached to timing a ball perfectly, which is one of the deep reasons for playing sport. It is the moment when you get something exactly right. But it isn't only a matter of timing; there's also placing. And a third element is repeatability. It is all very nice to time a shot right, but it's even nicer to feel one is doing it reliably as well. I remember playing a shot off Garry Sobers when the ball went like a rocket to the cover boundary, timing and placing both perfect, but actually I knew it was a fluke. I let my hands go in the direction of the ball, with minimal footwork, and just happened to hit it sweetly past the fielder; the ball bounced back off the wooden fence in front of where the old Tavern had been. The pleasure would have been greater had there been more sense that I might do it again when an opportunity arose.

DS: You're talking about timing *and* placing. You're talking about the aesthetic satisfaction which the poet gets, I take it, from finding exactly the right word for that rhyme, *the* word that you need for that line at that moment. You get the feeling that it's the only possible word. My question here is: to what extent is that experience echoed in the spectator? How does the spectator's pleasure in seeing it relate to the performer's pleasure in doing it? And does the painter, when he does it with a stroke of the brush, get that same satisfaction?

MB: Well, you'd have to tell me the answer to that last question. But I imagine he does. I imagine there must be something similar when, after a struggle, one finds the right thing. As to your other question, yes, certainly in sport, the spectator picks up, shares in, that satisfaction. There are two essential points of view in the aesthetics of sport, which you've raised at once: that of the performer and that of the spectator. I think the latter engages with, identifies with, and dis-identifies with the agent in the sport in a way parallel to what happens when we look at a picture. In a way the viewer is freer than the player because of the distance and detachment, which enables him to have a full range of thoughts and imaginings, whereas the player is pressed in upon by the exigencies of the next ball and by the flow of the game. Indeed one mistake a batsman makes is to be carried away by his own excellent form. In your own writing on art you take advantage of this freedom and space to identify and then dis-identify from the painter's activity. You allow yourself to imagine what he might have been up to. You also come back to the particular viewpoint of the watcher. A similar experience is available to the attentive spectator of sport.

Certainly watching sport gives people an experience of utter absorption in an event, inducing a certain identification with the player on the field. Spectators oscillate between partisanship and a more neutral point of view. Such a shifting of viewpoints is not unlike what I do in my work as a psychoanalyst. In that role I am constantly drawn by the patient to see things from his point of view. And this is essential . . . But I also need to dis-identify from this, and identify with others in the story that the patient is telling. I must also inhabit my own point of view, as his interlocutor, or as the person he is unconsciously trying to affect.

In art criticism there's room for an imaginative consideration of how the model is being used in the making of a painting, how the painter treats her (or him) visually. This opens up reflection on how she or he might feel in relation to such a mode of looking. (A crucial part of work with patients in psychoanalysis is how the patient feels looked at.) The critic/viewer enlarges his take on the picture by standing imaginatively in the shoes of painter, painted and spectator.

DS: When a goal is scored, there is a mixture of placing and timing. As the spectator there's no doubt that one's own reactions and the reactions of the scorer and of other players are almost identical. It's that mixture of placing and timing that causes the goalkeeper to miss the ball. He dives a millisecond too early or a millisecond too late. It can be either – we see penalties scored when the goalkeeper dives too early, and the guy shooting the goal puts the ball where he had just been. It's a mixture of timing and placing. In a painting, we get this tremendous satisfaction that a mark is in exactly *that* place and no other. Now, the first thing you did when I talked about timing was to bring in placing. My question is: can we talk about timing as distinct from placing? Are we not talking about placing/timing rather as if we were talking about space/time? Are spacing and timing not the same?

MB: Well, no, they're not. There is a space difference between playing a perfectly timed cover drive straight to a fielder; and next ball I play exactly the same shot but three yards to his right. The latter gives me more satisfaction, but the timing might be identical.

DS: Ah, and this is the key question. *Is* the timing the same? Isn't that placing completely tied up with the timing? Is the shot in fact perfectly well-timed if it goes straight to the fielder? Does the batsman feel the same satisfaction in his muscles when that happens?

MB: I think he does. But he's disappointed as well.

DS: He's disappointed, but is the feeling, the physical feeling, the same?

MB: I think I have two answers here. One is yes, it (often) is. I play the shot, feel the pleasure, look up, and am delighted or frustrated as the case may be. The other is when I have the picture of the field-setting properly in mind, and subliminally adjust my shot just right, so that it bisects the fielders. Then the full aesthetic pleasure, in muscles and mind, is as you suggest. But the other situation is common enough. In golf each action is simply you and the ball [DS: Yes and the hole.]

MB: You play a shot and you hit it dead right. You get that feeling through your hands of perfect timing, you look up, and you think, oh God, it's too high, or too far, it was the wrong club, it's in the bunker. You don't lose the feeling because the outcome is not the desired one. Perhaps there's a difference between the ordinary player and the top pro, though I'm not sure.

DS: Well this is crucial because, when I made the analogy with the brush mark that's in the right place, if it's not in the right place then what the hell is the timing?

MB: The funny thing about a painting is that although you can see it from different angles and from different distances, once finished it exists in a timeless way. It might deteriorate and so on, but it's there, that's it. From the point of view of the end product does it matter how it was constructed? Or is this an ignorant remark?

DS: Think again, because this is the crux.

MB: Well, the point I'm trying to make is that with a painting the thing you've got exists in space, but doesn't change through time. A piece of music obviously changes over time. A cricket stroke exists in time and place. You could take a photograph or film of a batsman without including the fielder; he's playing a perfectly correct stroke. And you could be sure of that, and agreeably pleased by that, without having to know whether the ball goes past the fielder or straight to him.

DS: Well, there is a point here which may be relevant. Of course, in music, a good example of timing is rubato. Whether the player gets the rubato right or wrong decides whether it comes out sounding poignant or sentimental, that's timing. And it's absolutely crucial to the writing and to the performance or to the combination of the two. But what I wanted to ask you – and this may be where sport and art are profoundly different – is: are art and sport profoundly different in that in sport there is a result, in a work of art there is no result? In sport there is a difference between the shot that produces four runs, and the one that produces none because cover-point stops it. The result counts.

MB: Yes I agree, that is a difference. And this may be partly why sportsmen characteristically underplay the aesthetic. They talk in terms of cost-effectiveness. They sneer at pretty play. Now of course one would sneer at pretty art as well, one might do that.

DS: Yes, exactly, exactly.

MB: But the sportsman would ask: 'How many runs could you get for that shot?' I learned a lesson many years ago, when I played a pretty late cut against an off-spinner. The ball turned, kept low, and hit my off-stump. M. J. K. Smith, the England captain at that time, asked me: 'How many runs would you have got if you'd played that shot exactly right?' I said, 'One.' And he said, 'So was it worth it?' You see what I mean? If the stroke would have been worth four if I'd played it properly, it just might have been worth the risk. But despite what I said before, aesthetics enters into this value-for-money business.

DS: Go on.

MB: If a batsman shovels a ball through mid-wicket in an ungainly way, with a lot of bottom hand, and manages to time it and place it right and the ball goes for four, this doesn't give us the same satisfaction as seeing Viv Richards, say, stroking the same ball through the same space, imperiously, with a sense of inevitability. And the reason for this satisfaction is partly that it is beautifully done, but also that it's more reliable. As a spectator or player you say to yourself, 'Ah, that man can play the shot at will.' I've known bowlers who dreaded bowling against Viv. But with the first man, the shoveller, you might as a bowler think, 'I'll try that again, a bit slower, and he might well miss it.' Cost-effectiveness is related to classical form or correctness of form. We can see intuitively that with a straight bat you're more likely to make contact with the ball than if you play across the line, or with a crooked bat.

First, there is this element of outcome that enters into how we enjoy and appreciate sport, which is lacking in a work of art. Nevertheless – second point – our pleasure in that outcome is partly aesthetically based. Classic form develops for the purpose of reliable effectiveness. There is a third point, which I touched on before, and that is that when a batsman has the whole field-placing in his mind, and is able to put the ball exactly where he wants to, this gives pleasure to him and to the spectator.

DS: Beautiful. But if so, what is the art equivalent of cost-effectiveness?

MB: I've tried to think about that and I don't know that there is one. There must be limitations in any medium. There must be difficulties in expressing what one wants to in that medium. Is part of what we appreciate in art to do with making the best of a bad job? Making something that should work against you work for you?

DS: I'm not forgetting this point about cost-effectiveness, but maybe we can get at it in this way. The other day I was watching a Sri Lankan batsman playing some good spin bowling and playing it with beautiful correctness. I was responding to the sheer correctness of his straight bat. Was that pleasure an academic intellectual recognition, or was it an aesthetic response to the correctness?

MB: Yes O Socrates!

DS: Both.

MB: I think so.

DS: It's not something that you would only recognize if you'd been coached as a schoolboy and learned how you're supposed to play?

MB: No, but you'd have to know the game. Just as you have to know something about painting to appreciate a work. You can't just listen to Bartók or Beethoven, or look at Pollock, say, and understand it without knowing something. Similarly with a game. Knowledge of cricket might not be coached, it might be learned just from watching or playing in the streets.

DS: It might be learned from watching?

MB: Yes, it might.

DS: But then it would feed back to effectiveness?

MB: It would. The two are indissolubly linked. There would be many other factors besides correctness in our appreciation. I too saw some of the recent Sri Lanka–England series on television, and I loved watching England's Graham Thorpe bat. He played many classical shots both defensive and attacking. But what he also was able to do was take a calculated chance, as a deliberate ploy. When Muralitharan, the great Sri Lankan spin bowler, bowled what were to him, a left-hander, vastly turning leg-breaks, Thorpe on a couple of occasions planted his front foot down the pitch, and smote the ball over mid-wicket against the spin. He played these unorthodox strokes for a specific purpose, as part of a strategy. He did it to persuade bowler and captain to take away close catchers, and put them in the outfield. If you saw this shot out of context, you'd say it was close to a 'cow-shot', too risky. You'd hope the youngsters weren't watching. But in fact it was an exceptionally good piece of batting. I thought he outwitted the opposition captain and bowler by this willingness to take a risk. The result was that Thorpe was then free to work ones and twos by pushing the ball with minimal risk into the big open spaces on the leg-side. These were big shots, on which a lot depended. That is an important part of batting skill.

DS: But in painting and music too, one of our great excitements lies in our response to risk.

MB: I agree.

DS: If the composer or painter can bring it off, risk makes it all more exciting. Risk in art and risk in sport are very close.

MB: Yes I agree. And in both activities there is the need to balance risk and safety.

DS: You know that a painter could have chosen an easier solution to resolve a compositional problem, but if he chooses the easier one, there won't be the same frisson.

MB: Yes. You know, there's another interplay, closely related but different, which these examples remind me of, and that's the one between spontaneity and planning. I'm reminded of the remark attributed to the old Nottinghamshire cricketer, George Gunn, that 'Most batsmen pay too much attention to the bowling. They don't go with the tide.' If you're batting at your best, there is a constant oscillation between absorption and relaxation, of freedom and at the same time prudence, care, planning. Thorpe's risk was based on a definite decision; he set himself to do just that when the ball was in the right spot, he'd worked out that the risk was worth the gamble. But at other times he, like others, would just do something without conscious planning or thinking. Even in the state I've described, he was on the go, on the look-out for a chance to do something different. Even in this mind-set there's this combination of conscious and unconscious. Donald Tovey, the music historian and critic, made the same point when he said that if you asked the centipede to concentrate on each of its legs, and move each one intentionally, it would immediately fall into the ditch. But at the same time, there will have been hours of focused attention on each finger's movements for a violinist, say. I imagine there is an analogy in art to having a game plan for an innings, or in having a strategy in the field.

DS: Of course. But the question is, do we actually get an aesthetic excitement as spectators from responding to that planning?

MB: I think the answer is, potentially yes. It's part of what the discerning spectator finds enjoyable. You can observe a batsman building an innings, going through an immense struggle in the early stages, let's say. You can see him gradually opening up, having phases in his innings, and you can get satisfaction in that.

DS: Such as you get from seeing a Henry Moore, or from reading a Henry James?

MB: Yes, the intelligence behind writing, behind the work . . .

DS: And the aesthetic satisfaction you get from the intelligence behind the writing.

MB: Yes exactly. One gets a sense of the person going about his work, doing his job. You describe this in some of your work. You imaginatively evoke how a painter has produced this thing that you have in front of you, what sort of processes may have gone on, and sometimes you confirm this by conversation with him. This leads into the range of human qualities one can perceive in someone's performance. Courage is an obvious example. In sport it's very obvious.

DS: Of course, you can see this in the way a group of actors works together as a team; it's like a team in sport. And you watch the interplay of those actors.

MB: That's right. And you get a sense of the director too, sometimes.

DS: And a sense of the director. Absolutely.

MB: I don't know how much that team-effort applies in art, where the work is usually done by someone on his own.

DS: It's something you get more of a sense of in collaborative art. Yes. We've been talking away about timing, ostensibly. What do we really mean when we say that the timing was perfect? Are we to apply it to making love? There are changes of rhythm when you're making love, which happen through the spontaneous interaction of two people, which give them both greater satisfaction. And there's a sense of the two together working towards an end. Is timing in love-making closely analogous – I think it is – to timing in the arts and sports?

MB: It's an interesting analogy. You bring in one of the most intimate two-person activities in life. A baby at the breast is another one.

DS: Yes.

MB: But the timing that we think of in sport is often both momentary and done by a single person in response to a challenge from an opponent. There's also the timing of a whole innings, or in the lengthening of stride in the last lap of a race, when someone beautifully surges past his rivals with something to spare. But as I say these are individual activities. It's not quite two people together. In a football team, players collaborate, and incisive and intricate passing movements call for perfect timing between players. I suppose one might try to include partnerships between batsmen and those between bowlers, but that's stretching it a bit. I'm not sure how that relates to making love. And I'm not sure if that captures what a painter does, either.

DS: When you talked about surging past, I thought of horse racing. Seeing a horse with a bit to spare coming through to win in the last few yards gives an unbelievable sense of excitement. But there is another ingredient, which comes over in art too, namely courage. When you see two horses battling it out, or two boxers: the tremendous aesthetic excitement that we get from courage! And this sense of courage gives us this powerful aesthetic reaction, yes?

MB: I think so.

DS: Yes I think we do get this sense of courage in art, in Beethoven, who, again . . . but there it comes back to risk.

MB: And uncompromisingness.

DS: And uncompromisingness.

MB: Think of Rembrandt's self-portraits – a clichéd example, no doubt. You get the feeling that here's a man who's painting himself without any illusions. He's facing the facts. I like the phrase, from the Yorkshire and England batsman Maurice Leyland, who had a rugged and busy style: 'Fast bowling keeps you honest.' Isn't that what we're talking about, a sort of integrity in facing whatever is thrown at you, whatever is an obstacle to your performance from within or without, and seeing it through? I think this gives enormous satisfaction. It's heart-warming. Which means I suppose that aesthetic pleasure can't be separated off from moral qualities and human qualities. Uncompromisingness, facing the facts, not turning one's face away, not giving up . . .

DS: All qualities that are used in praise of the arts.

MB: Yes I agree. I agree.

DS: Exactly analogous.

MB: In fact they're used in respect of every human activity. I mean, a doctor, let's say, or a mother, or someone faced with illness, or deprivation, and the way they courageously find the ways and means to survive it, stick it out, and make something of it. And by the same token, cowardice is betrayed as well, failings, weaknesses, tension, over-eagerness to please. It's not restricted to art and sport. But these personal qualities – dishonesty, cheating, honesty, courage – come through in sport and art.

DS: And this is what moves us in sport and art, that it is a paradigm of good qualities.

MB: Sport and art have something else in common. They are set aside from the absolute necessities, the bare necessities of life. And they have a frame round them. The painting with its frame, or the cricket ground with its boundary, or the boxing ring, or whatever. They are framed and set off from ordinary life. This wouldn't be true of everything, of architecture for instance, but it's true of many forms of art and sport. And yet within that frame, there's a possibility of finding many of the qualities in life that we admire or lack in concentrated form. What fascinates us is a moral dimension, in a broad sense of 'moral': the dimension of the revelation of human qualities.

Another quality that is revealed is freedom. How free am I? How much am I constrained by anxiety or by fear of failure? Or – here it's back to risk – how free can I be in my mind, with my fantasies? There's a difference here between sport and life, in that sportsmen tend to be conservative, whereas artists tend to be radical. In your book *About Modern Art* you quote Matisse saying to an American lady journalist:

> Oh, do tell the American people that I am a normal family man;
> that I am a devoted husband and father, that I have three fine
> children, that I go to the theatre, ride, have a comfortable home,
> a fine garden, and that I love flowers, etc., just like any man.

He says this to correct a cliché about artists. A sportsman wouldn't have to tell that story. He might have to tell the public the opposite story:

> Look, I actually enjoy doing something completely outrageous,
> I can enjoy a work of avant-garde music, and am not a complete
> freak as a result, or maybe I am, but I don't care.

374

DS: A bit earlier you were going to say something and stood back to let me say something that I wanted to say, to do with surging past another horse. Can you remember?

MB: I don't remember – except that what I now think of saying is that if someone merely scuttles past in the last lap, one admires their courage, but if someone lengthens his stride, and cruises past, one has different feelings. It's the same business we've been talking about, of outcome mixed with aesthetic pleasure. That comes back to economy of movement, to the classical, and to that aspect of beauty. We haven't used the word beauty much yet, have we? By the way, Wittgenstein in his conversation on aesthetics says that we use the word 'beauty' rarely; the notion plays little part in our appreciation of pictures or music or whatever. But beauty, nevertheless, is partly to do with making something look simple that isn't. Artists may make efforts to make what they do look easy.

DS: You introduced beauty, but in passing you mentioned something that is absolutely vital that we have not yet mentioned, though it was suggested by various things we've said: that nothing moves us more in the arts than economy of means. One example of which is when a string quartet can be given the richness of a whole orchestra. We get a sense of the person making more of the means he has, and this is one of the main preoccupations of the artist, who will pride himself on using the greatest economy of means. Now to what extent are we right, then, if we say that timing is of the essence, or is it one of several things? Is not the essence, perhaps, economy of means?

MB: No, I think it's one of several things. It's like a cake, you know, there are many essential ingredients. I think there are other elements than both these. Colin Cowdrey, the Kent and England cricketer who was noted for the graceful simplicity of his batting style, could move the bat a short distance and the ball would speed off – economy of means plus timing – he would just caress the ball. This gave satisfaction. Ian Botham, the fine England all-rounder, and a great hitter, simply heaved, and the ball went miles. There's something admirable and pleasing in both.

DS: Yes.

MB: They're very different things. Then again, the Trinidadian Brian Lara, a wonderful left-handed batsman, offers another element of pleasure; he plays with a little extra flourish, his bat twirls, he picks it up an extra few inches. His bat moves extraordinarily fast in playing a stroke. All three of these things are satisfying in different ways. They all have a shared basic structure; I mean, the bat comes down basically through the line of the ball, and they all hit the ball at more or less the same point in the pendulum swing. All are aesthetically pleasing. But the actual styles are different. Economy of means is one, but only one, of the many factors that appeal to us. I think it satisfies us because of its links with learning. Think of a baby learning to walk. At first it's impossible, incredibly difficult. The baby totters, falls, is caught by father. Gradually he or she can just do it. The same is true of skiing or batting. We gradually learn. So the capacity to perform naturally, with ease, without extraneous fuss, appeals at a deep level to us all.

DS: And the baby's satisfaction?

MB: Yes, enormous satisfaction. I think doing something with one's body that is difficult, but making it look easy, natural, must be firmly rooted in sport and the pleasures of sport. May I say something else?

DS: Of course.

MB: I was thinking about the layers of meaning in sport and art. I think with art one expects the artist to deal with, portray, central things in life. I don't know how far that can be taken with sport. But there are Oedipal and sexual analogies to what we do in sport, which link with what you said before about intimacy and timing. For example, isn't there a sexual analogy, a sexual meaning even, in piercing the field, when you push something into a small space or target, as when you score a goal in football? I'm impressed by the remark of Adrian Stokes – who was a psychoanalytically oriented critic and theorist of art – about batting as a matter of guarding one's 'castle' (jargon for wicket) like an Oedipal father against the sons who assault it and try to take it away. He's protecting his wife as well as his home. I think that's probably right, and of course there are a lot of rivalrous Oedipal elements which are upfront in sport. Two people, often, but not always, men, fighting each other in one form or another.

Stokes also writes of the more idyllic, pre-Oedipal, aspects of cricket. What takes place has a slow rhythm to it, extending over a long period of time. There are colours, green and white, the sun on the grass, originally a rural setting. Or take another aspect. Cricket consists of a series of somewhat disconnected mini-dramas. Each ball involves two protagonists pitted against each other. But one can see this in a more holistic way; as the bowler runs in, the fielders move in alertly towards the batsman. Then they relax, and drift back. There is an ebb and flow, like breathing, like waves breaking on the beach and then drawing back. The rhythm is of coming together intensely, and moving apart. I think that sort of rhythm echoes deep rhythms in life, including sexual ones. And it's part of the attraction, of the aesthetic.

DS: It's also part of the attraction of horse racing. The horses cantering to the start.

MB: Walking around in the ring.

DS: And walking around in the ring. And all those different rhythms relate to one another, and the pace changes. This offers an artful aesthetic experience, which relates, of course, to changes of pace in music.

MB: Absolutely. And indeed to silence in music.

DS: Indeed.

MB: I was talking earlier about sport as contest, and then of sport as beyond or other than simply contest. This ingress of fielders on the batsman can be seen as a form of hunting; a paranoid experience. One is hemmed in by these hostile fielders, Australians, in green baggy caps, perhaps, with Dennis Lillee, one of the greatest fast bowlers of all time, racing in to bowl, and the crowd baying. But one can see it too as a loving activity, moving close and drawing back, picking up a baby and putting it down, coming together and moving apart. Another thought: when we catch a ball at cricket, we sometimes have the conviction that we are certain to catch it before we do. And there is something containing, holding, being a safe pair of hands, being held by one's parents, or one's lover in this sort of experience. I wonder how much these thoughts apply also to art.

DS: Absolutely. In art things come to a rest.

MB: I want to make one more comment about intimacy and pairing in cricket. Most commonly, the bowler is experienced by the batsman simply as his enemy. Occasionally, if I was really feeling OK in myself as a batsman, I had an experience of the bowler as necessary for me, and me for him. I could realize in a full way, on the pulses, that we are both involved in a *joint* activity. He needs a good batsman to bring out the best arts of his bowling, and I need him as an excellent bowler to bring out the arts of my batting. At these rare times, I could feel this sort of oneness with my antagonist. Mostly I was too anxious, or pragmatic, for that, or too insecure; but there were these valuable experiences of a sort of union between us.

DS: As it is in chess.

MB: As it is in chess.

PART 11

BACK TO THE BEGINNING

49

SUMMER COUNTY

Soon after I started at the City of London School, at the age of ten, my father, who was in charge of cricket there, took me to Jack Hobbs's sports shop in Fleet Street. We went into a back room, where the great man himself was sitting – I have an image of an old man in a dark suit (in fact he must have been seventy, having been born in 1882), dignified, quiet and modest. There I got my first proper bat. I seem to remember that its name was Summer County (though now I am unsure; was it rather a brand of margarine?). And on the back, near the shoulder, was the signature – JB Hobbs – in neat, small, copperplate handwriting, slightly blurred as the ink from his fountain pen had bled at the edges into the surface of the wood.

I've no idea what happened to the bat. I was so proud of it, taking care of it in the then approved way – with liberal applications of linseed oil. The smell is with me now, as is the smell of cut grass at the cricket ground at Middleton-on-Sea when I saw it for the first time, with its row of poplars at the sea end, and its beautiful swathe of fine grass.

Our lives are short (if not necessarily nasty and brutish – perhaps I have Hobbs, and via him Hobbes, on my mind: it was Thomas Hobbes who described life as nasty, brutish and short) but I find it amazing that in 2018 I remember meeting the man known as The Master, who was born in 1882, the year of 'the death of English cricket' – and the birth of the Ashes – when England lost to Australia at the Oval by seven runs. (It was not long before the official County Championship began, in 1890.)

Sixty-odd years on from that moment of contact with The Master, I still enjoy the game (or a lot of it), and writing about it. I am more particular now about what I choose to watch. I prefer seeing close team contests between the best sides, and individual tussles between top bowlers and top batsmen. (The prospect of watching Virat Kohli batting against James Anderson, for instance, sharpens the appetite, as did seeing Shane Warne bowl to Brian Lara.) I like cricket best when the conditions slightly favour the bowlers, not outrageously, but allowing movement in the air, off the seam or for spin; I prefer seeing batsmen having to struggle, and sometimes finding a way to emerge on top.

As a passenger in a train, bus or car, I crane my neck to try to see the next ball in a game going on, though I'm usually frustrated. Not long after I retired I was persuaded to join a game being played in a small stone-paved space in the old city of Ahmedabad, with a large cow at silly mid-on and a fine left-arm over-the-wicket bowler running smoothly in along one of the feeder roads, with a taped and wetted tennis ball that skidded through off the hard surface; there was much excitement, especially when he bowled me first ball (they insisted on my continuing).

Nowadays, I am less partisan than when I was playing. I remember writing a piece when I retired, entitled something like: 'Put out my deckchair', in which I imagined a sort of dreamy relaxation, with little inclination to take sides. In fact I have not infrequently failed the Tebbit test, that crude measure of whether an immigrant truly belongs in the UK. I sometimes support England's opponents, perhaps when they are the underdog, or when it is not England who are playing the inventive, purposeful and gifted cricket.

So what did I miss when the deckchair came out? I was ready for it, I think. I was after all, forty. I had had a good innings, as they say, and I now had a new house, a new addition to the family, and an apprenticeship in a new career. There wasn't much time for deckchairs. On summer days, beavering in my basement, I would sometimes regret that I wasn't tossing up against some county rivals, perhaps at Headingley or the Oval, or playing in a pleasant country ground like Tunbridge Wells or Neath. Or going out to bat at Lord's. But there is a time for everything under the sun and the rain.

I began to think about cricket more psychologically. Cricket is capable of many forms of beauty (and ugliness) and also is a good example of the ways character shows itself through action on the field. Indeed, I often think about the complex aspects of C. L. R. James's question: 'What do they know of cricket who only cricket know?'

Cricket is a game of individual contests in a team context; as in other areas of life, the good team encourages unselfishness alongside realistic recognition that one has to perform individually, sometimes even playing in an unpopular way in the interests of the team (I recall Keith Fletcher telling his Essex team-mates off for 'Glory shots again').

I like arguments and discussions about tactics. I like thinking about how a bowler and captain might find resources to surprise or disturb even the most secure-looking batsman. I like the ability to 'read' a game or an encounter fluently. I like the humour shared with old cricketing friends, and the quick uptake of appreciation.

As one gets older, the thrill of the new is liable to be blunted or experienced more infrequently. But I was excited, even thrilled, to be keeping wicket to Shane Warne in that charity match in 1993. Another moment that comes to mind was when England beat Australia at the Oval in 1997 by nineteen runs, slow left-armer Phil Tufnell taking eleven wickets in the match. With its tense climax, the match did not finish until about seven-thirty on Saturday evening, past the deadline for my piece. So, from my seat in the Press Box I was composing the last paragraphs by speaking my excited commentary over the phone directly to the copy-taker. I felt like a genuine reporter.

I have been struck by the women's cricket matches that I have, too rarely, watched; there seemed to be a freshness of spirit and an enthusiasm of team-spirit, a less cynical take on the game. The culmination of the rise in recognition of women's cricket came in the remarkable World Cup Final in 2017, when England beat India in a close-run game in front of a full house at Lord's. I like the fact that the ECB have used some of their increased revenue for developing both women's cricket and the disability game.

My eleven years on the MCC's World Cricket Committee, six of them as chair, kept me up to date with developments in international cricket. I have been a strong supporter of DRS, of the proliferation of anti-corruption units, and of experiments in ways to protect and nurture Test cricket. I enjoy T20 cricket, and the innovations it has given rise to, while at the same time being alarmed at its proliferation and the threat it poses to international – particularly Test – cricket.

Hobbs himself once said that he would, on occasion, on good pitches, when he and Andy Sandham had put on, say, 150 runs for Surrey's first wicket, give his wicket away to the most deserving professional bowler; it was when Harold Larwood and Bill Voce were bowling for Nottinghamshire, or the pitch was spiteful, that he really had to earn his money. He would not have found it easy to see those leisurely days at the Oval and the razzmatazz of a T20 match there now as phases in the history of the same game.

Yet the continuity is there, the one-to-one contest in the team context. The pitch still twenty-two yards long, the ball hard and (sometimes) red, with leather outside, weighing five and a quarter ounces, and the crouching, predatory fielders closing in.

Long may it all continue . . .

NOTES & REFERENCES

'Are We Going to the Same Place?' (pages xi–xiii)
Written for this book.

1 The Football Cap (pages 3–13)
My father spent hours playing catch or cricket with me. He got me thinking about the game in a way that went beyond individual skills of batting, bowling or fielding. My mother supported us all. Michael Burns contributed his view of my father.

2 'Then I Knew We Had a Chance' (pages 14–21)
Richard Hutton invited me to speak at the 364 Society lunch on 23 June 2016, the centenary of his father's birth. It was also the day of the EU referendum. This chapter is based on the talk. Here, as elsewhere, I'm indebted to Stephen Chalke.

Colin Cowdrey, M.C.C.: *Autobiography of a Cricketer.* London: Hodder and Stoughton, 1976.
Alan Ross, 'Hutton departs' in *Cape Summer and the Australians in England.* London: Hamish Hamilton, 1957.

3 The Darling Buds of May (pages 22–29)
Based on an interview with Denis Compton on the occasion of his seventy-fifth birthday for the Observer *in 1993.*

William Shakespeare, *Sonnets.*

4 The Gnawed Umbrella Handle and the Burned Bail (pages 33–35)
Ian Botham, *My Autobiography.* London: Collins Willow, 1994.
    (I wrote the foreword to Ian's book.)
Mike Brearley, *Phoenix from the Ashes.* London: Hodder and Stoughton, 1982.

Scyld Berry and Rupert Peploe, *Cricket's Burning Passion: Ivo Bligh and the Story of the Ashes*. London: Methuen, 2006.

5 Raking Through the Ashes (pages 36–42)
Based on an article in the Observer, *May 2009.*

Mike Brearley, *Phoenix from the Ashes*. London: Hodder and Stoughton, 1982.
BBC: *Botham's Ashes*, 1981.
Wilfred R. Bion, *The Long Week-End 1897–1919*. London: Routledge, 1982.

6 A Late Developer (or: My Lucky Breaks) (pages 43–47)
Mike Brearley & Dudley Doust, *The Return of the Ashes*. London: Pelham, 1978.
Mike Brearley & Dudley Doust, *The Ashes Retained*. London: Hodder & Stoughton, 1979.

7 Almost Losing a Dominion (pages 48–59)
From my foreword to the 2009 edition of In Quest of the Ashes *by Douglas Jardine (1933).*

Douglas Jardine, *In Quest of the Ashes*. London: Methuen, 2005.
Gerald Pawle, *R. E. S. Wyatt: Fighting Cricketer*. London: George Allen & Unwin, 1985.

8 Four Images from the 2006–7 Series (pages 60–65)
England had had a disappointing tour of Australia. I was asked to comment by the Observer. *These four images stood out in my mind. Mike Hendrick and I had a recent conversation on selectors' and others' over-valuation of out-and-out fast bowlers. Rodney Marsh confirmed my views on Chris Read.*

9 Giants (pages 66–71)
Ever since Ian Botham made his sensational early appearances on the international stage, comparisons have been made. Is X the new Botham? How did Botham compare with his rivals from other teams? This new piece is based on an article for The Times *in 2017 after Ben Stokes scored a century against South Africa.*

10 What Makes a Hero? (pages 75–79)
Like many pieces here, this one was written for the book. As Fred Titmus once said, it's easier to get on top than to stay there. Once up, the one dramatic way to go is down. Heroes turn into villains.

George Eliot, *Middlemarch: A Study of Provincial Life*, 1871. London: Everyman's Library Classics, 1991.

E. M. Forster, *A Passage to India*, 1924. Penguin. London, 2005.

Sigmund Freud, 'On Transference Love' in *Standard Edition Vol. 12*, 1915. London: Hogarth Press, 1958.

11 'In My Opinion' (pages 80–83)

A palpable hero! Written without a purpose, except to put into words some feelings around the great man.

12 'Michael Boy' (pages 84–89)

We always had a playful rapport. The first version of this piece was published in Wisden Cricketers' Almanack 2008 *and reprinted in* Wisden Anthology 1978–2006: Cricket's Age of Revolution, *edited by Stephen Moss. I enjoyed conversations with Suresh Menon on Bedi.*

Suresh Menon, *Bishan: Portrait of a Cricketer*. India: Penguin, 2011.

13 From Wot To Fot (pages 90–99)

This piece is close to what I wrote as a contribution to Dennis Lillee's book. I'm grateful for his permission to use it here. I rate Lillee as the best bowler I faced. Dennis and Rodney Marsh were both helpful with this piece.

Dennis Lillee, *Dennis Lillee*. Melbourne: Affirm Press, 2016.

14 Whispering Death (pages 100–107)

Based on article in the Observer, *2013.*

See film: *Fire in Babylon* (2010), directed by Stevan Riley.

15 Caleb Garth: the Craftsman (pages 108–115)

Written for this book. I am very grateful to Stephen Chalke, who was generous with his help and ideas.

George Eliot, *Middlemarch: A Study of Provincial Life*, 1871. London: Everyman's Library Classics, 1991.

Stephen Chalke, *Tom Cartwright: The Flame Still Burns*. Bath: Fairfield Books, 2007.

16 Crises in Cricket (pages 119–123)

Written for this book.

Peter Hain, *Outside In*. London: Biteback, 2012.

17 'Batting like a Gorilla' (pages 124–127)

This piece is based on my talk at Doug Insole's Memorial Service, at St John's Wood Church, on 23 February 2018. I was helped by Doug Insole's daughters and grandson, Gwen Shawyer, Anne Nagle and Stuart Nagle.

Mike Brearley & Dudley Doust, *The Ashes Retained*. London: Hodder & Stoughton, 1979.

18 'Nice Bonking Pace' (pages 128–134)

Based on article for the Observer, *published in 2011. Basil D'Oliveira had died the day before. I am grateful to Peter Oborne, not only for his book, but also for his kindness and effort in helping me with this chapter and the next one. Also to Duncan Fearnley and Raymond Illingworth for their openness about D'Oliveira.*

Peter Oborne, *Basil D'Oliveira: Cricket and Conspiracy: The Untold Story*. London: Little, Brown, 2004.
Alan Paton, *Cry, the Beloved Country*, 1948. London: Vintage, 2002.
C. L. R. James, *Beyond a Boundary*. London: Hutchinson, 1963.

19 'We Picked Him' (pages 135–145)

Written for this book. I'm grateful to Peter Oborne and Stephen Chalke.

Peter Oborne, *Basil D'Oliveira: Cricket and Conspiracy: The Untold Story*. London: Little, Brown, 2004.
E. W. Swanton, *Gubby Allen: Man of Cricket*. London: Hutchinson, 1985.
Stephen Chalke, *At the Heart of English Cricket: The Life and Memories of Geoffrey Howard*. Bath: Fairfield Books, 2001.

20 'Half a Good Night' (pages 146–152)

The piece is partly based on what I said at David's funeral service, 17 March 2005.

David Sheppard, *Bias to the Poor*. London: Hodder & Stoughton, 1984.
David Sheppard, *Steps Along Hope Street*. London: Hodder & Stoughton, 2002.

21 Bible and Passion (pages 153–157)

Ben Howell and his sisters helped me with this piece.

22 The Zimbabwe Affair (pages 158–165)

This piece is a rewritten, more up-to-date version of what I wrote for the Financial Times *in 2003.*

Nasser Hussain, *Playing with Fire: The Autobiography*. London: Michael Joseph, 2004.

23 Cometh the Hour (pages 166–180)

This chapter is based on a talk I gave in Trinidad in 2010 at an event celebrating the fiftieth anniversary of Frank Worrell's appointment as captain of the West Indies. I have learned a lot about West Indian cricket from Clem Seecharan, and (of course) from my favourite cricket book, Beyond a Boundary.

C. L. R. James, *Beyond a Boundary*. London: Hutchinson, 1963.

Learie Constantine, *Cricket and I*. London: Philip Allen, 1933.

Clem Seecharan, *Muscular Learning: Cricket and Education in the Making of the British West Indies at the end of the 19th Century*. Jamaica: Ian Randle, 2006.

24 Not Common-or-Garden Cheating (pages 183–190)

This is an expanded version of the piece originally written for the Observer *in May 2001. Michael Atherton wrote with compassionate clarity about Mohammad Amir.*

Virgil, *The Aeneid*.

Marilynne Robinson, *Home*. London: Virago, 2009.

Mark Twain, *Following the Equator*. Hartford: American Publishing Company, 1897.

Tom Wolfe, *The Bonfire of the Vanities*. New York: Farrar Straus & Giroux, 1987.

25 Ball Tampering: Disenchantment (pages 191–197)

I first learned about the Australian reaction from Kate Fitzpatrick. Tom Derose and Ivan Ward added some depth to my final piece.

Charles Dickens, *Bleak House*, 1853. London: Everyman's Library, 1991.

Sigmund Freud, 'Analysis of a Phobia in a Five-year-old Boy' in *Standard Edition Vol. 14*, 1909. London: Hogarth Press, 1958.

26 The Sting: Lord's 2010 (pages 198–204)

Based on two pieces: one for the Observer *in August 2010; the other in* The Times *in 2016.*

William Shakespeare, *Richard II*.

William Shakespeare, *Macbeth*.

27 The Spirit of Cricket (pages 205–215)
A version of this chapter appeared in The Times *in 2017.*

28 Scoops, Switch-hits and Helmets at Short Mid-on (pages 219–226)
Written for this book.

Arthur Conan Doyle, 'The Story of Spedegue's Dropper,' 1916, in Peter Haining (ed.), *LBW: Laughter Before Wicket!.* London: Allen & Unwin, 1986.

29 Father of Reverse Swing (pages 227–233)
Written for this book.

Peter Oborne, *Wounded Tiger: A History of Pakistan Cricket.* London: Simon & Schuster, 2015.

30 The Doosra and the Splint (pages 234–240)
Based on a talk I gave at a dinner honouring Muttiah Muralitharan in 2010.

31 'Naaaaaagh, That's No Good!' (pages 241–248)
Written for this book. I found Gideon Haigh's book very helpful. Graham Gooch did his best to get me back to historical reality on his dismissal to Warne in 1993.

John Emburey, *Spinning in a Fast World.* London: Robson, 1989.
Gideon Haigh, *On Warne.* London: Simon & Schuster, 2013.

32 Supping with the Devil (pages 251–259)
Part of this chapter is based on a piece I wrote for the Observer *in 2002.*

W. H. Hudson, *The Purple Land that England Lost.* London: Duckworth, 1930.
Ashis Nandy, *The Tao of Cricket.* New Delhi: Oxford University, 2000.

33 'When I First Saw the English Bowling' (pages 260–266)
I found Suresh Menon's and Ramachandra Guha's books insightful and enjoyable.

Ramachandra Guha, *A Corner of a Foreign Field.* London: Picador, 2003.
Mansoor Ali Khan Pataudi, *Tiger's Tale: The Story of the Nawab of Pataudi.* London: S. Paul, 1969.
Suresh Menon, *Pataudi: the Nawab of Cricket.* India, HarperCollins, 2013.

34 The Indian Bradman (pages 267–272)
Based on articles in the Observer *in 2007 and 2008.*

35 The Bridge (pages 273–279)
Written for this book. Suresh Menon and Ramachandra Guha have written perceptively on Virat Kohli in various Indian newspapers and in Wisden Cricket Monthly. *Conversations with both men enriched my understanding and view of Kohli.*

36 From the Commentary Box (pages 283–284)
Written for this book.

37 'Desperately Good' (pages 285–292)
Parts of this piece appeared in my Sunday Times *obituary on John Arlott, who died in December 1991. A second and longer version appeared in* Wisden Cricketers' Almanack 1992, *and was reprinted in* Wisden Anthology 1978–2006. *Here I have added in further thoughts and reflections, some of them spoken at the launch of a posthumous book of Arlott's* (A Celebration of Cricket, Wine, Poetry and Place), *others at the Winchester Poetry Festival, 2015.*

David Allen and Norman Ackroyd, *Arlott and Ackroyd: A Celebration of Cricket, Wine, Poetry and Place.* Newnham, Gloucestershire: Christopher Saunders, 2002.
Stephen Moss, *Wisden Anthology 1978–2006: Cricket's Age of Revolution.* London: John Wisden & Co., 2006.

38 'Another Time, Another Time' (pages 293–297)
Written for this book. Antonia Fraser was supportive of my wish to publish Harold's poem.

'Poem' by Harold Pinter, taken from VARIOUS VOICES by Harold Pinter (Faber & Faber, 2009). Copyright © 1989, Harold Pinter. Reproduced by permission of Faber & Faber Ltd.
Harold Pinter, *The Caretaker.* London: Faber & Faber, 1991.
Harold Pinter, 'Arthur Wellard: A Tribute' (privately published by the author and available from www.HaroldPinter.org)

39 Endgame (pages 298–302)
The first version was published in: Mark Nixon and John Pilling (eds.), On in their Company: Essays on Beckett, with Tributes and Sketches; presented to Jim Knowlson on his 80th Birthday. Reading: Beckett International Foundation, 2015.

Wilfred R. Bion, *Experiences in Groups and Other Papers*. London: Tavistock, 1968.

James Knowlson, *Damned to Fame: The Life of Samuel Beckett*. London: Bloomsbury, 1996

40 'They've Not Got the Singles Going' (pages 303–307)
First published in The Times, *2018.*

41 What Do They Know of Cricket . . . (pages 308–320)
This chapter is based on a talk I gave at a conference in Glasgow on C. L. R. James's work in 2011. My piece will appear as 'Socrates and C. L. R. James' in David Featherstone, Christopher Gair, Christian Høgsbjerg, Andrew Smith (eds.). 2018: Marxism, Colonialism, and Cricket. Duke University Press. All rights reserved. Republished by permission of the rightsholder. www.dukeupress.edu

C. L. R. James, *Beyond a Boundary*. London: Hutchinson, 1963.

Jonathan Lear, *A Case for Irony*. Harvard: Harvard University Press, 2014.

K. S. Ranjitsinhji, *The Jubilee Book of Cricket*. Edinburgh: Blackwood, 1897.

42 Behind the Timbers (pages 323–325)
Written for this book, but including an excerpt from a piece for The Times *in 2016.*

43 Elegance (pages 326–331)
Sadly, J. T. Murray died in July 2018, shortly before the book went to the printers. This piece is based on an article in Wisden Cricketers' Almanack 1976, *marking his retirement the year before.*

44 'What Do You Think This Is, Randall?' (pages 332–337)
This chapter is similar to the one I contributed to Rod Marsh's forthcoming book. I'm grateful to him for permission to include it, and for his trust in me to say things as I see them.

Mike Brearley & Dudley Doust, *The Return of the Ashes*. London: Pelham, 1978.

Christian Ryan, *Golden Boy*. London: Allen & Unwin, 2010.

Rod Marsh, *Rod Marsh; 50 Years in Cricket*. Melbourne: Affirm Press, 2018.

45 The Flea (pages 338–344)
We named Alan Knott 'The Flea' for his hopping around and his perpetual exercising (not that fleas are noted for hip rotations). The original of this piece was published in Wisden Cricketers' Almanack 1986 *and reprinted in* Wisden Anthology 1978–2006: Cricket's Age of Revolution, *edited by Stephen Moss.*

46 Not Yet the King of Albania (pages 345–349)
One part of this piece appeared in the Observer *in 2011; another in* The Times *(2016).*

Kumar Sangakkara's 'MCC Spirit of Cricket Cowdrey Lecture' given
in 2011 is available on: https://www.lords.org/mcc/mcc-spirit-of.../
mcc-spirit-of-cricket-cowdrey-lecture/

47 The Art of the Masses (pages 353–360)
Written for this book.

David Sylvester, *London Recordings*. London: Chatto & Windus, 2003.
C. L. R. James, *Beyond a Boundary*. London: Hutchinson, 1963.
Simon Barnes, *A Book of Heroes*. London: Short Books, 2010.
Scyld Berry, *Cricket: The Game of Life*. London: Hodder & Stoughton, 2015
George Eliot, *Middlemarch: A Study of Provincial Life*, 1871. London:
Everyman's Library Classics, 1991.

48 The Beautiful Game (pages 361–379)
Interview with David Sylvester, a great art critic and commentator, who was also passionate about both cricket and psychoanalysis.

Interview with Michael Brearley by David Sylvester. Copyright © 2003, Estate
of David Sylvester, used by permission of The Wylie Agency (UK) Limited.
David Sylvester, *London Recordings*. London: Chatto & Windus, 2003.
Adrian Stokes, *A Game That Must Be Lost: Collected Papers*. Manchester:
Carcanet Press, 1973.

49 Summer County (pages 383–387)
Written for this book. My father again. And 'The Master'. It amazes me how far back our connections go, especially when we get old.

ACKNOWLEDGEMENTS

This is a book which has over decades involved input from many people, direct and indirect; though few in the recent writing and re-contextualizing of it.

I am grateful to various sports editors for their support, advice and comments, notably David Robson, Simon Kelner, Brian Oliver, Tim Hallissey and Matthew Hancock. Also, to fellow writers and thinkers about the game: Robin Marler, Vic Marks and Michael Atherton; and to Ed Smith, Mike Selvey, Steve James, John Inverarity, John Stephenson, Fraser Stewart, Neil Burns, Mike Gatting, Raymond Illingworth, Doug Insole and Duncan Fearnley. I could go on . . .

Several people helped with particular chapters, and I have acknowledged them in the Notes & References above. I should like to mention a few who have been particularly generous in this regard. Stephen Chalke read the whole text and made invaluable comments on small and large matters, correcting several mistakes; we also had many conversations about Tom Cartwright. Peter Oborne has not only given me a great deal through his books on D'Oliveira and Pakistan cricket, but also generously commented on my long section on 'Cricket and Race'. I would like to mention too Ramachandra Guha and Suresh Menon for stimulating conversations relating in particular to 'Game Changers' and 'Indian Batsmanship'. I am also grateful to my anonymous informant for the possible reconstruction referred to in 'We Picked Him'.

Kannan Navaratnem, Robin Sen-Gupta, Gabriella Braun, Mischa Gorchov Brearley and Hugh Brody have helped long-term and in overall ways. They have all read and commented on pieces I have written over the years.

I'm grateful for permissions to print pieces, versions of which were originally in the *Observer* and *The Times*; also for permission from *Wisden Cricketers' Almanack* for chapters 37, 43 and 45. I am grateful to Andrew Smith and Duke University for permission to use chapter 41, and to Dennis Lillee and Rod Marsh for their permission to use pieces I originally wrote for their books.

I would like to thank my agent, Matthew Hamilton – always encouraging, interested and shrewd. In the background are my parents, Horace and Midge; my sisters, Jill and Margy, who tolerated for at least a few years being asked, even perhaps expected, to field; my wife, Mana Sarabhai Brearley (who clear-mindedly dissipates anxiety on small and large matters as well as, on occasions when I'm complacent, salutarily increasing it), and my son and daughter (Mischa and Lara), and their lovely partners and children.

I thank people at Little, Brown, including the careful and considerate copy-editor Nick Fawcett, and Jo Wickham. Finally, there has been my editor, who has gone way beyond the call of duty, travelling to me for stimulating meetings early on Monday mornings. I recommend 'Start the Week' with Andreas Campomar.

IMAGE CREDITS

INDEX

Abbas, Zaheer 253
Accrington 175
Adelaide 20, 55, 57, 97, 98, 165
aesthetics 351–79
Afghanistan team 277
Agarkar, Ajit 259
Ahmed, Tauseef 88
Ahmedabad 384
Akhtar, Shoaib 87
Akram, Wasim 101, 232–3
Alam, Intikhab 241, 245
Alderman, Terry 96, 336
Ali, Abid 86
All Blacks 211
all-round players 69
Allen, 'Gubby' 26, 28, 53, 56,
    57–8, 87, 140, 141, 143, 316
Amateur Cup Final, Wembley
    1956 126
amateurism 318–19
Ambrose, Curtly 101, 106, 307
American football 312
Ames, Les 343, 345
Amir, Mohammad 189, 190,
    198–204, 233
Amiss, Dennis 44, 144
Anderson, Jimmy 101, 277, 278,
    305, 347, 384

Andrew, Keith 324
anti-apartheid movement 121
anti-corruption units 119, 386
Antigua 305
apartheid xii, 28, 110, 120, 121–3,
    128, 130–2, 136, 145, 150,
    154, 163, 206
Appleyard, Bob 20
Arlott, Jimmy 289–90
Arlott, John xiii, 25, 128, 285–92,
    294–5, 298–9, 301–2, 349
Arlott, Pat 290–1
Arlott, Robert 291
Arlott, Tim 291
Arlott, Valerie 290
Armstrong, W. W. 51
Arnold, Geoff 221
Arsenal FC 26
Ashby-de-la-Zouch 328
Ashcroft, Peggy 262
Ashes, the xiii, 31–71, 79, 93–4,
    101, 103, 200, 211, 220–1,
    243, 303, 336, 343, 384
Asia Cup 2001 264
Asif, Mohammad 189, 198, 201,
    203, 233
Atherton, Michael 193, 205–7,
    215, 315, 358

Australia 19, 25, 27, 35, 36, 45, 51–2, 62, 65, 95, 97, 120, 124, 137, 143–4, 163, 167, 179, 194, 196, 293, 358
  see also Western Australia
Australia national cricket team 12, 15–16, 20, 27, 33, 34, 37–41, 43–7, 50–5, 57, 59, 61, 87, 92, 100, 104–5, 129, 131, 136, 148, 149, 191, 193, 209, 220, 244–5, 279, 306, 325, 333–6, 345, 384, 386
Australian Cricket Board 46, 49–50, 120, 124, 195–6
Australian public 51, 55, 57, 93, 104, 192–3
Azharuddin, Mohammad 253

Bacher, Ali 186
Bailey, Trevor 16, 149, 319
Bairstow, David 220, 304
Bairstow, Jonny 323, 324
ball tampering 183, 191–7
ball tracking technology 119
balls 229–30
Bancroft, Cameron 183, 191, 195–7
Bangalore 88, 341
Bangar, Sanjay 258, 259
Bannerman 12
Barbados 168, 171
Barbados national cricket team 265
Barber, Bob 115, 241
Barenboim, Daniel 91
Bari, Wasim 325
Barnes, Simon 360
Barr, Charles 130
Barrington, Ken 230, 328
Bartók, Béla 368

Basil D'Oliveira Trophy 134
Bath 10
batsmen 70–1, 222, 225–6, 249–79, 313, 345, 379
BBC see British Broadcasting Corporation
BCCI see Board of Control for Cricket in India
Beckett, Samuel 290, 298–302
Bedi, Bishan Singh 78, 84–9, 155, 192, 235–7, 261–2, 341
Bedser, Alec 16, 18, 136, 142, 293
Beethoven, Ludwig van 91, 368, 372
Begum of Bhopal 261
Beldham, William 357
Bell, Ian 208
Bell, Ronnie 219–20
Benaud, Richard 16, 17, 40–1
Bendigo 27
Bennett, Don 25, 91
Berlin Wall, fall of the 122
Bermange, Benedict 101
Bernini 358
Berry, Scyld 163, 358–60
  Cricket's Burning Passion 34
Bhutto, Benazir 88
Binks, Jimmy 325
Bion, Wilfred 35, 298–301
Birtwistle, Sir Harrison 293
Bishop, Ian 205–6, 208
Blackheath 284
Blank, Victor 242
Blatter, Sepp 133
Bligh, Hon. Ivo 34
Blofeld, Henry 263
Board of Control for Cricket in India (BCCI) 277, 278
'Bodyline' series 35, 49, 51, 57–8, 261

Boer War 188
Bognor 5
Bognor Colts 5
Bolt, Usain 104, 255
Bondman, Matthew 356–7
Bonnard 288
Border, Allan 213, 224
Bosanquet, Bernard 234
Botham, Ian 33–7, 39–41, 46–7,
    62–3, 66–8, 70–1, 96, 101–2,
    200, 212, 229, 248, 261,
    286–7, 319, 336, 343, 359,
    376
Botham's Ashes (BBC video,
    1981) 40
Bowes, Bill 6, 54, 155
bowling 66–8, 90–1, 99, 100–4,
    111, 130–1, 168–9, 222,
    223–4, 225–6, 229–30,
    235–40, 267–8, 313, 339–40,
    359–60, 378–9
    underarm 219–20
    see also doosra; googlies;
    leg-breaks; leg-spin; off-tactic
Boyce, Keith 126
Boycott, Geoffrey xi, 17, 78, 95,
    136, 222, 272, 304, 315
Bradman, Don 27, 49, 52–4, 58,
    87, 94, 267, 268, 272, 276
Brahms, Carol 152
Bramall Lane, Sheffield 6
Bransgrove, Rod 247
Branson, Eddie 113, 115
Bravo, Darren 81
Brazil national cricket team 36
Brearley, Horace (Mike's father)
    4, 5, 6–7, 8–9, 10–11, 75–6,
    155, 383
Brearley, Joseph (Mike's paternal
    grandfather) 6

Brearley, Lydia-Anne (Mike's
    paternal grandmother) 6
Brearley, Margy (Mike's younger
    sister) 9
Brearley, Mike
    On Form xii
    The Return of the Ashes 332
Brearley, Mischa (Mike's son) 97
Brentham Club 4, 5, 9–10, 208
Brisbane 52, 62, 94, 98
British Broadcasting Corporation
    (BBC) 40, 168, 285, 287
British Empire 206, 251
Broad, Chris 347
Broad, Stuart 102, 199, 200–1,
    277, 305
Brown, Freddie 5–6, 16
Brown, Sid 11
Brylcreem 23
Bucknor, Steve 137
Buller, Syd 238
Burns, Michael 10
Burton upon Trent xiii
Butcher, Roland 317–18
Butt, Ijaz 198
Butt, Salman 190, 198, 201–3,
    233

Calcutta 137, 254
Cambridge Union 302
Cambridge University Cricket
    Club 8–9, 14–15, 28, 125,
    148–9, 219–20, 265, 323, 354
Cambridgeshire cricket team 7
Canterbury 340
Cape Town 191, 232
Cardus, Neville 176, 244
Carey, Michael 79
Caribbean 104, 129, 131, 168,
    170, 255, 305

Caribbean Premier League 107
Carr, A. W. 53
Carr, Donald 221
Cartwright, Tom 67, 77, 108–15, 121, 129, 136, 142, 224, 286, 356
Castagno 358
Cavaliers match 88
Centenary Test, Melbourne 1977 33, 44, 45, 92–3, 97, 120, 334
Central Lancashire League 289
Chalke, Stephen 8, 56, 112–15, 114, 142
Champions Trophy 273
Chandigarh 269
Chandimal, Dinesh 323, 324
Chandrasekhar, Bhagwat 85, 86, 241
Channel 4 165, 288–9
Channel Nine 120
Chaplin, Charlie 313
Chapman, Percy 56
Chappell, Greg 46, 92, 95, 97, 101, 315, 335, 354, 355, 359
Chappell, Ian 44, 97, 104, 210–12, 225, 265–7, 303–7, 315, 333, 335
Chappell, Trevor 209
cheating 181–215
Cheetham, Jack 140
Cheltenham 149
Chennai 269, 354
Chichester 5
'circus' scheme 120
Clark, Stuart 60
Clarke, Giles 198
Clarke, Michael 61, 102
Close, Brian 44, 104, 167, 242
coaches/coaching 99, 314–16
Cobham, Lord 140

Coldwell, Len 109
Colombo 239
colonialism 34, 177, 179, 251, 310
Combined British Universities 6
Combined Cadet Force 12
commentators 281–320
commercialization of cricket 121
Compton, Denis 6, 11, 12, 16, 18–21, 23–9, 75, 77, 126, 262, 266, 286
Compton, Leslie 327
Conan Doyle, Arthur 220
Condon, Lord 134, 184
Constant, David 96–7
Constantine, Learie 57, 104, 167, 171, 173–7
Constantine, Lebrun 167, 171, 173, 174
Contractor, Nari 264–5
Cook, Alastair 70
Coote, Cyril 148
Corinthian Casuals 126
corruption xiii, 119, 181–215
    see also anti-corruption units
Cosh, Nick 28
County Championship 112, 347
    1890 384
    1949 11
    1977 221
    2010 65
county cricket 187, 209, 264
Coventry 111, 113
Cowdrey, Colin 17–18, 84, 136, 138, 142, 144, 262, 375–6
Cowdrey Lectures 348–9
Coy, Arthur 139–40
Cricket Australia XI team 53
Cricket Board 150
Cricket Society 138

Cricketer, The (magazine) 283
Cricketers' Association 286, 289
Croft, Colin 101, 229
Cronje, Hansie xiii, 183, 185–6,
    188, 190
Crowe, Martin 207, 215, 276
Cumberbatch, Archie 171
Cunis 302

Daily Telegraph (newspaper) 79
Daniel, Wayne 101, 102, 105,
    156, 168–70, 229
Das, Shiv Sunder 258
Davidson, Alan 16
Davison, Brian 220
day–night cricket 121
Day–Night Test match 2016 80
de Klerk, F. W. 122
Delhi 89, 264, 341
Denmark 220
Denness, Mike 242
Derbyshire cricket team 109, 238,
    325
Derose, Tom 197
Dev, Kapil 66, 67, 68, 99
Dexter, Ted 148, 261
Dhaka 264
Dilshan 'scoop' ('ramp' shot) 222,
    223
Dilley, Graham 37, 201
Dilshan, Tillakaratne 223, 349
Dodemaide, Tony 99
D'Oliveira, Basil 121, 122–3,
    128–34, 136–44, 147–8, 289
D'Oliveira affair 1968 xii, 120,
    123, 131–4, 136–43, 146, 149,
    289, 302
Dominions XI 174
Donald, Allan 90
Donatello 358

doosra (bowling technique) 234,
    236–9, 243, 246
Douglas-Home, Sir Alec 139,
    146–7
Downton, Paul 343
Dravid, Rahul 253, 258, 272, 276,
    279
DRS *see* Umpire Decision
    Review System
Dubai 70, 80
Dujon, Jeffrey 166, 324
Dulwich College 12
Durban 126
Durham cricket team 347
Dymock, Geoff 46

Ealing cricket team 9
East Africa 111
East, Ray 156
Eastbourne 232
ECB *see* England and Wales
    Cricket Board
Edgbaston 37, 46–7, 278
Edmonds, Philippe xiii, 221–2,
    340
Edney, Harry 10
Edrich, Bill 6, 11, 23, 27, 29
Edrich, John 44, 94
Edwards, Mike 130
Edwards, Ross 94
Eliot, George, *Middlemarch* 77,
    108, 356
Elizabeth II 34
Emburey, John 37, 46, 79, 97,
    220, 244, 340
Engel, Matthew 293
England 104, 119, 122, 129, 132,
    165, 168, 177, 189, 195,
    200–2, 256, 257–8, 261, 271,
    273, 288–9, 299, 335, 337, 347

England Coaching Academy 336
England national cricket team
  5–8, 13–17, 20, 24, 34, 36–40,
  41, 43, 45–7, 50–7, 61–3,
  66–8, 70–1, 77, 79, 83, 86–7,
  98, 100, 102–6, 113, 120,
  128–9, 131–2, 134, 138, 143,
  145, 147, 149–50, 155, 159,
  163, 165, 173–4, 178, 184,
  189, 193, 198–202, 212, 214,
  224–5, 239–40, 244–5, 251–2,
  258–9, 261, 268–9, 273,
  277–8, 284, 296, 304–5,
  308–9, 314–16, 323, 327, 336,
  342–6, 355, 366, 368–9, 376,
  384–6
England national football team
  133
England and Wales Cricket
  Board (ECB) 165, 198, 207,
  209, 386
English Schools tours 28
Enron 185
Essex cricket team 124–6, 129,
  156, 163–4, 385
Evans, Godfrey 343
Evening News (newspaper) 12

Fagg, Arthur 220
Fearnley, Duncan 142–3
Federer, Roger 355
Fellows-Smith, Jonathan 220
Fenner's, Cambridge 148
Fingleton, Jack 16, 52, 53
Finn, Steven 102, 323
Fire in Babylon (film, 2010) 101
First World War 35, 299–300
Fishwick, Herbert 358–9
Fitzpatrick, Kate 193
Flavell, Jack 109

Fletcher, Duncan 61, 64
Fletcher, Keith 47, 94, 315, 385
Flintoff, Andrew 38–9, 60–1, 62,
  66, 68, 70–1
Flower, Andy xii, 123, 158–65,
  315
Flower, Danielle 159
Flower, Grant 161
Fonteyn, Margot 262
football 3–4, 36, 133, 353
Forest School 11
Forster, E. M., *A Passage to India*
  78
Fowler, Graeme 232–3
Freud, Sigmund 78, 194, 355
Fry, C. B. 252, 349

Gandhi, Mahatma 261
Ganguly, Sourav 253, 257, 258
Garner, Joel 101
Gatting, Mike 24, 37, 41, 83, 224,
  241–3, 297
Gavaskar, Sunil 88, 253, 268,
  271, 279, 315, 355, 358
Germany national cricket team
  36
Gibbs, Herschelle 190
Gibbs, Lance 238
Gilchrist, Adam 210, 345
Gilchrist, Alan 324
Giles, Ashley 63
Gillette Cup 85, 329
  1963 16–17, 119
Gilligan, Arthur 140
Glamorgan cricket team 109,
  112, 325
Gloucestershire cricket team 149
Golden Age of cricket 28, 155
Gooch, Graham 21, 41, 68,
  244–5, 315, 319

Goodwin, Keith 228
googlies (bowling technique) 7,
    11–12, 26, 86, 92, 155, 228,
    234, 241–2, 293
Goose 33
Gough, Darren 114, 200
Gower, David 114, 271–2, 319,
    357, 360
Grace, W. G. 172, 174, 175, 253,
    309
Grade cricket 196
Graveney, Tom 109
Gray, Simon 296
Greenidge, Gordon 166
Greig, Tony 43–4, 56, 66, 69, 71,
    87, 94, 97, 104–6, 179, 208,
    210–11, 214, 231
Griffith, Billy 6, 140, 141
Griffith, Charlie 130–1, 264–5
Griffith, Mike 6, 8, 220, 265
Grout, Wally 325, 329
Guardian (newspaper) 244, 287–8
Guha, Ramachandra 263, 278–9
Gunn, George 370
Gupta, Mukesh 183, 185
Guyana 231

Hadlee, Richard 66–8, 96, 101
Haigh, Gideon 246–7
    On Warne 244
Hain, Peter 121–2, 133
Hales, Alex 323
Hall, Wes 130–1
Hammond, Wally 27, 58, 358–60
'Hammy' (fictional Bajan fast
    bowler) 169
Hampshire Club and Ground
    286
Hampshire cricket team 28, 29,
    109, 114, 247

Harare xi, 158, 159, 162–3, 164,
    220
Harlem Globetrotters 189
Harmison, Steve 38, 60, 61, 268
Harris, John 121–2
Harris, Lord 252
Harris, Ryan 101
Harrison, Leo 286
Harvey, Bagenal 23
Harvey, Neil 17
Hawke, Bob 56
Hawke, Lord 178
Hayden, Matthew 61, 62
Hazlewood, Josh 307
headgear 44–5, 220–1, 334
Headingley 7, 33, 35, 37, 39, 41,
    45, 46, 96, 149, 184, 222,
    244–5, 257–9, 343, 385
Headley, George 123, 167, 179,
    309
Healy, Ian 65
Heckmondwike 8
Hendren, Patsy 6, 57
Hendrick, Mike 62–3, 109
heroes 73–115
Hicke, Graeme 245
High Commissioner for Sri
    Lanka in London 349
Hill, Eric 296
Hirst, George 51
Hobbes, Thomas 384
Hobbs, Jack 153, 383, 384, 386–7
Hobbs, Robin 228, 241
Hogg, Quintin 110
Hogg, Rodney 94, 96, 199, 323,
    332
Hoggard, Matthew 61
Holder, Vanburn 105
Holding, Michael 44, 77, 100–7,
    167, 231, 315

Holland 220
Hollies, Eric 25
Hook and Southborough club 296–7
Hotson, Mr 49
Hove 26, 104, 178, 232, 263, 264
Howard, Geoffrey 18, 141, 251
Howell, Gill 156
Howell, Peter 130, 153–7
Howell, Susan 157
Hudson, W. H., *The Purple Land* 256
Hughes, David 85
Hughes, Kim 96, 335–6
Hurst, Bob 13
Hussain, Nasser 163
Hutton, Dorothy 21
Hutton, John 112
Hutton, Sir Leonard 6–8, 14–21, 119, 126, 149, 159, 178, 214, 296
Hutton, Richard 14–15, 16–17, 112, 265
Hyderabad 264

ICC *see* International Cricket Council
'ideal cricket match' 50
idée fixe 62
Illingworth, Raymond 43, 109, 131, 143–4, 155–6, 247–8, 303, 315, 319, 343
India 64, 70, 86, 87, 88–9, 155, 192, 214, 230, 251, 255–6, 270, 271, 273, 299, 341
India national cricket team 21, 87–8, 136, 155, 189, 193, 200, 208, 234, 257–9, 261–2, 264–5, 273–4, 277–8, 325, 341, 355, 386

India Under-19s 275
India XI team 279
Indian cricket style 86–7, 249–79
Indian High Commissioner 273, 275
Indian Independence 251, 273
Indian Premier League 119, 121, 247
Ingleby-Mackenzie, Colin 28–9
innovation 119, 217–48, 252, 386
Insole, Barbara 135
Insole, Doug 21, 55, 122, 124–7, 129, 135–8, 141–2, 144–5, 150, 209, 293
Insole, Geoff 135
Insole, Susan 135, 136
International Cricket Council (ICC) 119, 162, 193, 194, 195, 207, 237
  Anti-Corruption Unit 134, 184
Inverarity, John 63
Irani, Ronnie 163
Iraq War 163
Ironmonger, Bert 58
Irons, Jeremy 297
Italy national cricket team 36
ITV 94
Iverson, Jack 8

Jackson, Archie 52–3
Jackson, Les 109
Jamaica 39, 88, 104, 171
James, C. L. R. xii, 104, 123, 130, 167–8, 170, 172–6, 179–80, 308–13, 316–17, 385
  Beyond a Boundary 308–11, 356–7
Jan, Yasir 225
Jardine, Douglas xiii, 35, 48–59, 200

Jayawardene, Mahela 253, 346
Jenkins, Roly 12
Jennings, Keaton 278
Jennings, Terry 94
Jessop, Gilbert 253
Jesus 214–15, 223
John Player League 119, 126, 288
Johnson, Mitchell 98–9
Jones, Allan 84–5
Jones, Eifion 325
Jones, Geraint 38, 61, 63–4
Julian, Brendon 245
Jumadeen, Raphick 167

Kallicharran, Alvin 208
Kallis, Jacques 69, 345
Kanpur 262
Karachi 88
Karim, Saba 264
Karunaratne, Dimuth 324
Kasprowicz, Michael 38
Kelly, Brendan 81
Kennedy, John 279
Kent 2nd XI 10
Kent cricket team 8, 26, 168, 221,
    223–4, 284, 342, 343, 345
Kenya 111, 158
Kenyon, Don 136, 141, 142
Key, Rob 336
Khan, Imran 66, 67, 101, 229,
    231–2, 261
Khan, Saif Ali 263
Khan, Zaheer 259
King Commission 183
Kipling, Rudyard 308
Kippax, Alan 53
Kirkegaard, Søren 311
Kirmani, Syed 325
Knight, Barry 129, 138
Knott, Alan xiii, 64–5, 69, 85, 97,

210, 223, 324–5, 327, 333,
    338–44
Knott, James 344
Knott, Jan 344
knowledge of cricket 308–20, 368
Knowlson, James 298–9
Kohli, Virat xiii, 251, 253, 273–7,
    278–9, 346, 384
Kumble, Anil 234, 244, 259, 264,
    279

Lahore 228, 230, 348–9
Lancashire cricket team 8, 85,
    109, 232, 238, 241, 244
Lancashire League 128, 173
Langford, Brian 126
Lara, Brian 233, 267–8, 272, 345,
    376, 384
Larwood, Harold 49, 51–5, 57,
    200, 386
Latchman, Harry 7
Laws of Cricket 205–7, 215, 221
Lawson, Geoff 96
Laxman, V. V. S. 253
Lear, Jonathan, *A Case for Irony*
    311
Lee, Brett 38–9
leg before wicket (lbw) 27, 46,
    51–2, 232, 242–3
leg-breaks (bowling technique) 7,
    11–12, 86, 92, 155, 228, 230,
    234, 236, 241, 247, 355, 369
see also doosra
leg-spin (bowling technique) 6,
    7–8, 10, 12, 51, 94, 155, 228,
    234, 241–6, 248, 293, 324
'leg-theory' 49–53, 55, 57
Lehmann, Darren 193, 196
Leigh-Breeze, Mr 5
Lever, John 62–3, 192

Lewis, Arthur 179
Lewis, Tony 14, 87
Leyland, Maurice 58, 358, 373
Lillee, Dennis 40, 45, 77–8, 83, 87, 90, 90–9, 101, 184, 229, 287, 333, 335, 336, 378
Lillee, Helen 98
limited-overs cricket 119
Lindwall, Ray 15–16, 20, 27, 229
Lions rugby 36
Lloyd, Clive 105, 106, 167, 228, 243, 287
Lodha panel recommendations 278
Long, Arnold 325
Lord's 7, 10, 12, 13, 21, 24–7, 34, 44–5, 57, 81, 87, 91, 102, 110, 124, 126, 138–40, 143, 154, 156, 167–8, 173, 198–204, 221, 238, 260, 265, 273, 289, 297, 298, 323–4, 327, 331, 336, 346–8, 385–6
Lord's Nursery Ground 25, 91
Luckhurst, Brian 224
Lumb, Richard 44

MacLaren, Archie 244
Mahmood, Mazher 201
Mailey, Arthur 52
Majeed, Mazher 202
Malan, Dawid 278, 304
Malden Wanderers ground 9–10, 12
Malik, Sajida 202
Mandela, Nelson 122
Manjrekar, Vijay 265
'Mankading' 206, 208
Mann, George 24, 301–2
Mann, Tufty 301–2

Marks, Vic 293
Marlar, Robin 148, 262
Marsh, Mitchell 306
Marsh, Rodney 37, 45, 65, 91–2, 95, 96, 184, 287, 288, 315, 332–7
Marshall, Malcolm 83, 101, 107, 166
Martindale, Manny 57
Marylebone Cricket Club (MCC) xi, 13, 18, 26, 35, 44, 48–9, 57, 59, 87, 94, 97–8, 111–12, 121–3, 129–30, 133, 136, 138–41, 143–8, 150, 159, 171, 205–7, 261, 264, 289, 302, 326–7, 334
and ball tampering 192
Brearley's presidency of 293, 298
Carol Service, 2016 138, 139, 142
Easter classes 155
and the Nawab of Pataudi tribute dinner 260
Special General Meeting, 1968 146–7, 153
tour of Australia, 1946–7 293
tour of Holland and Denmark, 1962 220
tour of India, 1950s 251
tours of South Africa xi, xii, 122–3, 129–30, 133, 289
see also MCC Committee; MCC Under-25 team; MCC World Cricket Committee
masculinity 82–3
Masood, Asif 228
Master, The 384
match-fixing 119, 183–5, 188
Matisse 374

May, Peter 136, 142, 148, 149, 245

MCC *see* Marylebone Cricket Club

MCC Committee 28, 139, 141, 146, 148

MCC Under-25 team 228

MCC World Cricket Committee 337, 386

McCabe, Stan 53, 55

McCosker, Rick 92

McDonald, Ted 175, 360

McGrath, Glenn 37, 60, 237, 245, 307

McIntyre, Arthur 16

McKenzie 265

Melbourne 53, 56–7, 60–1, 92, 97, 210, 265, 333, 339
see also Centenary Test, Melbourne 1977

Menon, Suresh 155, 276

Michelangelo 175, 357

Middlesex Committee 120–1

Middlesex cricket team xii, xiii, 5–7, 10–13, 23–8, 76, 79, 83, 86, 91, 94, 102, 109, 121, 143, 155–6, 168, 178, 213, 220–2, 227, 238, 244, 286, 317, 327–8, 330–1, 336, 343, 354

Middlesex II team 10, 26, 178

Middlesex Second XI team 4, 13

Middlesex Young Amateurs 13

Middleton Sports Club 5–6, 8, 128

Middleton Sunday XI team 5

Middleton-on-Sea Sunday Eleven 263

Milburn, Colin 319

Miller, Geoff 46

Miller, Keith 15–16, 20

Misbah-ul-Haq 225

Mohammad, Mushtaq 228, 231, 241

Monckton, Lord 28

Monroe, Marilyn 262

Moore, Henry 370

Moseley, Ezra 168

Moss, Alan 109, 330

Mozart, Wolfgang Amadeus 319–20

Mugabe, Robert xii, 159, 163

Mugabe regime 158

Mumbai xi, 70, 260, 265, 269–71

Muralitharan, Muttiah 87, 224, 234–40, 243–4, 246, 345, 368–9

Murray, Deryck 167, 255

Murray, John 7, 326–31, 336

Murray, Mike 24

Mushtaq, Saqlain 234, 238, 244

Naipaul, V. S. 179

Namibia team 158, 161

Nandy, Ashis 259

Narwaz, Sarfraz 358

Nation, The (Trinidad newspaper) 123, 167, 172

national character 254, 258, 259

Nationalist Government (South Africa) 122

Nationalist Party 129

Nawab of Pataudi ('Tiger') xiii, 5, 56, 57, 251, 260–6

Nawaz, Sarfraz 67, 227, 228–33, 237, 243

Neath ground 385

Nehru, Jawaharlal 175

Nelson 167, 173

New South Wales cricket team 17

New Zealand 36

New Zealand national cricket team 209, 339

News of the World (newspaper) xiii

sting 2010 198, 201, 202

Nijinsky, Vaslav 19

Northamptonshire cricket team 86, 231, 325

Nottingham 44, 167, 214, 334

Nottinghamshire cricket team 53, 65, 370, 386

Ntini, Makhaya 267–8

Oborne, Peter 133, 136–41, 144, 230, 232

Observer (newspaper) xii, 198, 258

off-theory (bowling tactic) 52

O'Keefe, Kerry 241

Old, Chris 40–1, 62, 210

Old Trafford 27, 47, 96, 129, 232–3, 245, 287, 332

Oldfield, Bert 359

Olivier, Sydney 171

Olonga, Henry xii, 123, 158, 159, 163–4, 165

Oosthuizen, Tienie 141

O'Reilly, Bill 58

orthodox (conventional) swing 229–30

Osborne, Peter 229

Oval 15, 70, 100, 102–3, 105–6, 141, 273, 355, 384–7

Test 1882 34

Test 1930 52

Test 1968 131

Test 1981 336

Test 1998 239

Test 2011 189

Owen-Smith, 'Tuppy' 6

Oxford cricket team 263, 265

Pack, Roger Lloyd 297

Packer, Kerry 44, 46, 105, 120, 121, 136, 289, 335, 342

Pakistan 88, 228, 232, 241

Pakistan Cricket Board 198, 203

Pakistan national cricket team xiii, 64, 88, 137, 155, 165, 198–204, 225, 227–31, 234, 273, 325

Palairet, R. C. N. 48

Palmer, Charles 220

Panesar, Monty 60–1, 63, 64, 269

Paranavitana, Tharanga 348–9

Parfitt, Peter 330

Paris 300–1

Parks, Jim 324

Patel, Parthiv 200

Paton, Alan 132, 133

Peirce, Gareth 202

People's National Movement 172

Peploe, Rupert, *Cricket's Burning Passion* 34

Perth xi, 17, 35, 53, 61–3, 95, 98, 124, 199, 255

Test 2017 304, 306, 307

Phidias 357

Philip, Prince, Duke of Edinburgh 254

Pietersen, Kevin 224, 245, 277, 304, 354

Pinter, Harold xiii, 293–7, 298–302

pitches 103–4

Plunkett, Liam 347

Pollock, Graeme 133

Pollock, Jackson 368

Ponsford, Bill 52, 53

Ponting, Ricky 62, 267, 345
Powell, Robert 297
Prabhu, K. N. 255
Pradeep, Nuwan 323
Prasanna, Erapalli 86, 341
Preston, Ken 127
Price, John 330
Prideaux, Roger 129
Prior, Matt 324
Procter, Mike 101, 229, 267
Professional Cricketers'
    Association 331
professionalism 318–19
Pujara, Cheteshwar 253
Punch (magazine) 148

Qadir, Abdul 155, 241, 244
Qasim, Iqbal 88
Queensland 95
Queensland cricket team 92

racial issues xii–xiii, 117–80
racism 121, 131–4, 156, 162, 174,
    177, 251
Radio 3 285
Radley, Clive 168, 221, 317, 318
Raj Singh Dungarpur Lectures
    260
Raja, Rameez 80
Ramadhin, Sonny 8, 148, 167,
    241
Ramprakash, Mark 114, 304–5
Randall, Derek 45–6, 71, 92–3,
    125, 332–4
Ranjitsinhji xiii, 251–3, 309, 314,
    359
Rayment, Alan 114
Read, Chris 61, 63–5
Redpath, Ian 44
Reiffel, Paul 245

Rembrandt 373
Rest of the World 144
Retford 333
'reverse' swing *see* 'switch-hit'
    sweep
Rhodes, Harold 238
Richards, Barry 126
Richards, Viv 77, 80–3, 92–3,
    101–2, 166, 168, 212, 261,
    271, 340, 367
Richardson, Arthur 53
Richardson, David 194
Richardson, Peter 284
Rist, Frank 151
Roberts, Andy 44, 101–3, 105,
    107, 167, 169, 214, 229, 305,
    340
Robertson, Jack 11, 12, 75–7, 126
Robin, D. H. 329
Robins, Walter 6, 24–6
Robinson, Emmott 178
Robinson, Marilynne, *Home*
    186–7
Root, Joe 15, 70, 276, 305, 306,
    346
Rose, Brian 209
Ross, Alan 18–20
Routledge, Reg 12
Royal Air Force (RAF) cricket
    team 327
Rudder, Joshua 167, 177
rugby 36, 122
Russell, Bertrand 175
Ryan, Christian, *Golden Boy* 335
Ryder, Jack 52

SACA *see* South African
    Cricketers' Association
St Hill, Wilton 173
Salahuddin 228

Salisbury (Harare) xi
Samuel, John 287–8
Sandham, Andy 386
Sangakkara, Kumar xiii, 235, 238–9, 277, 345–9
Sargant, William 247
Scholar, Richard 35
Schubert, Franz 290
Second World War 15, 111, 156
Seecharan, Clem 172, 174
Seenigama 235
Sehwag, Virender 239–40, 253, 276, 279
Selvey, Mike 105, 221
Shackleton, Derek 109–10
Shakespeare, William 203
Shankly, Bill 115, 295, 353
Shannon 170, 173, 310
Sharp, Harry 24, 26
Shepherd, Don 109–10
Sheppard, David 121, 123, 130, 139, 146–52, 261
Sheppard, Grace 152
Silk, Dennis 115
Sims, Jim 6, 12–13
Singh, Harbhajan 259
Singh, Maninder 88–9
Singh, R. P. 189
Sivell, Dale 79
Sky 106, 284
Sky Sports 101
slavery 177, 179
Smith, M. J. K. (Mike) 94, 96, 168, 220, 317, 318, 330, 354, 366
Smith, Steve 183, 191–3, 195–7, 276, 306, 346
Smith, Ernest James 'Tiger' 315
Snow, John 5
Sobers, Garry 71, 167, 354, 362

Socrates 49, 311, 318, 368
Socratic approach 311
Solkar, Eknath 86
Somerset cricket team 67, 102, 113, 209, 286, 296, 325, 344
South Africa 28, 36, 110, 121–2, 128, 134, 136–7, 139–43, 145, 147–8, 150, 158, 161, 163–5, 172, 185–6, 193, 197, 206
    English tour 1968–9 129, 130, 131–2
    exclusion from world sport 133
    MCC tours xi, xii, 122–3, 129–30, 133, 289
South Africa national cricket team 70, 183, 185, 191
South African Breweries tour 1982 342
South African Cricketers' Association (SACA) 139–40, 147
South African Government 121, 122, 130, 147
South African Nationalist Government 122
South African rugby team 122
South Australia cricket team 164
Southampton cricket team 347
Spirit of Cricket 205–15
Spofforth 12
Sporting Times (newspaper) 34
Sri Lanka 255, 348–9
Sri Lanka national cricket team 239, 323, 345, 346, 368–9
Sri Lankan civil war 349
Statham, Brian 17, 18, 20, 109, 238
Steele, David 44
Stephenson, Lieutenant Colonel John 81, 142

Stewart, Alec 345
Stewart, Micky 15
Stockwood, Mervyn 151–2
Stokes, Adrian 377
Stokes, Ben 66, 68, 70–1, 306
Strauss, Andrew 336
Strudwick, Herbert 327
Sun (newspaper) 168
Sunday Times (newspaper) xii
Surrey cricket team 10, 15, 213,
    221, 277, 325, 328, 344–5,
    386
Sussex cricket team 12, 25, 26,
    49, 106, 148, 219–20, 261,
    314
Sussex II team 178
Sussex XI team 261–2
Sutcliffe, Herbert 6, 15, 58
Sutherland, James 196, 197
Sutherland, Joan 262
Swann, Graeme 199, 269
Swann, John 4–5, 10
Swann, Paul 4
Swansea 10
Swanton, E. W. 26, 140, 223,
    224, 283, 284
Swanwick, Bill 44
Sweetman, Roy 325
'switch-hit' sweep ('reverse'
    sweep) 222, 223–4, 226,
    227–34, 243
Sydney 17, 45, 46, 65, 94, 125,
    200, 220, 261, 265, 342, 358
Sylvester, David 288, 355, 356,
    360, 361–73, 375–9
    London Recordings 361
Symonds, Andrew 60, 62

T20 cricket 82, 87, 107, 119, 121,
    324, 386, 387

Tagore, Sharmila 262
Tanzania 111
Tasmania 220
Tate, Maurice 27
Taunton 286
Tayfield, Hughie 126
Taylor, Bob 325
Taylor, Brian 127
Taylor, Derek 325
Taylor, Ken 8
technology 119
Telegraph, The (Kolkata)
    (newspaper) 279
television rights 120
Tendulkar, Anjali 270–1
Tendulkar, Sachin xiii, 137, 245,
    251, 253, 258–9, 267–72, 276,
    279, 345, 354
Terry, John 133
Test and County Cricket Board
    (TCCB) 120, 136, 221
    Cricket Committee 209
Test cricket 6–7, 10, 12, 17–18,
    20, 26, 34, 38, 52, 82, 87–8,
    97, 98, 100, 102–4, 107,
    109–10, 120–1, 125–6,
    129–31, 133–4, 136–8, 141,
    144, 148–9, 159, 166–7,
    169–70, 184, 189, 191, 195,
    198–200, 202–3, 208, 210,
    214, 224, 231, 234, 238–9,
    242, 244–6, 258–9, 261–2,
    264–5, 268–9, 276–8, 287,
    304–7, 309, 323, 327–8, 330,
    334, 336–7, 339–43, 345,
    346–9
    see also Ashes, The
Test Match Special (Radio 3
    show) 285
Thatcher, Margaret 28

Thomas, Bernard 87, 192
Thomson, Jeff 93, 94, 101, 333
Thorpe, Graham 239–40, 368–70
Times of India (newspaper) 255
Times, The (newspaper) xii, 156, 203–4
timing 355, 362, 364–6, 371–2, 375, 377
Timms, Brian 286
Titmus, Fred 10, 24, 26, 27, 109, 257, 327, 330
Tovey, Donald 370
Tremlett, Chris 102, 347
Trent Bridge 41, 208
Trinidad 167, 170–1, 173, 174, 176, 208, 255, 309, 356
Trinidad Indoor Cricket School 255
Trinidad national cricket team 114
Trott, Jonathan 199, 200
Troubles 1947 261
Trueman, Fred 8–9, 17, 39, 40, 212, 229, 263
Trustee of the Foundation of Goodness 235
TUFF acronym 98–9
Tufnell, Phil 386
Tunapuna 176
Tunapuna recreation ground, Trinidad 356
Tunbridge Wells ground 385
Turnbull, Malcolm 193
Twain, Mark 186
Tyson, Frank 17, 18, 20

Udal, Shaun 247
Umpire Decision Review System (DRS) xii, 386
umpires 119

Underwood, Derek 46, 85, 245, 333, 339–40, 342, 360
United Arab Emirates (UAE) 80
University of West Indies 171

Valentine, Alf 167
Vallance, Peter 262–3
Vaseline incident (MCC tour of India, 1976–7) 87
Vaughan, Michael 15, 36
Vengsarkar, Dilip 253
Venkataraghavan, Srinivasaraghavan 86
Verity, Douglas 56
Verity, Hedley 6, 56, 58
Virgil, *The Aeneid* 185
Vishwanath 88
Viswanath, Gundappa 253, 279
Voce, Bill 53, 54, 57, 386
Vorster, Johannes 129, 136, 140

WACA ground, Perth 99
Wadekar, Ajit 86
Wadsworth, Ken 339
Wainwright, Ted 252, 254
Waite, Dennis 105
Walcott, Clyde 167
Walcott, Derek 179
Wales national cricket team 112
Wales Under-16s 112
Walker, Keith 10
Walker, Tom 219
'walking' 187
Wallace, Mark 112
Walsh, Courtney 101
Ward, Brian 126
Ward, Ivan 197
Wardle, Johnny 7, 8
Warne, Shane 212, 234, 241–8, 355, 384, 386

Warner, David 82, 183, 191, 195–7
Warner, Pelham ('Plum') 26, 57, 171
Warr, John 25, 26, 28, 330
Warwickshire cricket team 25, 113
Washbrook, Cyril 8
Watson, Shane 102, 247
Waugh, Steve 45, 213, 245
Weekes, Everton 167
Wellard, Arthur 296–7
West Indies 87–8, 93, 104, 130, 131, 137, 144, 147, 171, 174–6, 231
West Indies Federation 171
West Indies national cricket team xii, 39, 43–4, 57, 80, 88, 100–1, 104–6, 123, 129, 148, 166–8, 171–3, 179–80, 214, 220, 243, 309, 315–16, 319, 336
West, Sam 297
Western Australia 255, 335
Western Australia cricket team 62–3, 92, 335
Whitelaw, Billie 156
wicket-keepers 321–49
Williams, David 99
Williams, Dr Eric 172
Williams, Lawrence 96
Williams, Rowan 152
Willingdon Club, Mumbai 251
Willis, Bob 36, 37, 41–2, 45, 46, 62–3, 92, 101, 102, 105, 229
Wilson, Don 142
Wilson, Rockley 59
Wilson, Vic 18
Wilton, Penelope 297
Winchester College 58–9
Winchester College 'Lords' XI 261–2

Wisborough Green team 5, 262–3
Wisden Almanack 128
Wittgenstein, Ludwig xii, 375
Woakes, Chris 102
Wolfe, Tom, *The Bonfire of the Vanities* 185
Wood, Graeme 99
Woodcock, John 15, 262, 263
Woodfull, Bill 49, 55, 57
Woods, Joseph 'Float' 171, 174
Worcester 11, 209
Worcestershire Club 12, 109, 128, 140, 142–3, 284
World Cricket Committee 80, 207, 348
World Cup
    1987 224–5
    2003 158–62, 164
    2008 275
    2017 386
World Eleven 228
World Series Cricket 44, 45, 46, 93, 104, 106, 119–20, 119–21, 136, 305, 342
Worlock, David 151
Worrell, Frank xii, 104, 123, 167, 168, 172, 174–5, 179–80, 220, 309, 310
Wright, Doug 8, 16, 293
Wyatt, Bob 55, 316
    Fighting Cricketer 49, 53

Yorkshire Annual General Meeting 178
Yorkshire cricket team xiii, 6–8, 11–12, 14, 17, 51, 56, 76, 109, 155, 178, 212, 221–2, 263, 312, 325, 328

Yorkshire Evening News
    (newspaper) 155
Yorkshire Seconds 6
Younis, Waqar 101, 232, 233

Zanu-PF party 164

Zimbabwe xii, 123, 158–65
Zimbabwe affair 158–65
Zimbabwe national cricket team
    158, 163
Zimbabwean civil war 220